Linguistics in language teaching

Linguistics in language teaching

D. A. Wilkins

Senior Lecturer in the Department of Linguistic Science, University of Reading

 Edward Arnold

© D. A. WILKINS 1972

First published 1972 by
Edward Arnold (Publishers) Ltd.,
41 Bedford Square, London WC1B 3DP

Reprinted with corrections 1973
First published in paperback 1974
Reprinted with corrections 1974
Reprinted 1975
Reprinted 1977
Reprinted with revised Further Reading 1978

ISBN: 0 7131 5748 8

Printed in Great Britain by
Richard Clay (The Chaucer Press) Ltd
Bungay, Suffolk

Contents

Preface

I have written *Linguistics in Language Teaching* for teachers of foreign languages including English as a foreign language. It is not an introduction to linguistics, nor is it a book on methodology. It is an attempt to bridge the gap between the two, to investigate how legitimately knowledge of linguistics contributes to the taking of decisions about language teaching. I have assumed that the reader has some familiarity with the methodology of language teaching but no previous knowledge of linguistics. It is most suitable, therefore, for the teacher about to start a course in linguistics or applied linguistics, or who wishes to see whether such a course is worth undertaking. I hope that it can also be read with benefit by teachers in training and with interest by students and teachers of general linguistics.

In order to give a balanced view of the field of linguistics, I have been deliberately eclectic. Parts of the discussion owe much to early structuralism, some to later developments in transformational generative linguistics, and others to Hallidayian linguistics. I hope I have managed to do this while still retaining overall coherence. Choice from among the different viewpoints—if choice be necessary at all—can only be made from a detailed study of each, and that is not attempted here. Inevitably I have had to be highly selective in the topics I have chosen. No one book could cover the whole of linguistics. This means that some aspects of linguistic enquiry, which could certainly be of interest to teachers, have been omitted. Since I have not been writing about linguistics as such, I have explained the linguistic points only as far as suits my purpose. For fuller treatment readers should turn to the literature on linguistics.

My approach is deliberately naive, in that I take the linguistic point first and then ask what value it has, if any, for language teaching. I do this *not* because I believe that decisions in language teaching follow linguistics in this way, but because I think it makes the issues clearer. In this way we can meet the question of the practical applicability of linguistics head-on. A further advantage of this approach is that it enables me to give the book a conventional linguistic arrangement so as to give the reader some idea of the field of linguistics.

The principal language of exemplification is English. This reflects my own interests and experience, but also the fact that I hope the book can be read both by teachers of English as a foreign language and by teachers of other foreign languages in English-speaking countries. Other examples are from the teaching of French, Spanish and German.

I must acknowledge my debt to all those who contributed to this book whether directly or indirectly. I have incorporated numerous suggestions made by my colleagues at the University of Reading and owe a particular debt to Ron Brasington, Roger Bowers, David Crystal, Malcolm Petyt and Peter Roach. I must also thank Frank Palmer, who gave me great encouragement from the beginning. My final thanks are to my wife. She bore the brunt of my preoccupation with various versions of this text over about three years and must have seen the last of the typescript with a great sense of relief.

1
Linguistic attitudes to language

1.1. Introduction

A person with no knowledge of linguistic science who picks up a modern descriptive Grammar and glances through it, even in a fairly superficial way will be struck by the very strangeness of much that he sees.[1] No doubt he will notice first the new symbols and terminology, which will be quite unlike anything that he remembers of grammar from his schooldays. On a closer reading he may discover that the attitudes to language too are different from those that he himself acquired in the course of his education. If he comes to the conclusion that there is little resemblance between linguistics and 'grammar', we should not be surprised, because for a long time linguists[2] themselves defined their subject by the ways in which its principles were a rejection of principles followed in traditional grammatical descriptions. In the fifty years or so since this conscious break with tradition, linguistics has developed with considerable vigour. The attempt to start again from scratch, to re-examine all the assumptions and to develop techniques of description that have been thought out afresh, has aroused so much interest in language that linguistics is becoming an autonomous academic discipline. Yet there is little doubt that in retrospect this development of the twentieth century will be seen less as a complete innovation than a fairly violent change of direction in a continuing tradition of language study that stems from the Greeks. Even the conclusions that linguists reach about aspects of the structure of language are not always so very different from those reached by earlier scholars, even if they are presented in new ways. On the other hand, some of the new attitudes are bound to produce new information and new analyses. The

---

[1] Throughout, the word 'Grammar' is used to indicate a book in which the *grammar* of a language is described.

[2] By 'linguist' is meant *linguistic scientist* not *polyglot*. 'Linguist' is used consistently in this sense throughout.

focusing on spoken rather than written language, for example, has brought additional data within the range of linguistic study. This range has been extended in other directions by the contact with sociology and psychology. So diverse are the developments in language study that the boundaries of linguistic science are impossible to define.

Linguistics is not about language teaching. It does not follow that because there have been changes in the scholar's study of language there should be related changes in the teaching of foreign languages. But since both linguistics and language teaching have language as their subject-matter, the possibility that each can learn something from the other must be considered.[3] If it proves that linguistics does have implications for language teaching, these implications must be fully understood so that they can be used to evaluate our language teaching practices. Language teaching methodology has for centuries been a matter of fashion, because of the very great difficulty of studying it objectively. Linguistics is one of the fields to which language teaching may be referrable, if we are to attain this objectivity. Just how important a place linguistics has in the evaluation of language teaching is something that must be left to the final chapter.

For the moment I want to begin the discussion of how legitimately and in what ways linguistics and language teaching might be related by looking at some of the linguist's attitudes towards language. The attitudes that I shall be referring to are those that represented the break with tradition. The issues are close to many of the assumptions made in language teaching too. We shall see that in some cases the influence of linguistics has been felt directly. In others it is still potential, while elsewhere direct results in language teaching are not to be expected. There are four sections, one on speech and writing, one on form and meaning, a third on descriptive accuracy and the final one on *langue* and *parole*. These are by no means the only issues that characterize the linguist's general view of language. Others will arise in subsequent chapters. The approach adopted here and in other parts of the book, where appropriate, is first to explain the linguistic point as briefly and as simply as possible and then to examine its validity and relevance for language teaching through some fairly detailed exemplification.

[3] In practice the assumption is widely held that language teaching stands to gain something from an acquaintance with linguistics. I do not know of any discussion of the other possibility—that linguistics can learn something from language teaching.

1.2. Speech and writing

Linguistics has brought to the study of language a revaluation of the relationship between the spoken and the written forms of the language. Traditionally in the description of languages a much higher status was accorded to the written than to the spoken. It is not difficult to see the reasons for this. In cultures where only a minority was educated, literacy was the significant indication of the educated mind. The educated man was revered for the knowledge to which his literacy gave him access and for the social prominence that his learning gave him. Since, by definition, a literate man is one who can understand written language, it follows that the high regard that attaches to the individual should also attach to the form of the language that only he appreciates. Something that only few people have access to becomes the most valued. What is more, the written language is the repository of the finest literary achievements of a society. If one wishes to discover what is 'finest', what is 'most beautiful', what is, quite simply, 'best', it is to the written literature that one looks. It is not surprising, then, that language of all sorts is evaluated against the norm of the literary language. To the scholar this written language has one further asset. It is permanent. The scholar's references are accessible to all. The literature is a goldfield in which he can hunt for precious samples. Speech is transitory and in the past there was no means of seizing it, of reliving speech events and of making them available to others. It is difficult to assign as much importance to the fleeting as to the permanent and in a literary culture the matter must have seemed beyond question. Grammars have usually been Grammars of the written language.

This is not just a historical point. The attitudes which are the product of the above situation still exist. They are perpetuated by much school teaching and they are widely held by both the more and the less educated. School-teachers devote much energy to eradicating the influence of speech on writing, commonly asserting that the forms produced by pupils are grammatically incorrect. At times children have been required to produce prose modelled on the style of some literary master. Literary masterpieces, it is claimed, embody all that is best in the language and the best most of us can do is to come as close as possible to them in our own style, as a means of improving our control of the language. Written language is held up as a norm for all our uses of language, so that a working-class child is likely either to reject the forms which he associates with his home or to come to think of language as something which he learns about in school and which can be dismissed from all considerations of serious practical use. That this is the case is suggested by the popular use of the word *language* to mean *written language*. For many people what they speak is not language. It is in some way unworthy of the name. Their speech is a departure from the standard that language represents. Language, in this sense, may be considered as of concern to 'them', but not to 'us'.

Such attitudes towards speech and writing of the mother tongue are not confined to a generally European culture. If one looks elsewhere, there are situations similar to those that now exist or have existed in the past in Britain. In some countries of Asia, Africa and Latin America the level of literacy, though improving, remains low. The attitudes that prevail among literate and non-literate are just those that are described above. Social and economic advancement are obtained through education. Educated men are those that can read and write and, it is believed, one undergoes education in order to be able to read and write. This has consequences for the teaching of foreign languages in such countries. The teacher may well meet the attitude in his pupils that they are not really learning anything until they are being taught to read and write. The teacher who believes in an oral-based methodology or, worse, who may believe that since his pupils' need is to speak the language, they should be taught only speech, may get serious resistance from his pupils, who want to be able to produce the evidence that they are learning a language. For them, being able to speak it does not constitute valid evidence. They know illiterate individuals who have learned to speak the foreign language, especially English, to a degree that permits reasonable communication without any formal instruction at all. Yet they are uneducated men. They are not considered to have learned the language since they remain illiterate. The only evidence that seems acceptable is an ability to read aloud from the text-book or to write a few words. The attitudes to be found reflect mainly the stage of economic and educational development of the country, but this may be complicated by other factors. In Moslem countries the written language has additional status because of its religious significance. The Arabic language is to be found in its 'purest' form in the Koran and the particular forms of Arabic found there have religious sanction. Current spoken forms are perhaps further removed from this than Spanish is from Latin, yet it is the classical form which is considered the model of correctness rather than modern spoken dialects. To question the importance of the written word is sometimes seen as an attempt to undermine the religious authority stemming from the Koran. In such a case, the teacher ignores his pupils' opinions at his peril.

In the present state of education one doubts whether the reasons for these attitudes are still considered valid. The ability to read and write in the industrially advanced countries is now so general that no special status attaches to it. It is not true either that one of the principal uses of written language is the expression of or exposure to literature. Literature remains the interest of a minority and the majority has chosen to ignore those aspects of language which, at school, they were told to value highly. Indeed there is probably a conscious rejection of literary uses of language precisely *because* they were held up for appreciation in the schools. While it is known that many educated people have an interest in literature, it is also known that many do not and it is certainly well known that material success does not depend on high education. So, written language has lost much of its status.

It was said at the beginning of this section that linguistics had produced a revaluation of the relationship between writing and speech. We have seen that the old attitude involved the elevation of written language. The linguistic attitude attaches the greater importance to speech. For the linguist speech is the primary manifestation of language, and writing is both secondary to it and dependent on it. This is not the place for an extensive discussion of the linguist's reasons, since only the conclusion is relevant to language teaching, not the reasons for it. However, they may be stated briefly as follows:

1. It is part of man's biological nature that he should speak, just as it is that he should walk. Men do not necessarily learn to write. There are many societies where writing is unknown. With physiological, neurological and psychological normality a child will talk.

2. While it cannot be proved that human beings spoke before they wrote at some point on the evolutionary trail, it seems much less plausible to make the contrary assumption.

3. Every individual learns to speak before he learns to write. Indeed he learns to speak whether we 'teach' him or not. It would be much more difficult to learn to write without help. In fact when writing is learned, it is as a representation of speech which has been acquired previously.

4. Languages change and the most potent force for change is

speech. Sound systems seem to be permanently in a state of flux and grammatical systems are not completely stable either. Where change has occurred in speech, the written language may eventually be changed to accommodate it. Where the changes are not made, an increasing difference develops between writing and speech so that the one serves less and less as an accurate guide to the other. Society often resists the change by saying that the new forms are wrong, but whether or not there is any justification for this resistance, it is rarely successful. It is true that certain forms, being restricted in occurrence to written language, may be said to produce change too, but the structural development of a language is much more influenced by speech than by writing.

The linguist, then, has speech as his main subject-matter, and although he would not dismiss written language from his field of study he would relegate it to a secondary position. In describing a language he will be more occupied with its spoken than with its written form. Of course, his description may in some instances be as true of speech as of writing, but we are not entitled to assume that this is the case and rarely is an aspect of the language identical in its two forms.

The primacy of speech is of some importance to the language teacher. Many people have argued that since linguists have shown that 'the speech is the language' and since, as teachers, we aim to teach 'the language', we must set out above all to teach speech even at the risk of excluding written language altogether. Not many people would go as far as that, but it is a characteristic of much modern teaching that the greatest emphasis is placed on speech. Even though this view is not always directly derived from the 'speech is language' base, current language teaching practice has been strongly influenced by a number of people who were both linguists and language teachers and their views on the aims and methodology of language teaching were closely related to their views on the nature of language itself. Believing that speech is language, they advocated the teaching of oral language at a time when few teachers would have done so. War-time and post-war teaching programmes in Britain and the United States were conducted along lines suggested by linguists. The teaching of English as a foreign language especially has long followed an oral approach whose origins might be found in the work between the wars of teacher/linguists like H.E. Palmer.

Still, in spite of the apparent historical influence of such a view, one is entitled to ask whether the fact that linguists see speech as primary is of any decisive relevance to matters of language teaching at all. Linguistics is concerned with the nature and form of language and even where linguists interest themselves in the ways in which a language is acquired, it is a first rather than a second language that they have in mind. The linguist's interest in language is not in discovering the most efficient means by which a foreign language might be acquired, but in attempting to describe the very complex structure that is the ultimate goal of the learner. The linguist is not qualified to voice an opinion on the means by which the target which he describes should be reached, since different kinds of research are needed to resolve problems of strategies for teaching. Nor does it prove that speech is the only acceptable goal of foreign language teaching. As will be seen in a later chapter, social and personal factors enter into the definition of the goals of language teaching, so that even the target itself is not a matter for the linguist alone. Initially the aims of learning will probably be expressed in sociological and behavioural terms. If the learning of written language is for some reason more important, the fact that speech has a unique status for the linguist is irrelevant. He cannot say that *because* speech is the primary form of language, it should be the major target of language learning. What he can ensure is that the possibility of speech as a valid goal for teaching is given full consideration. Since there have been times when language teaching has been principally *written* language, there is value in the clear articulation of the alternative possibility. In the last three decades linguistics has provided this alternative and has thereby contributed to the redefinition of the goals that has led to the increase in the teaching of spoken language.

Spoken language now has a status in education which it did not previously possess. In the teaching of both the mother tongue and foreign languages the principal goal, I have suggested, has rarely been anything other than proficiency in the written forms, perhaps because speech was not commonly thought of as language. Now in both cases there is a realization that the improvement of skill in spoken expression and understanding is a legitimate goal of language teaching. Pupils developing a facility in oral expression are genuinely improving their mastery of language. Linguistics must take a good deal of the credit for making speech a respectable element in teaching. It would not be surprising to find that the new confidence in self-expression resulting from teaching is of benefit in writing and other areas of education. To consideration of whether the child expressing himself orally in class is doing something worthwhile, the linguist has something to contribute.

Since the linguist is primarily interested in speech, the Grammars or fragments of Grammars that he produces will be Grammars of the spoken language rather than Grammars of writing. Most people are not accustomed to thinking of grammar as something that is variable. Indeed they do not usually apply the term *grammatical* to speech at all, but think of it as essentially *ungrammatical*. Giving prominence to speech, as he does, the linguist believes that the forms of speech should not be judged by their degree of deviance from written forms, but rather have a grammar of their own which is distinct from the grammar of written language. Now it is obvious that there will be broad similarities in the spoken and written forms of language, but they are not as close as most people would expect. A linguist's description of a language, that is of speech, will therefore be different from the descriptions which are usually available to a teacher, which are, of course, descriptions of writing. This can best be shown by examining an example.

1.2.1. French adjective gender

The common formulation of a rule about the gender of adjectives in French might run as follows. 'Feminine adjectives are formed from the masculine by the addition of an -*e*. Masculine adjectives which already end in -*e* do not change.' To this information one would need to add additional rules concerning adjectives which show further changes such as doubling of the final consonant before suffixation of the -*e*, certain consonant changes, insertion of a further vowel before the -*e*, and placing of an accent on the preceding vowel. In practice these are often learned not as rules but rather as isolated forms when they occur. The following orthographic examples illustrate these rules.

Masculine	Feminine
laid	laide
rouge	rouge
bas	basse
frais	fraîche
long	longue
léger	légère

Such rules relate to the written forms, and as soon as one looks at speech one can see that the rules are quite inapplicable there. You cannot talk about final -e's which are not said, nor the doubling of consonants which were not there in the first place.

So, to show what forms are to be handled we must express them in a manner which reveals the sounds which actually occur in speech. In speech the above words occur in the following way:

Masculine	*Feminine*
[lɛ][4]	[lɛd]
[ruʒ]	[ruʒ]
[ba]	[bas]
[frɛ]	[frɛʃ]
[lɔ̃]	[lɔ̃g]
[leʒe]	[leʒɛr]

From this one can see that what is happening is not the addition of any vowel, nor the doubling or changing of a consonant, but essentially the addition of a consonant. The formulation of a rule would be more along the lines of: 'certain adjectives do not change for the feminine, but others add a consonant.' (We can ignore certain complications for the sake of this discussion.) In practice such a rule would produce an unnecessarily long-winded grammar. There would be no way of predicting which consonant was to be added, so that the grammar would have to list all the adjectives according to which consonant was suffixed to form the feminine.

In fact there is a far more economical way of doing it. There is no powerful reason why we should consider this area in terms of deriving the feminine from the masculine at all. The whole description becomes very much simpler if we take the feminine as the base form and derive the masculine from it. In this case the principal rule for the variable forms would be: the masculine form of the adjective is formed from the feminine by the omission of the final consonant. So the grammar of this aspect of French will be something like this: (still incomplete)

  a Regular form: these adjectives do not change for the masculine:

$$[ruʒ] \rightarrow [ruʒ]$$
$$[ʒœn] \rightarrow [ʒœn]$$

---

[4] All transcription will be enclosed in square brackets until bracketing conventions are explained on page 48.

    b Irregular form: the masculine is formed from the feminine by the omission of the final consonant:

    b1

[plat]	→	[pla]
[griz]	→	[gri]
[bas]	→	[ba]

    b2 Where the omitted consonant was /n/, the resulting final vowel is nasalized.

[plɛn]	→	[plɛ̃]
[bryn]	→	[brœ̃]
[fin]	→	[fɛ̃]

    c Second irregular form: final voiced labio-dental fricatives, [v], are not omitted but are devoiced, [f].

[aktiv]	→	[aktif]

1.2.1.1. *Pedagogic considerations.* For foreign language teachers this analysis, though interesting, would be of no particular consequence unless it had pedagogic implications. However, it fairly clearly has. If a course is preparing pupils solely to be able to read and write French, then this analysis may not be relevant. If, on the other hand, a course aims to teach pupils to be active both in writing and in speech, then we must give consideration to the different analysis provided when we study speech. The teacher may choose to present language initially in its written form, in which case the usual presentation of adjective gender need not be changed, since the rules by which the pronunciation can be derived from the orthography are not particularly complex. Alternatively, he may choose to present language orally first and practise it without the aid of written forms. This is what many methodologists recommend. In this case the grammar of written French is quite irrelevant. It is pointless to claim to be teaching speech if one is in fact teaching the grammar of written French in an oral form. The organization of teaching would need to be based on the fragment of grammar above. The issues can be most clearly discussed if we imagine a purely oral course, that is, one which is designed to teach spoken French and in which written forms are not employed.

    If, in this situation, pedagogic organization follows the grammar of written French—and assuming we follow a pedagogic principle of presenting and practising one thing at a time—then our teaching will consist broadly of two units, one devoted to adjectives whose forms are not variable, the other to adjectives whose feminine is produced by adding -*e* to the masculine. This second unit, based on a perfectly sound orthographic rule, may include items such as *laid*, *léger*, *gris*, *plein*, *brun*, *plat* all of which add an *-e* in the feminine. The unit might also contain words like *actif* and *bas* which have an additional, but not difficult modification to the final consonant. The fact that they are presented in one unit should indicate that an identical or very similar process is involved, yet, as we have seen, these adjectives have to be placed in three different sub-classes if we are to describe adequately the regularities involved. The matter would be further complicated if we included words like *antérieur* or *général* which belong to the invariable class in speech but to the variable class in writing. The object of placing items in a unit together is that they are realizations of a particular rule, and that by practising use of these items in association the pupil learns the rule either consciously or unconsciously according to the method. By basing our oral teaching on the grammar of written French we have made the job of the learner far more difficult. We are leading him to believe that he has one thing to learn when in fact he has three. If he is told the written rule, then he can only learn successfully by divorcing his conscious from his unconscious knowledge. He is in any case going to have a struggle remembering feminine forms since, in speech, they are quite unpredictable from the masculine.

If, however, the teaching of speech is organized along the lines of a linguistic grammar of speech, then these inconsistencies are overcome. Our simplified grammar fragment gives us four classes of adjective, which are, to summarize:

(1) Forms which do not change, e.g. *rouge*.
(2) Forms which change by omitting the final consonant, e.g. *grise*.
(3) Forms which omit the final consonant and nasalize the vowel, e.g. *pleine*.
(4) Forms which change the final consonant. e.g. *active*.

These then constitute four separate teaching points, four units of teaching. How will the need to separate these teaching points influence the teacher's overall strategy? He could restrict the initial presentation of the adjective—when the main concern might be the position of the adjective in relation to the noun—to the feminine form. This would permit him to introduce words from any one of the four classes above. When the time came to learn the masculine forms, the members of the first class of adjectives which were already known would be taken and practised and then each of the other classes would be presented and practised in sequence. A problem with this solution might be that when the adjectives of all classes were first taught, it would be very difficult to stop pupils trying to use them to modify masculine nouns, and thereby making undesirable errors. One could avoid this by restricting the *nouns* taught to feminine nouns, but no doubt other criteria for selection would render this impracticable.

Rather than this, the initial presentation of adjectives might be restricted to those which have identical masculine and feminine forms.[5] In this way adjective *position* can be learnt without undue additional complications or restrictions. Pupils will be producing correct sentences whether they attach the adjectives they learn to a masculine or feminine noun. This allows some freedom of expression to the pupils. The other classes can be learnt subsequently in sequence. The disadvantage of this approach will lie in the restriction placed upon the choice of adjectives to be introduced at first. It might prove difficult to find adequate frequent and useful words for this stage of the course.

This brief example of the relation between linguistic description and pedagogic organization shows how a description of *speech* can lead to a radically different sequence of teaching. It shows too the interconnection of different parts of the sequence, so that a change in one part entails related changes elsewhere. The analysis of adjectives here results in limitations either in choice of noun or on vocabulary selection. Linguistics does not often provide analyses that are so surprisingly different or so evidently applicable to teaching as this one. But even where changes are small, they may be significant for the repercussions that they have on other parts of the teaching.

I have argued that the significance of speech is not that its importance in linguistics provides a justification for an oral method of teaching or for the adoption of spoken language as the goal of teaching. Its status helps the educator in arriving at decisions on what should be taught, but no more. Its influence on teaching is legitimate and direct when it is speech that is being taught and the analysis of speech that is being used as the basis for the linguistic organization of courses. I have illustrated this with a grammatical example where a different analysis has to be made if speech, not writing, is taken as the data for analysis. Such differences are not confined to

[5] This is the approach adopted in *En Avant*, the Nuffield French Course for primary schools, (E.J. Arnold, Leeds, 1966). In Unit 5 four invariable colour adjectives are introduced—*rouge, bleu, noir* and *jaune.* Not until Unit 14A—nine units and many lessons later—is adjective agreement taught through *gros* and *petit.*

the grammar. As the second chapter will show, there is much in the phonetics and phonology of languages that is not reflected in the written forms. We shall also see that the choice of the spoken or written channel of communication, and therefore of the preferred grammatical and lexical forms, depends in part on the social function of an utterance.

1.3. Form and meaning

A second characteristic of linguistic study of language is that it makes a clear distinction between statements about the use to which we put language (its meaning) and the actual shape which units of language have and the relationship which exists between them (its form). It is, of course, the function of linguistic forms to convey meaning, so that in describing these relationships one is also saying something about one aspect of meaning. However, there is a good deal concerned in our use of language that is not accounted for when we describe the forms. If the description of a language makes any claim to be comprehensive, it must account for both the forms and the meanings of that language.

This may seem rather obvious, but for as long as scholars have been studying language, for more than 2,000 years of which we have direct evidence, they have adopted varied views on which aspect of language most deserved their attention, and especially on the necessity or otherwise of a formal basis for their study. So, some have assumed that whatever language we speak, a universal conceptual system underlies our use of that language. In describing a language, therefore, they have sought to categorize its forms in terms of a universal system, which did not have to be justified each time one made a description. In contrast, others have believed that far from there being a universal system of grammar, every language should be examined with a minimum of preconceptions and its regularities explained only on the basis of observable evidence. Thus, for every language there would be, potentially at least, a different descriptive framework.[6]

[6] Scholars have differed on other related issues too. Some have assumed that, whatever our language, we use it to refer to external reality in broadly the same way, and that therefore forms in two languages can be equated. Other scholars have concentrated on the meaning of distinctions that are implicit in different formal systems, and have suggested that forms in different languages cannot be equated and indeed reflect perceptions of reality so different that translation from one to the other might prove impossible. While some scholars have taken the regularities of a language for granted, and have been occupied with pointing out the irregularities, others have had as their purpose the establishment of the regularities and may have neglected what was not so regular.

Although these approaches to language are clearly different, each has contributed towards a cumulative increase in our understanding of language and languages. In this sense it would be true to say that linguistics is scientific. In many respects linguists accept what has gone before and build on it. The very detailed examination of European languages and the greater knowledge of non-European languages has led to a much greater understanding of the kind of structure that a language may have and an appreciation of the kind of theoretical framework that is needed to describe it. On the other hand, in spite of the existence of this body of generally accepted knowledge, fundamental disagreements about our purpose in study-ing language persist. The preoccupations of scholars at different periods of history are now reflected in a sharp division among linguists as to the aim of their discipline. As the conflicting attitudes have such deep historical roots it would not seem unreasonable to assume that the division will remain unresolved in the foreseeable future, and to refrain from attempting to predict the eventual outcome. At least this is not the place to chart the opposing views, nor to state our preference for the one or the other. However, differing opinions as to the aims of linguistics produce different linguistic method-ologies, and since this is marked by attitudes to form and mean-ing it is worth our examining the consequences of one of these views.

Although this section begins with an outline of the characteristic attitude of the linguist towards form and meaning, it is not a very precise statement. Had this book been written fifteen years earlier a much closer statement of the relation between form and meaning would have been possible. At that time it was the predominant view that in studying language one should be concerned primarily with actually occurring forms. One should aim to discover the regularities of the forms themselves, their arrangements and relationships. Such a view was felt almost to be a defining characteristic of linguistic study of language and was commonly believed to be in contrast thereby with more 'traditional' attitudes to language.

The origins of this principle lay in the belief that statements about language should be based on evidence that was available to all. Only in this way could linguistics be an objective scientific study. If the linguist starts from pieces of language which he knows have actually occurred, then makes his analysis and predicts on the basis of it, anyone can check the statements he makes against language which is actually produced. It is sometimes said that a statement is only worth making if it is clear by what means we might attempt to disprove it. The forms of language can be studied in this way.

Meaning, however, is not susceptible to such an approach. Evidence of the meaning of language is not available to all. The meaning of items of language is compounded of the internal states of both speakers and hearers, of the context, physical and linguistic, in which the language is produced and received, of the uses to which the recurring items have been put in the past, of the biographical experience of the individuals concerned in the language event, and so on. It is not surprising that linguists have felt that it is impossible to make precise statements about meaning, or that such statements as are made are little more than expressions of opinion and are not particularly valuable since there is no objective way of evaluating them. Bloomfield expressed his doubts in the following way:

> The statement of meanings is therefore the weak-point in language study, and will remain so until human knowledge advances very far beyond its present state. In practice, we define the meaning of a linguistic form, wherever we can, in terms of some other science. Where this is impossible, we resort to makeshift devices.[7]

It was Bloomfield's ideas on the study of language that dominated linguistics until the 1950s. Bloomfield would never have said that meaning should not be studied, but for some that followed him semantics was a field outside linguistic science and it was considered somewhat disreputable to be interested in it. Even if not everyone went so far, at least it was agreed that considerations of meaning should not be allowed to influence the analysis of language, which should be based on the forms alone. A linguist might ask himself whether forms conveyed different meanings, but he would not enquire as to what these meanings were.[8]

The rejection of meaning as an unsure basis for linguistic decisions sometimes results in radically new analyses, but more often produces minor adjustments and on occasions even identical conclusions. Following a notional definition of what comprises a class of words called nouns in English will produce a list very similar to that produced by the application of formal criteria, in spite of the very different ways of arriving at it. Much the same thing could be said of verbs. However, a formal analysis would never permit one class of words to include all that is included in the traditional class called

---

[7] L. Bloomfield, *Language* (London, Allen & Unwin 1935), p. 140.
[8] Not a principle that was much adhered to in practice.

adverbs. The membership of this class—something of a dustbin in traditional grammar—contains items such as articles, negative particles, some question-words, sentence adjuncts, intensifiers—all of which function in quite different ways. A formal analysis of such words, an analysis of their syntactic functions, will result in their being classified and sub-classified quite differently. Indeed, by far the most important criterion for the establishment of classes of word, phrase, or clause in a language is similarity of function in the structure of a sentence. Nouns are classes of words that typically behave in certain ways. We can sub-classify them further in terms of certain differences of behaviour within the general similarity. Such a means of classification is far more reliable than using the internal similarity of language units,[9] or than classifying according to meaning, which proves in practice almost impossible to do.

I said above that a linguistic definition of *noun* would produce a list of words very similar to that which the teacher will already be familiar with. I suspect that this happens not because the earlier semantic definition was adequate but because, in practice, it was ignored. Instead, one used one's intuition to identify parts of speech, and that intuition was based on the very formal criteria that the linguist now employs. Any attempt to identify classes of words on semantic grounds alone seems doomed to failure.

Using a formal approach, then, is an attempt to eliminate the conscious or unconscious use of one's intuition. In this way decisions about structure and the process by which these decisions are arrived at are clearly displayed and open to examination. This is not to say that the linguist's intuition has no part to play, but even where he employs it in formulating hypotheses about the structure of a piece of language he must provide formal evidence to justify it. Neglect of one's semantic intuition and overdependence on formal analysis can lead to dubious conclusions about the structure of a sentence.[10]

1.3.1. Pedagogic considerations

When we write language teaching materials, we base the content on what we know of the language we are teaching. We obtain this knowledge from a variety of sources—from what we learned about the language as pupils ourselves, from what we were told about it

[9] Although morphology may prove a sound guide to class membership on occasions.
[10] This point is expanded in Section 3.2.

when we were being trained as teachers, from the manner in which language is taught in other text-books, and, finally, from descriptive Grammars of the language. All of this is derived ultimately from the work of grammarians, but often it has passed through many hands before reaching us. Since in practice, and probably rightly, we do not base our teaching on a single description of the language, our teaching will at some points reflect different attitudes towards language than at others. This suggests the probability of inconsistencies and even theoretical contradictions in the implications of our approach to teaching. Part of the value of studying linguistics is presumably that it brings these implications into the open. Our decisions should be taken in full awareness of the linguistic significance of what we are doing. This applies to the form/meaning dichotomy as it does to other aspects of language. It is a dichotomy which can operate both in the teacher's analysis of his teaching aims and by influencing the content of learning through the type of description on which the teaching is based.

The effect of identifying the object of language learning as the mastery of the ways of communicating certain semantic notions and relations, or of using a grammar which has a largely semantic basis for its categories, will be to equate some formal categories which are different and to divide others which are alike. It will produce an approach to teaching which denies the pedagogic benefits of using a language's formal regularities in the organization of teaching. It is the opposing view—the one based on a Bloomfieldian approach to language—that has tended to be dominant in language teaching in recent years. In this case the aim of learning is seen as mastery of the formal arrangements of a language. The related language descriptions are preoccupied with matters of form and tend to neglect both the semantic relations that the forms express and the social function of the language. Since the view is well documented and has been applied to language teaching quite explicitly, we will look at the pedagogic implications in more detail.

There is one example of an experimental course which was produced as a conscious application of the view that language is best described in formal terms and indeed that learning a language consists only of the mechanical acquisition of a skill in the production of its structural devices.[11] It is worth looking a little more closely

---

[11] These two views are distinct but often jointly held. Bloomfield's views on meaning were mechanistic, and that language is a response to some kind of stimulus is, or was, a common assumption in linguistics.

at the course produced by F. Rand Morton.[12]

Morton wrote a course in Spanish for American college students. The course assumed no previous knowledge of the language. His aims were to permit students in one semester to attain 80 per cent fluency, to permit most learning to take place outside the classroom— that is in a self-instructional situation—and to favour no particular type of student. Accepting as he did a sharp distinction between linguistic form and meaning in language description, he decided that as far as was practical they should be *taught* separately too. Mastery of the forms of the language would precede meaningful use of these forms. 'Language itself is all mechanical skill', he says, thus suggesting that meaning is not an aspect of language at all. This impression is reinforced by the analogy he draws between learning to speak a language and learning to type. Learning to type is essentially a skill. *Using* a skill, using a typewriter for some *purpose*, is not normally part of the process of learning to type. As in typewriting, so in language. Teaching must be directed at developing in the student a skill in control of forms of the language. Enabling the student to use the language, that is to convey and receive meaning via linguistic form, is not the principle function of the teacher.

Morton's course was divided up in the following way:

1. *Phonematization.* This stage aims to develop in the student an ability to discriminate the sound system of Spanish. The student is not required to produce any sounds. His only activity is to write symbols in a work-book as a response to what he has heard. The sounds are presented to the students in words which are all actual Spanish words. However, the meaning of these words is not given, so that they might as well be nonsense words for all the difference it makes at this stage. The 180 exercises are divided into 7 sets. The amount of time required by the students to attain a score satisfactory enough for them to move on to the next stage varied from 28 hours in the language laboratory for the fastest students, to 56 hours for the slowest.

2. *Sound Reproduction.* Here the discriminative ability taught in the first stage is developed into a productive ability, but still with effort 'undissipated' by any concern with meaning. There are 230 exercises divided into 4 sets. As well as simply imitating isolated

[12] F.R. Morton, *The Language Laboratory as a Teaching Machine* (Ann Arbor, University of Michigan Press, 1961).

sounds, the student has to carry out various manipulations, such as substitution, addition and inversion. In doing this the student quite unconsciously conjugates each of 16 irregular verbs one hundred times and covers one-third of the 105 model patterns to be taught.[13]

3. *Structural Cues.* The students learn to respond automatically to the important grammatical devices of Spanish (morphology), including subject and object pronouns, verb inflections, certain tense forms, negation, number, articles, interrogative pronouns and adjectives and so on. The student produces verbal and gestural responses to verbal and gestural cues. The gestures, although arbitrarily determined, do often attempt to relate to the meanings conveyed. For example, to point forward indicates that the form just heard or sought from the student is a future form. To point back indicates 'past'. In some cases the form of the cue itself determines the form of the response. Where neither of these means is practicable English equivalents are used. This stage consists of 10 sets, each made up of two hours of recording.

4. *Model Patterns.* By the end of this stage the students should be able to respond meaningfully to 105 'basic model patterns' and 1500 vocabulary items. Meaning additional to that learned in the previous stages is conveyed by 'broad hints in English'. A good deal of this stage appears to be devoted to imitation and learning by heart of fixed sentences. Even where the student has to answer questions on a text or dialogue, he is permitted to listen as many times as he wishes to model answers first. The questions are therefore not a test device. The material is made up of 10 sets totalling 40 drills.[14]

5. *Vocabulary Building.* An additional recognition vocabulary of 1000 items is taught. Meaning is usually clear from the context, but if not, explanations in Spanish are used. The 7 sets are made up of 14 drills.

6. *Allied Skills—Reading, Writing, Translation.* These are not integrated into the course at all.

It can be seen that such a course represents a very different approach from that usually found in our classrooms. The first three

---

[13] Morton does not say how long students spent on this and later stages.

[14] At this stage we can see that Morton's approach is not only mechanistic and formal, but also applies the sequence of linguistic description by teaching first the phonetics and phonology, then the morphology, and finally the syntax of Spanish. The validity of basing pedagogic sequence on descriptive sequence is discussed in the final chapter.

stages, in which meaning is almost totally excluded, could well occupy a whole year of an average English school class. Even in the later stages it appears that meaning is not taught with any precision. The students are unable to produce original sentences, since these require the presence of a teacher and all that is described above is controlled by a teaching machine. It is claimed that the experiment was successful in that it resulted in high oral proficiency in the students.

Before concluding this section on form and meaning, it is worth noting that the distinction is present in much present-day language teaching, but not in a way at all as revolutionary as that described briefly above. A common classroom practice activity goes by the name of structure drill or pattern practice. This is a technique designed to give the maximum opportunity for the pupil to produce sentences which are examples of the particular structure being taught. The aim of the drills is to ensure that the pupil can produce the correct grammatical forms with promptness, accuracy and minimum conscious thought. This has sometimes been described as 'automatizing speech responses', but this is rather misleading, since a drill of this sort lacks some important features of natural language use. Still, the point is that it is with *forms* of language that pattern practice drills are principally concerned, and if one looks at examples one can see that it is often *only* forms that they practice.

Example 1[15]
Practice Drills
Change the following sentences as in the example.
    Example: Les rues sont larges. Que les rues sont larges.
  1. Elles sont larges.   Qu'elles sont larges.
  2. Les magasins sont grands. Que les magasins sont grands,
                             etc.
  3. Ils sont grands.
  4. La ville est belle, *etc.*

Example 2[16]
(A substitution drill to practise the Present Progressive form of the verb in English. The substitutions are cued by a set of pictures.)
    I'm looking for a comb.

[15] F. Huss, *Pas à pas* (London, University of London Press, 1967), p. 46.
[16] R. Lado and C.C. Fries, *English Pattern Practices* (Ann Arbor, University of Michigan Press, 1962) p. 46.

I'm looking for a watch.
I'm looking for a key, etc.

Example 3[17]

(A drill which is in the form of a question and answer, but in which there is considerable similarity of structure in the stimulus and response. The items for substitution are cued by the words to be inserted themselves.)

1. What do you want me to do?
   (come here) I want you to come here.
2. What do you want me to do?
   (go away) I want you to go away.
3. What do you want me to do?
   (move) I want you to move. etc.

Each of these drills has a specific linguistic aim. In Example 1 the structure of the original sentence is changed by the addition of the same single word at the beginning of each sentence. Example 2 requires not the addition but the substitution of a word. In the third a sentence is transformed from a question to a statement with the appropriate and fixed change of pronouns and the substitution of a given verb phrase, which is alternatively transitive or intransitive. These given are just some of the many techniques available for this kind of drilling. We might ask what is required of the student for him to be able to perform the drill correctly. In each case it is that he make some change in the form of the sentence. In no case is it necessary that he should understand either the cue sentence or the sentence that he actually utters. It is perfectly possible to produce a string of sounds in an entirely mechanical way without any thought of the meaning of what is being said. The only element of choice is in the second drill where the student has to find the correct word when pictures of a comb, a watch, a key, etc., are presented to him. However, this is only one aspect of meaning. The student may respond correctly without understanding the lexical item *look for* and without being aware of the significance of the Present Progressive. It is, in fact, for mastery of the latter that the drill is designed. It may be said therefore that such pattern practice drills are intended to practise the forms of the language and not the meanings.

This is not the place to evaluate such an approach to language teaching, but there are two points which seem worth making. In the

---

[17] M.A. Tatham, *English Structure Manipulation Drills* (London, Longmans, 1968) p. 79.

first place, it is possible to produce drills which, while giving the opportunity for intensive practice of particular grammatical structures, remain fully meaningful for the student. They do require considerable ingenuity on the part of the writer, however, and it has not yet been shown that all aspects of grammar can be practised in this way. Secondly, some teachers would hold that some areas of grammar are best taught by means of mechanical drilling even when other means are available. These areas might include concord, case, number, gender and, to some extent, word order, for example. Such teachers would consider Example 2 above satisfactory as one of a set of drills practising the *form* of the Present Progressive. It does not help the student to decide *when* to use it, of course. The distinction between form and meaning, which is made by some linguists, does therefore have its counterpart in language teaching. It is manifested in an extreme case by the attempt to separate the teaching of form from the teaching of meaning—even to the point of excluding the teaching of meaning or delaying it until the formal apparatus has been acquired. More moderately it is found in the belief that there is value in some kinds of language practice which have virtually no semantic content for the learner.

It is with the dominance of form in the form/meaning dichotomy that linguistics has until recently been most associated. The dominance of meaning, as I suggested above, would seem likely to lead to a downgrading of the importance of linguistic structure in the organization of teaching materials, an emphasis on the communicative function of language and a rejection of any attempt at purely mechanical practice. The soundest view would seem to be that neither should dominate, but that language teaching should be based on a full understanding of both the formal and the semantic nature of language.

1.4. Descriptive accuracy

There are certain principles of linguistic study that lead us to expect particularly accurate information about a language in its current usage. The first of these principles distinguishes clearly between descriptions of the language in its contemporary form and descriptions of its historical development. The linguist believes his first task must be to describe the actual state of the language without reference to the historical processes which have produced it. He would not be concerned to chart historical derivations, changes in the meanings and forms of grammatical and lexical items, nor even to 'explain apparent anomalies as being the survival of parts of earlier grammatical systems.

This is not to say that historical study of language (so-called *diachronic* linguistics) is not a legitimate field. Rather, historical study must be kept distinct from study of the state of the language at any one stage in its development (so-called *synchronic* linguistics). Grammars which aim to describe 20th-century or 16th-century English should do so without reference to the state of the language at any other time. Indeed many linguists would feel that synchronic descriptions are prerequisites for diachronic descriptions. In practice descriptive linguists have concentrated upon the present form of the language rather than older forms, and the intense scrutiny to which languages like English have been subjected in the last fifty years has resulted in a better knowledge of some aspects that were known partially before and the discovery of regularities in the language that were scarcely known at all previously. Of course, the languages of Europe have been examined for centuries and much of a linguistic description is very familiar in spite of the new principles being followed. Descriptive linguistics has been most revealing in its application to the lesser-known languages. Since they are rarely taught, however, these languages need not concern us here.

A second principle stems from the dissatisfaction of linguists with the fact that examples cited in some older grammars seemed somewhat far removed from current usage and could not be verified. Examples given in support of a particular analysis may have been constructed by the grammarian himself. By contrast there were other features of language which were known to occur and yet which found no place in the grammars, perhaps because they could not be conveniently included within the analysis, perhaps because the grammarian, unaccustomed to looking closely at the language in use, was unaware of their existence.

If linguistics was to be made a rigorous study, then nothing as subjective as this could be permitted. The evidence for linguistic statements should be available to all who cared to consider it. It should not be locked away in the mind of the grammarian. Only in this way could any degree of objectivity be attained. If the linguist was to make a hypothesis about the structure of a language, both the data on the basis of which the hypothesis was formulated and the further data against which it was checked should be available to the outsider. This was necessary if the validity of his conclusion was to be evaluated. It is largely in this sense that linguistics can be called a science. It was believed by some linguists that all linguistic descriptions should be based on data obtained from a corpus of recorded language. They set out to record extensive examples of speech (since they considered speech primary) and to produce an exhaustive description of the language in that corpus. Fries's 'The Structure of English' was based on recorded telephone conversations and the spoken part of Quirk's 'Survey of English Usage' is similarly based on recordings. Such a requirement forces the linguist to observe the way people really do speak their language. He avoids basing his description on what he or they *think* they say. In practice the need to use a defined corpus as the material for description is no longer entirely accepted. No corpus will contain everything that the linguist should include in his description. In any case, to emphasize the necessity for starting the analysis of a language from a collected corpus is to imply a belief in inductivism that has scarcely ever been adhered to in practice. Most linguists would now accept that this principle is satisfied if the linguist supports his analyses with extensive data. To have a corpus available might be valuable for the linguist who needs to check his hypotheses, but he does not need to restrict himself to examples drawn from it. It is in any case probably more fruitful for him to submit his analyses to other linguists. They are more likely to produce examples that will require him to modify or abandon his analysis. The principle requires then that language analysis should be closely related to reliable data.

The third related principle demands that, just as the linguist should not be subjective in his choice of data, neither should he be subjective in his attitude towards it. That is to say, it is not the function of a linguist to evaluate the language that he is describing. He is a descriptive linguist and his name implies that he is not there to lay down norms, at least not norms based in any personal opinions about the beauty, correctness, logicality or otherwise of some part of the language. That grammarians have in the past tended to do just this is reflected in the popular notion of the meaning of the word 'grammar'. For most people, educated and uneducated alike, grammar means 'correct usage'. Such a belief may be traceable more to schoolmasters and school grammars than to scholars' grammars, but most grammars have aimed to describe a 'standard' form and to preserve it against influences which would be considered harmful. Forms found in written language have been especially valued. Rules of correctness have been established by the use of arguments based on

Latin grammar. With the historical bias of many grammars, dying forms have been defended and current usage has been condemned as corruption. Efforts have been made to defend the language against the natural process of change. Since speech is most productive of change, it has been commonly thought of as 'ungrammatical'. Education has often been devoted largely to the attempt to eradicate the regional and social variations, which occur principally in speech.

These are the attitudes characterized by the linguist as *prescriptive*. He objects to them because they generally introduce non-linguistic evaluations into linguistic discussions. Objections to the use of certain forms and the encouragement of other forms are usually based on social judgments, even where they are rationalized in linguistic terms. For the linguist all occurring forms, whether spoken by few or many, by educated or uneducated, by Americans or Englishmen, are equally legitimate as subjects for his attention. He will see the varieties of English as different but no one variety as superior. Again, most linguists devote themselves to a standard educated form of the language, but this does not imply any belief in its superiority. It ensures a continuity of research and deals with the forms of widest use and of greatest interest to those learning English as a foreign language. The linguist, then, observes language in use, records it and tries to discover the structure that it has. He does not pass judgment on the language. It follows that he cannot reject any part of what he finds. If he is truly descriptive, he must include in his description all that he has recorded.[18]

While all linguists would not attach equal importance to each of these three principles—data-oriented, synchronic, descriptive study —all linguistic descriptions accept one or more of them. From our point of view as teachers they are important because they all tend to draw the linguist's attention to contemporary language, and to lead him to observe all aspects of language more closely than has ever been the case in the past. The observation will be made the more efficient by the availability of modern equipment which enables the linguist to preserve speech which, in the past, was transitory. As the number of linguists carrying out descriptive research increases, we can hope for an increasing flow of information about the way in which the languages we teach are used. Our present knowledge may not be

---

[18] This statement requires some modification, since the linguist does not normally attempt to describe false starts, changes of structure, hesitations, repetitions, pauses and other 'distortions' which are a feature of natural speech. Even linguistic science normalizes its data to this extent.

wrong so much as incomplete, and as gaps in our knowledge of a language are slowly filled in, so we as language teachers should be able to increase the degree of systematization of our teaching.

1.4.1. Phonetics

It is perhaps in the area of phonetics that misconceptions about language are most commonly found. If one was to ask people certain questions about their pronunciation, they would almost certainly give answers that would not coincide with a recording of their actual speech performance—at least as long as they did not know that they were being recorded. If one asked about *their* pronunciation of certain words and subsequently about the 'correct' pronunciation of those words, we would find that the two answers would be the same. Most educated speakers have some sense of what is 'correct' and the conviction that this correctness is found in their own speech.

1.4.1.1. '*Dropped aitches*'.   This can be illustrated by two examples from English. Most English speakers would defend passionately the statement that *him* is pronounced [him]—that is with an 'h'. The suggestion that they might 'drop the "h" ' would be taken as implying that their speech was generally sub-standard and they, therefore, uneducated. Yet the fact is that in the stream of speech *him* is almost always pronounced [ɪm], and indeed to pronounce 'h' would be to risk sounding unnatural. Part of the problem lies in the fact that when we are talking about the word *him*, when we are using it in isolation, it is inevitably stressed and this fact is the clue to the way in which we say this word. Personal pronouns are very commonly unstressed in English and when this is the case *him* is pronounced [ɪm]. However, we may put the sentence stress on the pronoun for special emphasis. In this case the usual pronunciation for educated speakers is [hɪm]. So we may contrast:

(1)   I gáve it to him.
            [ɪm]
and
(2)   I gave it to hím.
            [hɪm]

1.4.1.2. *Weak forms in English*.   These two sentences also provide examples of another aspect of English pronunciation well-known to linguistics and some teachers but quite strange to the man in the street. There are a number of monosyllabic words whose pronuncia-

tions are usually quite different from what they are commonly thought
to be. The word *to* is thought to rhyme with *too* and *two* and indeed
if this sentence was now read aloud the three words would be homo-
phonous—[tu:]. However, in (1) and (2) above, *to* is not pronounced
in this way. In fact there are two distinct pronunciations.

In (1) it is [tʊ]—the vowel being like that in *good*—[gʊd].

In (2) it is [tə]—the vowel being like that in *a*—[ə].

The word *to* is one of many in English which have one pronunciation
when they are stressed and another when they are unstressed. This
example is complicated by the fact that there are two unstressed
pronunciations. The vowel in *to* is [ʊ] when it is followed by a
vowel and [ə] when it is followed by a consonant. Where a word
has a stressed and unstressed form like this the unstressed form is
known as the *weak form*. There are at least 50 monosyllabic words in
English which have one or more weak forms. They include auxiliary
verbs, *can*, *was*, *were*, *must*, personal pronouns, *them*, *you*, prepositions, *to*, *at*, *from*, the articles, *a*, *an*, *the*, and conjunctions, *and*, *but*.
As with *him* the key matter here is whether or not the word in question is stressed. In by far the majority of their occurrences these
words are not stressed and therefore have their weak form. Yet what
is commonly thought of as the correct pronunciation is what is in
practice the stressed form. The 'correct' form therefore is that one
which occurs least.

We can see that where the linguist observes current speech closely
he discovers that the facts are very different from what they are
popularly held to be. An educated native speaker of English asked to
read aloud a written text—even a dialogue—is likely to be dominated
by his notions of what the correct pronunciation should be. The
result will be something quite unlike natural speech. The teacher
who asks a native speaker of the language he is teaching to record
his tapes for him cannot be sure that he is going to get an accurate
model for his pupils—indeed it is more likely that he will not. The
need for teachers to be fully aware of how the language is really
spoken is the greater. If one is to teach speech then it is necessary
that the model of speech one is aiming at should be the natural
speech of native speakers of that language. If the teacher has the
wrong ideas about English pronunciation in the two areas mentioned
above, if he aims to get a 'correct' pronunciation of these words
whenever they are used by his pupils, then his pupils are going to
acquire a pronunciation which to the ordinary Englishman will
sound foreign in some indefinable way. Since many languages do not

have vowel reduction even where they have different degrees of stress, as in English, this is an aspect of English which students find particularly difficult and which therefore requires strenuous attention from the teacher and a good acquaintance with the facts.[19]

1.4.1.3. *French nasal vowels.* We can mention briefly another example of the usefulness, indeed the necessity, of accurate observation of language use. It was pointed out above that languages change, and a recent survey of French pronunciation charted the degree of change in the French vowel system.[20] The survey was really sociolinguistic, being concerned to establish the most common pronunciations in the different regions of France. It is not easy to find clear discussion of what model of pronunciation is used in English schools in the teaching of French. Perhaps there is not sufficient awareness of the range of educated pronunciations in France for the issue ever to have been raised. But if we assume that educated Parisian French is our model, then this survey produces one striking piece of evidence for change in the target that is usually set for our pupils. In our teaching we usually distinguish between the sounds [ɛ̃] and [œ̃] as in *brin* and *brun*. Since neither of these nasal vowels occur in English they both present problems to the English learner of French. First he has difficulty in producing nasal vowels at all—rather than $a+n$, $e+n$ and so on. Secondly, even when he can produce a nasal vowel he has the problem of distinguishing between these two, rather similar vowels. Yet if Deyhime's facts are accurate then this second problem need never arise, for of educated Parisians only 24 per cent actually make the distinction between [ɛ̃] and [œ̃]. For the remainder there is one nasal vowel only—[ɛ̃]. The pronunciation taught to our pupils could well be simplified therefore, and not only will this make the learning of French one little bit easier, it will also result in the acquisition of a more accurate variety of French.

1.4.2. Grammar

In the field of grammar new information is harder to come by. This is largely because scholarly grammars of the principal European languages have been available for a long time and they represent very detailed study, so that totally unexamined areas of grammar are

---

[19] There is more discussion of this point in the next chapter, pp. 38–41.
[20] G. Deyhime, 'Enquête sur la Phonologie du Français Contemporain' (*Linguistique*, 1 and 2, 1967).

rare. Much linguistic work on these languages may be a reformulation of what had already been described. Details of analysis, organization of description, even theoretical principles may be different from more traditional approaches, but when looked at from the point of view of the teacher, the resulting description may seem very familiar. For the teacher's practical purposes there may not be much in a linguist's description that he did not already know. We need not be surprised at this. Some linguists may have seen the so-called traditional grammarians as very wrong-headed, but they were well able to discover the important structural elements of the languages they examined.

1.4.2.1. *Description not prescription.* So, what can one expect from the linguist's careful observation of the language in use? In the first place, and least importantly, the linguist will stand out against some of the absurder prescriptions of the grammarians. The familiar and popular discussions of the correctness of certain usages have no place in linguistic circles. The linguist will accept whatever is the most common usage. He would not wish to exclude any of the following from his description of English:

He is taller than me	(He is taller than I)
The girl that he is interested in	(The girl in whom he is interested)
We will be there soon	(We shall be there soon)
The thought of him dying upsets me	(The thought of his dying upsets me)

There is little point in discussing such examples at length. It is obvious that the content of teaching will be changed if it is based on truly descriptive grammars. Whether English is taught as a mother-tongue or as a foreign language, there is little justification for repeating the old prescriptions. Indeed for the native speaker of English the whole thing is, of course, something of a joke.

1.4.2.2. *Tense and adverbs in English.* What may be more useful to the teacher are the linguist's investigations into aspects of grammar that have hitherto received very little attention. Since the foreign language teacher is concerned to convey the regularities of a language to his pupils, the range of what he can teach systematically is extended if new regularities can be discovered. As was mentioned above, there may not seem to be much scope for this kind of study, since the languages with which we are concerned here have already received very close attention. But an example of newly available information about English can be cited to show what is possible.

In the teaching of English as a foreign language by oral, inductive methods it has long been the practice to introduce the verbal system by presenting the tense forms one at a time and working successively through the different meanings of each tense form by practising it in co-occurrence with certain adverbial expressions which brought out the chronological relations of the verb form. Where adverbial expressions like *now* (i.e. present), *yesterday* (past), *to-morrow* (future), were not used, then the situational context was so arranged as to make the chronological meaning of the verb equally unambiguous. The presence of the adverbials was seen, not as being required if the sentences were to be samples of natural English, but as a peda- gogic device to bring out the meanings that were potentially present in the verb forms whether or not an adverbial was present. The pupils learn that a tense has certain meanings. The adverbials are used as an aid to comprehension.

A recent piece of research examines the co-occurence relations which exist between the various types of temporal adverbials and the tenses of English.[21] The research is based on an actual corpus of material. It challenges the view that the meanings lie in the verbs alone and suggests that the time relations are specified by the verb and adverb forms together—that the verbs alone often cannot carry the features of time. Indeed if it is not dominated by an adverbial, or if the chronological significance is not clear from the situation, then the verb is very likely to be ambiguous. A verb may be dominated by an adverbial which is not actually in the same sentence, but which may have occurred several sentences previously and not have been cancelled, as it were, by the subsequent occurrence of some contrary expression of time. If a tense does not have a chronological meaning so much as certain possibilities of co-occurrence with time adverbials, the teacher must ask himself, not 'What meanings of these tenses shall I teach and what adverbials shall I select to highlight these meanings?' but 'What patterns of co-occurrence of adverbials and tense do we find in English?' Given the answer to this question, the teacher can then arrange them in some order of priority for teaching purposes. Not all of them will be of equal importance.

The information about this provided in Crystal's article cannot easily be summarized here. It is shown that for each tense examined—

[21] D. Crystal, 'Specification and English Tenses' (*Journal of Linguistics*, 2/1, 1966).

present, past, perfect, pluperfect, conditional, future—certain chronological meanings do not *need* any specification by an adverbial, though it may occur, but that in each case most of the meanings require the presence of an appropriate adverbial. For example, the so-called present tenses (simple and progressive) may be unmarked for time, one might say they are *timeless*, in which case no adverbial is necessary. On the other hand where they are used to refer to past, present or future events they must be accompanied by a temporal adverbial. What is surprising is that 70 per cent of the temporal meanings established *do* require adverbial specification. The information provided here is clearly most valuable for the teacher of English as a foreign language. As well as giving him a different view of the relationship between tense and temporal adverb, the article provides him with a comprehensive list of temporal meanings of verbs and the adverbial expressions which specify those meanings. Simply as a reference list for the teacher this is very useful. He will choose to ignore some of the meanings—they are often used for particular stylistic effects—but with the aid of this information the teacher can ensure that he has omitted nothing that is important.

1.5. *Langue* and *parole*

Most linguists accept a distinction that was first made explicit by the Swiss linguist, F. De Saussure, namely, that there is a difference between language as the speech act and language as a system by which we succeed in understanding or producing utterances. For de Saussure a language (*langue*) is shared by all the members of a particular speech community. It is an institutionalized element of their collective consciousness, and only because everyone shares in it is it possible for them to understand one another. If one was to examine the actual utterances of a group, everything that was common to their speech would be *langue*. If one took away what was idiosyncratic or innovational, *langue* would remain. *Langue* must, by definition, be stable and systematic. Society conveys the regularities of *langue* to the child so that he becomes able to function as a member of the speech community. *La langue* 'est l'ensemble des habitudes linguistiques qui permettent à un sujet de comprendre et de se faire comprendre'.[22] The habits are essentially social, although every individual participates in them.

By contrast each utterance, each act of speaking, is a unique

[22] F. de Saussure, *Cours de Linguistique Générale* (Paris, Payot, 1916).

event. There is a complex and changing relationship between the language and situational and personal features, which means that no one act of language—whether productive or receptive—is ever quite like another. The act of speech is distinguished by much that is the product of our personality, our temperament, or our physical incapacities and by those distortions in our speech which are not part of the system of language. It is because there are elements that are not shared by all the speech community that the act of speech is considered distinct from the *langue* and is termed *parole*. Given that there is a good deal that is idiosyncratic or not fully institutionalized, *parole* cannot be stable and systematic. It is, therefore, not considered suitable as the subject of the linguist's study.

A distinction of a similar sort has recently been made by a contemporary linguist, N. Chomsky. His terms are competence (*langue*) and performance (*parole*). They are not exact equivalents, since Chomsky would not accept that competence could be described in terms of collective consciousness. On the contrary, competence is seen as a set of processes possessed by the individual and developed in him as part of his maturation. The function of the community in this process is little more than that of a triggering mechanism. Nonetheless it is under the heading of competence and *langue* that we shall find all that is most systematic about a language. Both Chomsky and de Saussure would say that it is this systematic and stable element of language that the linguist must set out to describe. *Parole* (performance), being unstable, is not susceptible to adequate description. For Chomsky at least, there is no point in looking at *parole* since much that needs to be said about *langue* cannot be observed there. For de Saussure, while *parole* might not be the object of the study, it does provide the data from which statements about *langue* can be made.

In practice the study of *parole* for its own sake is not excluded by linguists, but such study will inevitably produce different kinds of descriptions from those which are produced as descriptions of *langue*. Most linguists, like earlier grammarians, have concerned themselves with *langue*—with the shared regularities of the language—even where they have based their study on a corpus of some kind. In spite of other differences grammarians, structural and generative linguists are all alike in this respect. However, some linguists, by definition from within the ranks of those who have looked closely at *parole*, have sought to establish rules that do not have the general application of the rules of *langue* but are restricted in ways that can be related to non-linguistic criteria. These are regularities of which we are rarely conscious even as native speakers of the language. They cannot, therefore, be discovered by introspection but are only revealed by close examination of language in use—*parole*. They would emphasize the linguistic variations relatable to regional and social factors, to the medium of communication, to the situation, to the purpose and personality of the participants, to matters of pathology and physiology and so on.[23] In a sense in examining these aspects of language the linguist takes for granted the existence of the general rules of *langue*.

1.5.1. Parallel decisions in language teaching

All this may seem rather far from the world of language teaching and yet it is not, for the teacher has always been faced with a very similar dichotomy and therefore a similar choice. It is the degree of predictability of the language learner's future needs that will determine the extent to which the teacher can adopt a *parole*-based approach to teaching. What the language teacher has traditionally done and in most cases what he still does—although by more modern methods—is to teach what the grammarian or linguist has described: the *langue*. He sets out to enable the pupil to acquire a practical mastery of the rules by which we receive and construct correct sentences in a given language.[24] He disregards the use to which the pupil will eventually put the language. It is supposed that anyone who has mastered the system will be able to learn how to apply it to the situations in which he finds himself. Teaching starts from the language and the syllabus gives the highest priority to linguistic criteria. Wherever accurate prediction is difficult, and this is most typically the case with language teaching in schools, there is probably a strong argument for orienting the content of language teaching to descriptions of *langue*. In schools predictability is at best limited. We have already replaced a literary by a more practical vocabulary and we have recognized a need for the teaching of spoken language, although what we teach is still not a very true sample of speech. Pupils in schools will, however, be so diverse in their eventual use

[23] The social parameters relevant to the analysis of language use are described more fully in Chapter 5.

[24] Many traditional approaches seem aimed not so much at a practical mastery of the rules as revealed by fluent performance as at an explicit knowledge of the rules governing language performance.

of the language they are learning that more precise predictions than these will be difficult to achieve. It seems likely that descriptions of *langue* will always have an important function in school language learning.

More accurate prediction is most typically achieved where languages are learned outside the school system. Adult learners, for example, frequently have a clear purpose in learning a foreign language. In this case the teacher's approach can be close to that of the linguist who sets out to describe *parole*. He asks what notions this learner will have to express, what channel of communication he will employ, what restrictions are imposed on his choice of language by the topics and by features of the situation. When the aims of the learner have been defined, it will be seen that some parts of the language system are functionally more important than others. By referring to the linguist's descriptions of *parole*, the teacher will be able to ensure that he is teaching those parts of the *langue* which have the greatest practical value for his pupils. What is more, instead of teaching the language in a situationally neutral context, he can present it in a context which replicates as closely as possible the one for which the language is being learned. It is no longer necessary to teach the entire system. The priorities of a language course may be reversed and items of language may be included or excluded solely because the needs of the pupils, and not the overall structure of the language, have been taken as the starting-point. What is learned may be smaller in quantity and greater in relevance.

The idea of specialized language courses is not, of course, a new one. What is new is the realization that has come with greater linguistic sophistication that the special languages are differentiated not only in their vocabulary but also in their grammar. We can look forward to the time when the linguist provides us with detailed analyses of the forms of language needed for special purposes. As for the general courses usually provided in schools, while it may never be possible to adopt a *parole*-based approach, it should not be beyond our ingenuity to construct materials that enable the learner to acquire the general system of the language through examples that have high practical value.

1.6. Summary

We have already seen that there are different relationships between linguistics and language teaching. There are points at which the two must arrive at their conclusions quite separately, however tempting it may be to argue that one follows from the other. In places, issues before the linguist and the teacher seem to parallel and reflect one another, and here the language teacher may benefit from an understanding of the linguist's view. Finally, the linguist can be of more substantial use to the teacher by making available descriptions of newly studied aspects of language or new and better analyses of more familiar areas. In this case the new information will be useful in extending our definition of the linguistic content of language learning and in helping to determine the most effective pedagogic segmentation and sequencing. These differences have arisen from our discussions of the linguist's view of the nature of language, but as our investigation extends into the whole field of linguistics we shall find that the relationships are similarly varied throughout.

2
Phonetics and phonology

2.1. Introduction: the teacher as a model

Linguistics attempts to make accurate statements about the system of language currently in use in any speech community. We have seen that in the area of phonetics this may result in the correcting of certain common misconceptions about the pronunciation of a language and an up-to-date charting of the changes in the sound system. Of course it is not the aim of phonetics simply to rectify false notions. Rather, this is what is achieved in the attempt to provide a comprehensive and exhaustive description of the forms in which the grammar and lexis of a language are realized. It is this description which is of great value to the language teacher, since it is in effect a precise analysis of the model of pronunciation to be presented to the learner and to be acquired by him. It provides the teacher with an inventory of items and also with a detailed description of the articulations by means of which the sounds are produced. It is in this respect that phonetics provides the teacher with information that goes well beyond what he is likely to know informally about the pronunciation of the language. Without training in phonetics and lacking a phonetician's description, one would have only the most rudimentary ideas about the articulation of sounds in a particular language. If he does not know or have access to information on the articulatory phonetics of the target language, the teacher is strictly limited in what he can do in the teaching of pronunciation. He can require of his pupils the most accurate imitation of his own pronunciation, but since achievement rarely measures up to aims, this is likely to result in persistent pronunciation error, especially in those areas of pronunciation where difficulties are known to occur.[1] Without further knowledge remedial pronunciation teaching is difficult. There is, however, an important point to be made about the teacher's own pronunciation.

If we can anticipate that the achievement of learners will fall short of the model that is put before them it is all the more important

---

[1] See Chapter 7, *Error and the Mother-Tongue.*

that that model should be as accurate a sample of speech as possible. The teacher who is relatively uninformed about phonetics risks transmitting quite serious errors to his pupils, especially in the earlier stages of language learning where a defensible case can be made out for slowing one's articulation below a normal conversational rate. The danger lies in the phonetic consequences that may result from a slow articulation if the teacher is not fully conscious of what else besides rate of speech needs to be controlled. English provides an excellent example here. It is possible to slow speech in English to a small degree while still retaining accuracy elsewhere in the phonetics. On the other hand, it is very easy even for a trained teacher to make mistakes of several kinds in doing it. In the first place he may disturb the rhythm of English speech. It is a characteristic of English that in uninterrupted speech it is the accented syllables that occur at more or less regular intervals of time. The period of time between the accented syllables will tend to be the same however many relatively less accented syllables occur. Two sentences having the same number of syllables but a different number of stressed syllables may be of different duration:

The first six have all won a prize.

There were prizes for six of them.[2]

Alternatively different numbers of syllables may occupy the same period of time:

I told you to lay it on the floor.

I told you to lay it down.

When one deliberately slows speech there is a tendency to reduce the distinction between the time spent on stressed and unstressed syllables, and if the time on each becomes more or less equalized then the teacher has turned English into something much closer to a syllable-timed language, that is, one in which the syllables, not the stresses, occur at regular intervals. If we may assume for a moment that the learner is a native speaker of such a syllable-timed language— French, for example—then the teaching itself will be reinforcing his tendency to try and speak English as if it too was syllable-timed. The

[2] See A.C. Gimson, *An Introduction to the Pronunciation of English* (London, Edward Arnold, 1962) p. 237.

difference is, of course, one that regularly causes difficulties for the English learner of French.

In the second place, and closely related to this first point, the stress system itself also becomes distorted. Analyses of English stress generally agree that there are at least three levels of stress. If speech is slowed down excessively it may have the effect that each syllable comes to be produced rather as if it was occurring in isolation. The levels of stress will then not be distinct from one another, since a syllable or monosyllabic word occurring on its own is given primary stress. The sentence will in this extreme but not uncommon case contain a sequence of primary stresses. In itself it is undesirable that levels of stress should not be learned from the beginning, but resulting from this is a third distortion. As we saw in the first chapter there are many words where the vowel quality depends on the stress given to the syllable. If it has primary stress then a full vowel is used; if it is unstressed then it may be weakened. So *can* may be [kæn] when stressed but [kən] or even [kn] when unstressed. What is more, the distortion may occur not only in words which do commonly have different pronunciations but also in those which in normal speech are unchanged. The word *interesting* is commonly [ɪntrəstɪŋ] but in bad teaching may become [ɪntrestɪŋ] or even with the addition of a syllable [ɪnterestɪŋ]. Clearly the orthography has had some influence here but also perhaps the feeling that the [ə] represents a weakened [e].

Every English teacher has to judge what speed of speech he should adopt. Many will feel inclined to speak more slowly in the classroom than they would in natural conversation. If they are not to present a completely distorted model to the learner, they will have to control very carefully their rhythm, stress pattern and vowel qualities. When any of these mistakes are made, it is interesting that they go unrecognized because they are not what are conventionally thought of as 'pronunciation errors'. One too readily thinks of error either in terms of a sound foreign to the language being spoken—the Englishman's [ɜ], as in *bird*, being substituted for [œ] in French *sœur*—or of choice of the wrong sound—pronouncing *her* as if it was *hair* in English. The problems that arise when speech is slowed are problems of connected speech, not of isolated word pronunciation. Even a teacher for whom English is the mother tongue will make the mistakes that have been described above unless he is conscious of the phonetics of connected speech. The distortions that would occur would pass unnoticed because they are appropriate to slow speech and single word utterances. Yet it is very doubtful whether we want the learner to acquire the forms of slow speech, since he will not recognise that his phonetics has to change when he is speaking at a more normal pace. It is far safer to reduce speed only to the point at which phonetic accuracy can be retained. To enable him to do this the teacher must have available an adequate description of natural speech. Without it he will find it difficult to judge what is correct and what is not correct. Too many teachers have been trained to believe that pronunciation involves little more than a list of sounds.

2.2. Intonation

In talking of phonetics so far the emphasis has been on what have been called the 'sounds' of a language, and probably what has been said has been familiar to many who have no knowledge of linguistics, because phonetics has long existed and been taught independently from linguistics. Information has been available for incorporation into teaching for quite a long time. This is not true of another aspect of phonetics—intonation. This is an aspect of speech in which the question of *what* exactly it is that one wishes to teach has been undescribed and indeed is still thought by many teachers to be undescribable. It is by no means uncommon to meet the point of view that intonation is idiosyncratic to a large degree and certainly not systematic enough for anything approaching a comprehensive description to be attempted. That we can understand the significance of different patterns of intonation is firm evidence that intonation *is* systematic. Because we share the system with other members of our speech community we are able to understand what they attempt to convey through intonation. We do misunderstand the meaning of intonation patterns in a foreign language, and this shows that intonation is a conventional system shared by a particular speech community. This is not to say that it is easy to discover what the regularities are, but a good deal more can be and is being achieved than might have been thought in the past. Earlier, approximate statements of somewhat doubtful validity are being refined as a result of having been tested against language data, with the result that descriptions for the teacher are becoming available.

This is not the place to attempt detailed descriptions of any one system of intonation, but one can indicate just what kind of information might be found in such a description. In English any study of intonation must be able to describe the movements of pitch which occur in the uttering of a sentence. Whatever the descriptive framework that the linguist will choose to employ, he will have to be able to show the characteristic pitch movement on one stressed syllable, commonly a falling or rising movement, but also often falling-rising or rising-falling. This stressed syllable, often called the *nucleus*, may occur at any point in the sentence, although it is frequently the last stressed syllable. In addition, the description must include the common patterns of pitch on stressed and unstressed syllables preceding the nucleus itself. In fact the alternative combinations are numerous and complex. Through his description the linguist sets before the teacher the formal potentialities that the speaker can employ, and this will constitute an inventory of items that the pupil has to learn, whether in a controlled fashion or not.

However, the form of intonation contours is only part of what the teacher would like to know about the target language. He must also have a clear understanding of the meaning(s) of particular contours. When we compare languages, we may see that similar stress and pitch sequences function differently in each language, and that one language may contain patterns of intonation that do not occur at all in the other. In English, intonation may be grammatical or attitudinal. It may be grammatical in two senses. The function of a sentence may be modified by intonation to achieve a meaning that could have been achieved by giving the sentence a different grammatical form:[3]

He often mows the lawn.

This is grammatically a declarative sentence and is here functioning as a statement.

He often mows the lawn.

This is grammatically declarative but is here functioning as a question in just the same way as the grammatically interrogative sentence:

Does he often mow the lawn?

There is a second sense in which intonation may be grammatical. It may happen that a sentence is grammatically ambiguous and only

---

[3] The markings in the following examples should be interpreted as follows:

\	High fall
/	High rise
v	Fall-rise
ı	Non-nuclear accented syllable (head)
ı	Tone group boundary

by means of intonation can we be clear of what grammatical structure we should give the sentence and thereby disambiguate it.

We didn't go to the museum because it was raining.

The different structures can be revealed by paraphrase.

(1) We did go to the museum (but not because it was raining).

(2) We didn't go to the museum (because it was raining).

However, such paraphrases would be unnecessary in speech.

(1) We ˈ didn't go to the museum because it was ráining.

(2) We ˈ didn't go to the museum | because it was ráining.

It is relatively rare in English for the grammatical structure of a sentence to impose restrictions on the intonation in this way, although it might be true to say that certain grammatical structures are commonly associated with certain intonation patterns.

It is not particularly difficult to assign meaning to intonation patterns in the functions so far described. Precision is more difficult to achieve when intonation has an attitudinal function. In this case intonation is not changing the grammatical function of the sentence, nor is it disambiguating its structure. It is rather adding something to the meaning already conveyed by grammar and lexis. Typically what is added involves the attitudes and emotions of the speaker towards his subject-matter, towards the hearer and even towards himself. By selecting the place of the nucleus, the type of pitch movement and the overall contour of the sentence, the speaker displays emphasis, doubt, surprise, determination, shock, sarcasm, incredulity and so on in varying degrees and with a variety of nuances, which are not often difficult to understand but usually very difficult to describe exactly. One has only to consider the different ways of saying a monosyllabic word like *yes* and then to imagine the different contexts in which each may occur to realize how difficult it is to generalize about the meaning of a particular intonation pattern. It would be safer to say that the meaning of an English intonation can only be determined with any precision when taken with the sentence with which it is used and indeed with the entire linguistic and situational context. Much confusion has arisen in the past from attempts to describe the attitudinal function of intonation, with careless use of labels for attitudes, no control of other factors such as facial expression, gesture, voice quality etc., and inadequate checking of the phonetician's judgment with the feelings of other speakers of the language. In spite of the difficulties a considerable body of descriptive material—on English at least—is now available, and even a certain amount of pedagogic material.

2.2.1. Intonation in language teaching

Once such descriptions are available the question arises of how use can be made of them in foreign language teaching. The production of teaching materials involves decisions on the selection of items to be taught and their ordering. So far this has been done on the basis either of the grammar of the language or of its vocabulary, the reason being that only here has research been done that is adequate to enable one to make the decisions. To a limited extent phonetic criteria have been used too. But the question of teaching intonation systematically, attempting to make general decisions on teaching content open to criteria concerning intonation, has been almost completely ignored. The justification for this has been that the necessary descriptions were just not available. This argument can hardly be employed now. There is no reason, *a priori*, why the general structuring of a foreign language course should not be attempted with the controlled introduction of intonation patterns, just as there is already controlled introduction of grammar and lexis. It would increase the number of variables to be manipulated and we would have to settle the priorities between the different levels of language and indeed between these and non-linguistic criteria. Still, even if course grading entirely in terms of intonation might prove impracticable, a deliberate restriction on the range of intonation patterns introduced in the early stages and subsequent presentation of new intonation patterns one or a few at a time might prove to be a practicable application of descriptions of intonation. The alternative is to leave intonation uncontrolled in general oral teaching, as it is largely at present, but to make provision for systematic practice drilling as the course proceeds. In this way the importance of intonation is not neglected and yet the general course content need not depend on what is desirable by way of intonation. In point of fact the trend towards greater use of dialogue in language teaching, and the attempt to make drilling resemble natural language use, make it possible to integrate intonation and grammar practice to an extent that suggests great potentialities for the teaching of intonation in the future.

It may be thought by some readers that more importance is being attached here to intonation than is justified. But perhaps such an attitude does no more than reflect the extent to which intonation has in the past been ignored in language teaching. In situations where people are learning a spoken language with a view to fairly extensive social contact in that language, intonation assumes major importance. I would place the need for accurate intonation above the need for accurate sounds.

A foreigner speaking English may not be able to pronounce the *-ng*, [ŋ], sound. For *thing*, [θɪŋ], he may always say *thin*, [θɪn]. As we look at this example we may think that the hearer will believe he has said *thin*. In practice he is most unlikely to interpret what he hears in this way. In a sentence like:

What's that thin over there?

the fact that *thin* is an adjective and could not appear after *that*, the general semantics of the sentence and the gestures and other para-linguistic features that might accompany the utterance would make it quite clear that the intended word was *thing* not *thin*. The hearer may not even be aware that he has had to disregard a faulty pro-nunciation. Communication is scarcely ever impaired by the mis-pronunciation of a single sound.

With intonation the position is quite different. Errors of two kinds may be made. A pattern may be used which is clearly not one that occurs in the target language. In this case the hearer will either simply not understand or will interpret it according to that intonation in his own language that shares some feature with it. He may or may not arrive at the right interpretation. The other kind of mistake is perhaps more probable. The hearer may not even be aware that there is an error in the speaker's utterance. Most people probably think that all intonational features are universal. They are not on their guard for possible error and will not notice when one occurs. Instead they will put their usual interpretation on what they have heard and understand something quite different from what the speaker intended to convey. Nothing in the grammar and vocabulary of the utterance, nor in the context, will rectify this, since, in English at least, none of these things determine the intonation of a sentence. Intonation is largely additive. In many languages it does not cast doubt on the validity of a statement to raise the pitch on the last stressed syllable, but in English it does. It may even turn the statement into a question. Especially in the attitudinal functions of intonation, the speaker may convey a meaning which is quite different from that intended, the effect of which he may not be aware of. How many foreigners have been thought to be rude and uncouth when in fact they were probably employing an intonation pattern which had a perfectly acceptable meaning in the mother tongue, but unfortunately had connotations of rudeness and uncouthness in the foreign language? It is easy to be humorous about a foreigner's intonation. In fact, incorrect intonation may seriously hamper communication at any levels. That is why intonation deserves more serious attention than it gets.

2.3. Phonetics and phonology

Many language text-books contain a list of the sounds of the language being taught. Often for each sound a symbol is given in a phonetic transcription. The transcription used for English in this book shows that English has twenty vowels, twenty-two consonants and two semi-vowels, while French has sixteen vowels, seventeen consonants and three semi-vowels.[4] The list of symbols appears to be for the sound system what the alphabet is for the orthography. Most people without training in phonetics would assume that just as there is a fixed number of letters for their language to use, there is also a fixed number of sounds. The number of sounds would usually be larger than, but comparable to, the number of letters.

In fact, it is a quite mistaken belief that these lists really represent all the different sounds of the language. We cannot even get by with the use of a word as imprecise as *sound*, although I have so far been using it myself. If one was to listen to the language being spoken and if one wrote down a fresh symbol for every different sound that one heard—if it were even possible to do this—we would end up with an inventory many times larger than the two mentioned above. Many of the noises that we think of as one 'sound' are different both acoustically and in their articulation. An English [b] may be voiced, voiceless or partially devoiced, according to whether it occurs between vowels, finally after a vowel, or initially before a vowel or consonant. The air-pressure that builds up in the articulation of a plosive consonant is normally released through the mouth, but if the [b] is followed by an [m], that is, a nasal consonant with the same place of articulation, the pressure is released through the nasal passage instead. From this it is clear that there is not just one [b] in English.

---

[4] These transcriptions are given in full on pages 231–2. They are *phonemic* rather than *phonetic* transcriptions, but the distinction is not made until page 48.

A close investigation of the vowels and consonants of any language would reveal a similar degree of variability.

Each of these variations is strictly speaking a different sound and the trained ear can hear the differences. If a different symbol were to be used for each sound, they would number hundreds, not forty-four or thirty-six. For an accurate picture of the pronunciation of a language we need to have this kind of detail, and when a phonetician is describing what he observes this closely, he is said to be providing a description of the *phonetics* of the language. Such a description will give us a very comprehensive picture of the native speaker's pronunciation, and since it is presumably the teacher's aim for his pupils to attain a pronunciation like that of the native speaker, he would, ideally at least, wish them to master all that is described. In practice, however, he might not find a description in this form all that usable. Amid such detail it would be very hard to know just where to start. At this stage there is no way of determining what would be most important and what most difficult for the learner. The question of what is most difficult is discussed in Chapter 7. The answer to the question of what is most important is to be found in the fact that the linguist believes that not everything has been said about the pronunciation of a language when the phonetics has been described.

The linguist/phonetician does not stop short at the phonetic statements that we have been discussing so far. He attempts to discover some kind of system operating within the great diversity of sound that occurs in any one language. There is good reason to believe that analyses of pronunciation systems proposed by linguists are not just a construct imposed by them on the data. Most native speakers are quite unaware of the variety of their own pronunciation. Their intuition tells them that the number of significant sounds is far fewer than the hundreds that the phonetician can observe. The lists of the 'sounds' of a language which were produced before the conscious effort was made to develop scientific procedures bear a close resemblance to the lists of *phonemes* that linguists eventually proposed. This suggests that the system has a psychological significance for both the user and the learner of the language.

To investigate the *phonology* or the *phonemics* of a language is to enquire how the different sounds are used to operate the grammar and vocabulary of the language and thereby to convey meaning. If the linguist finds two words which are identical in pronunciation except for one sound, he will accept that the pair of sounds are significantly different and will be satisfied that they constitute separate *phonemes*. On the other hand he will also come across sounds that are phonetically distinct from one another and yet never contrast with each other in such a way as to distinguish one word from another. As long as the two sounds have a reasonable phonetic similarity they will be considered realizations of the same phoneme.

This is most easily understood through an example. The words *pat* and *bat* in English are the same except for the first sound. *pat* begins with [pʰ], a bilabial, voiceless plosive, immediately followed by the puff of air known as aspiration; *bat* begins with [b̥], a bilabial plosive with partial voicing and no aspiration. This is the only difference between the two words, but it is enough to make the two words utterly distinct for any native speaker. We therefore know that /p/ and /b/ are separate phonemes in English.[5] Our examination will also reveal that there are other sounds in English that are rather like this [b] but not quite the same. In a word like *robber* there is a b-like sound between the vowels, only it is voiced throughout. In *mob* the last sound is completely voiceless [b̥]. These are just three phonetically distinct sounds that could possibly be thought of as *b*s. In order to establish that these differences were significant in English, we should have to find pairs of words that were distinguished from one another by such differences in the way that *pat* and *bat* are distinguished by /p/ and /b/. If we substitute [b] or [b̥] for the [b̥] of [mɒb̥], we do not change it into another word, nor would we do so if we substituted the different *b*s for one another in any words. Furthermore, as we look through the language, we observe that there are plenty of other words that begin with a partially voiced [b̥] and still others which end with a voiceless [b̥]. There seems to be a pattern, which we first found in *bat*, *robber* and *mob*, but which is repeated throughout the language. This will lead us to the conclusion that what we have are not different phonemes, but different variations of the phoneme /b/. To these varied realizations of the same phoneme we give the name *allophone*.

From the orginal undifferentiated list of sounds—from the phonetics—the linguist has abstracted a much more limited number of significant sounds, each of which may itself occur in a number of forms. However, in the way they enable the language to operate they

---

[5] Up to this point square brackets have been used for all transcriptions. There is a convention that slanting brackets enclose a phonemic symbol, e.g. /p/, and square brackets a phonetic symbol, e.g. [pʰ]. From now on this convention will be followed throughout.

may be thought of as the same and the differences may be disregarded. In any case the differences go unheard by the native speaker, although he produces them. To acquire a reasonable pronunciation the foreign learner has to develop a mastery of these significant sound distinctions. The aim of pronunciation teaching should be to ensure that the learner has a command of those features that enable the native speaker to perceive phonemic contrasts.

Is it possible to say that instead of teaching the hundreds of sounds of the language, the teacher need only teach the forty-odd significant sounds—the phonemes? Unfortunately it is not as simple as that. Phonemes are essentially abstractions, not concrete entities. If a phoneme always occurred in an identical form, one would be able to talk about teaching a phoneme. We have seen that the symbol /b/ represents several phonetically distinct sounds and the differences may be just as important as the similarities.

This can be seen if we look in still more detail at English plosives. The consonants /b, d, g,/ in English are still often referred to as *voiced* consonants and are contrasted with the *voiceless* plosives /p, t, k,/. From this labelling one might suppose that the crucial phonetic difference between them is one of voicing and that if one taught a group of learners always to voice the one set and to make the other set voiceless, one would have done all that was necessary to establish the phonetic contrast in their speech. A closer analysis of the various ways in which the contrast between these plosive consonants operates will reveal this to be a very superficial and dangerous solution.

In initial position the opposition between voiced and unvoiced often does not exist at all. The first sounds of *tome* and *dome*, for example, may each be voiceless. The distinctive feature here is the aspiration of the /t/ and the lack of it on the /d/. The foreign speaker of English may pronounce these two sounds in quite different ways, but the English-speaking hearer will be listening for the presence or absence of aspiration not for the degree of voicing. Where he hears no aspiration he will believe that he has heard /d/, even if the sound was completely voiceless. *Tome* will be mistaken for *dome*. Voicing is a more important feature where the plosives occur intervocalically. In *writer* /t/ is voiceless, whereas in *rider* /d/ is fully voiced. Here too, however, there is aspiration on the voiceless plosive, weak aspiration in a word like *writer* where it is in initial position in an unstressed syllable, but strong aspiration in a word like *pretend* where the syllable is stressed. In final position voicing is again irrelevant.

In *mat* and *mad* /t/ and /d/ are both voiceless. Since final consonants are often unreleased there is no aspiration to distinguish them either. The native speaker does not hear any difference between these final plosives. What he does hear is a difference in the length in the vowel, /æ/, which precedes them.[6] The /æ/ of *mad* is distinctly longer than the /æ/ of *mat*. It could be said that in final position the phonemic distinction between /t/ and /d/ is realized, not by voicing, but by vowel length. If the learner voices the /d/ his pronunciation will, at the least, be inaccurate. At the worst his utterance may be heard as *madder* or *man*, depending on whether he releases the final voiced consonant or not. To be acceptable the pronunciation of *mad* requires a voiceless final plosive, preceded by a long vowel.

There is no single way of pronouncing each of the six plosives that will lead to a largely accurate pronunciation of English. If a simple solution is demanded, probably the best is to insist that the fortis consonants[7] are always aspirated. This means that final consonants would always have to be released, but learners have a tendency to do this anyway. In view of this, the learner's pronunciation would still have a clear accent, especially since he would be aspirating strongly on unstressed syllables and on /t/ in words like *stem* where there is no aspiration in normal speech. This strategy involves deliberately teaching a faulty pronunciation and many teachers (and linguists) would baulk at going this far in an effort to simplify learning. Ultimately it might prove to have complicated the pupil's task.

If one looks at plosives in French the picture appears a good deal less complex. /p, t, k,/ are always voiceless and never aspirated. /b, d, g,/ are fully voiced in all positions. Each of the phonemes has a more or less consistent pronunciation. The target is simple but the learning is not necessarily so. The English learner of French might appear to have a relatively easy task, since even in his own language he produces fully voiced plosives in intervocalic positions. It is only necessary to teach him to produce this sound in the other positions. It is precisely this that he will find difficult to do, because pronuncia-

---

[6] The reason why the vowel is longer before /d/ than before /t/ is probably that the /t/ is produced with greater muscular energy than the /d/. It is the greater tension required for /t/ that results in the preceding vowel being shorter. The difference in tension between the plosives cannot be heard by ear in the plosives themselves. Although the tenseness of /p, t, k,/ cannot be directly observed, it is thought more accurate to characterize them as more tense than /b, d, g,/ which require less muscular energy. /p, t, k,/ are known as *fortis* consonants, /b, d, g,/ as *lenis* consonants.

[7] See the preceding footnote.

tion problems are not caused only by strange sounds with unaccustomed articulations, but also by familiar sounds in unfamiliar places. Following his English habits, he will produce a voiceless /b, d, g,/ at the beginning and end of words and these will be heard as /p, t, k,/ by the Frenchman, who will be looking for lack of voice as the distinguishing features and will be unimpressed by the existence of another, aspirated set of plosives in the Englishman's speech. To be satisfied by the learner's apparent ability to produce a voiced set of plosives would be to be quite misled as to his ability to pronounce French accurately. The full picture of what needed to be taught would only become clear when allophonic variation was taken into account.

We can see from these examples that it is impossible to know what the really significant features of a phoneme are without examining the relation of contrast with other phonemes. This is very well brought out in the analysis of vowel systems. If we were to hear a single vowel sound, we would have no idea of how to interpret it unless we knew something of the system in which it operated. English has twenty vowels but there are other languages with only five. The same sound would have a different value in each of the languages, even though there might be no phonetic difference. Even languages which have approximately the same kinds of vowel systems do not necessarily draw the boundaries between vowel phonemes in the same places. What is more, the phonetic realizations of one phoneme may overlap those of an adjacent phoneme. The degree of overlapping will certainly vary from one language to another. In brief, vowel phonemes are mutually defining and, as we shall see below,[8] this is important for the teaching as well as the description of vowel systems.

Oral vowels are distinguished from one another principally by vowel quality and length.[9] The relevant articulatory features in vowel production are the relative height of the tongue, the part of the tongue, front or back, engaged in the articulation, and the relative rounding or spreading of the lips. Each of these parameters is a continuum phonetically. The French phoneme /y/, as in *tu*, is pronounced with the front of the tongue high and the lips rounded. It contrasts with /u/, as in *tout*, which has the *back* of the tongue high and the lips rounded, and with /i/, as in *lit*, which has the front of the tongue high, but the lips spread. If the phoneme is to

[8] Pp. 56–7.
[9] The following discussion applies equally well to nasal vowels.

be perceived as /y/ by the hearer, it has to be sufficiently fronted to be distinct from /u/ and sufficiently rounded to be distinct from /i/. Provided these conditions are met, precise phonetic accuracy is probably unimportant, at least as an intermediate goal. Because to the English ear /y/ is auditorily closer to /u/ than to /i/, most English learners of French will probably substitute /u/ for /y/ in the early stages. The spelling will reinforce this tendency. Where in English /u/ follows the semi-vowel /j/, as in words like *duty* /djuti/ or *puma* /pjumə/, the allophone of /u/ is further forward because the front of the tongue has been raised to form /j/. The resemblance of this allophone to French /y/ will lead many English learners to substitute /ju/ for /y/. Words like *tu, du, nu* will be pronounced [tjü], [djü], and [njü].[10] One of the possible strategies in teaching an acceptable pronunciation of /y/ to English speakers is to make use of this existing English allophone.

A complex interaction of quality and quantity is shown in the opposition between /iː/ and /ɪ/ in the English words *bead* and *bid*. When the vowels are followed by a lenis consonant, such as /d/, or by no consonant at all, there is both a qualitative and a quantitative difference between them. /iː/ is a little further forward and closer, the lips a little more spread, the whole articulation rather tenser than with /ɪ/. /iː/ is also noticeably longer. In the words *beat* and *bit*, where the vowels are followed by a fortis consonant, there is no significant length difference, but the quality difference remains. Many foreign learners will bring from their own language a single vowel in this area which may be close in quality to /iː/ and in quantity to /ɪ/. They will find the English phonemes very difficult to separate because they are phonetically close together, perhaps closer than are some sounds that we consider allophones of the same phoneme. As we have seen, it is not the phonetic distance between two sounds that decides whether they are the same or separate phonemes. The learner will probably first succeed in making the distinction where quality and quantity reinforce each other. Working on the hypothesis that /iː/ is a long, tense vowel and /ɪ/ a short lax vowel, he will master the distinction between *bead* and *bid*. But, having learned to associate /ɪ/ with short duration, he will then produce /ɪ/ instead of /iː/ in words like *beat* where the final fortis plosive demands a short preceding vowel. He now has to learn to dissociate the vowel quality from vowel length. It would be quite impossible to know which features

---

[10] The diacritic ¨ indicates that it is the centre of the tongue rather than the back (or front) that is involved in the articulation.

are the most important to acquire, if one did not know the whole system of oppositions.

It is clear from the above that one cannot arrive at an understanding of the task that faces the learner without going into allophonic variation. Neither the 'sounds' with discussion of which I began this section nor the phonemes which were subsequently proposed to replace them can alone provide the basis for an acceptable pronunciation. Certain features of allophones must be insisted upon if phonemic distinctions are to be adequately drawn. Not all allophonic variation will be of equal concern to the teacher. A distinction has been proposed between *intrinsic* and *extrinsic* allophones. Broadly, the difference is that intrinsic allophones are 'natural' (i.e. predictable from their environment without knowledge of the phonology of the language in which they occur), while extrinsic allophones are not. We can generally account for allophonic variation in terms of position in the syllable and influence of adjacent sounds. The latter particularly seem the more predictable. The contact between the tongue and the roof of the mouth in producing /k/ is much further forward in *king* /kɪŋ/ than in *dark* /dɑːk/. This is because in *king* the articulation of the vowel /ɪ/, which involves raising the front of the tongue, is already being anticipated. The reason why such allophonic variation may not be very important to the teacher is that the learner can be expected to produce it without being taught or, indeed, without being aware of the different ways in which he is producing the same phoneme. He will not have to learn to produce a more palatal /k/, because the nature of articulation is such that he will do it automatically before a front vowel.

Other allophones are not natural, in this sense. They therefore have to be learned. The English word *little* contains two distinct kinds of /l/. They never contrast in English and the difference is not phonemic. In /lɪtl/ the initial /l/ is clear. That is to say it has something of the quality of a front vowel. In final position /l/ is said to be *dark*, because it has more the quality of a back vowel. It is perfectly possible to produce a clear /l/ in this position, as is shown by French. The word *table* ends with a dark /l/ in English, but with a clear /l/ in French. Since this sort of variation is not the result of any general conditioning factor, it is to be expected that it will present greater difficulties to the learner than that which we find with intrinsic allophones. Whether this distinction will prove to be of widespread application to language teaching will depend on how satisfactorily rather less obvious examples than these can be handled.

The importance of a phonological level of analysis for the language teacher is that it gives a clear understanding of the phonetic features that a learner must acquire if he is to make the phonological distinctions on which the language operates. Teaching that is based on no more than a list of phonemes or 'sounds' will prove unsatisfactory because it ignores much significant variation in pronunciation. It may seem that by aiming at allophonic accuracy one is returning to the complexity of a purely phonetic description. This is not so. Only through a phonological analysis can one determine what the most significant features are. A phonetic description will attach equal importance to all features. A learner must learn to make the phonological contrasts but this can be done with less than complete phonetic accuracy. The value of a phonological description is that it indicates the targets of pronunciation teaching.

2.3.1 Techniques of pronunciation teaching

Before enquiring into any possible relation between linguistics and the techniques of teaching pronunciation, I should like to consider just how important it is for a learner to acquire an accurate pronunciation. The obvious argument in favour of pronunciation teaching stems from the techniques adopted by linguists in making a phonological analysis. When we look at the contrast between a minimal pair like *sang* and *son* in French, /sɑ̃/ and /sɔ̃/, we can see that mastery of the difference between the phonemes /ɑ̃/ and /ɔ̃/ is necessary if the two words are to be adequately differentiated. If, like many English learners, a pupil only manages to master one of these segments—probably /ɑ̃/—his attempts to say *son* will sound like *sang*. Thus far the argument is indisputable. What one cannot go on to say is that the learner must master the difference because, if he does not, he will be *understood* to have said *sang* when he was attempting to say *son*. This is nonsense. The inability to master a phonetic distinction is most unlikely to lead to misinterpretation. What if the Englishman does say to his French friend: 'Je suis allé voir le spectacle de sang et lumière au château de Saumur.' How likely is it that a Frenchman will fail to understand? If one had to justify the need for accurate pronunciation in these terms, one would be hard put to it.

A more convincing argument is to be found in the general characteristic of natural languages that this example demonstrates—their redundancy. *Redundancy* is a technical term from communication engineering relating to the amount of information carried by the units in a message. Where each unit carried the maximum amount of information there is no redundancy because no unit can be omitted without loss of information. Where several units carry the same information or no information at all there is redundancy because units can be omitted with no loss of information. Language is naturally and necessarily redundant. At the level of phonological systems every language has more phonemes than it needs to express the number of words in the language and more phonetic features than it needs to realize the phonemes. The loss of a single phoneme or feature from a message will rarely mean the loss of any information. Up to 50 per cent of a message can be lost and it will still be understood.[11] If there were fewer features and fewer phonemes, but if these were more fully exploited, communication would actually become more difficult. It would become essential for us to hear every sound in order to understand the message. If there was any distortion —as there almost always is—we should not know which phoneme had been used, nor should we be able to work out what it was we should have heard. As a result some of the information being transmitted would be lost. With many of the possible words of languages not used—*spen*, *spon*, *spone*, *spoin* and *sparn* could be perfectly good words in English, for example—there is little necessity to hear every segment accurately. What is lost in the malperception of one phoneme in a whole utterance is readily replaced by the information carried by the rest of the phonology, the grammar, the vocabulary and even non-linguistic aspects of the situation.

The significance of redundancy is not that it shows accurate pronunciation to be unnecessary. It may not be necessary for a learner to master every phonemic distinction, but languages need to be redundant. Redundancy makes communication under normal conditions more efficient. The learner whose pronunciation contains numerous faults, however insignificant each of those faults may be in itself, cannot produce language with a level of redundancy that will ensure that he can communicate under conditions of noise. If he is also making mistakes in grammar and lexis, redundancy is further reduced. Most conversation takes place with interference from many sources. The biggest justification for pronunciation teaching is to ensure that the foreigner's language is fully redundant.

The teacher probably has more complete descriptions of the phonetics and phonology of the commonly taught languages than of

---

[11] See J.H. Greenberg (ed.), *Universals of Language* (Cambridge, Massachusetts Institute of Technology Press, 1966) p. xviii.

any other aspect of them. Descriptive material is not presented in a way that is pedagogically useful for the learner, although many detailed descriptions are written with the language teacher much in mind. How the teacher will use the descriptive information is still something that he must decide for himself.

The most evident influence of phonetics on foreign language teaching comes in the use of transcriptions, charts and articulatory descriptions. These aids are by no means new. The popularity of 'the phonetic method' of teaching followed the development of phonetics as a science and dates from early in this century. The introduction of transcription adds to what has to be learned in a way that some teachers find unacceptable. It seems best to think of transcription as a way of indicating the pronunciation of words in a language, like English, which has a difficult orthography. I find it doubtful that transcription assists the *learning* of a pronunciation system, since the symbols can only be interpreted by someone who has already mastered the sounds. If they can produce the sounds, the greatest part of pronunciation learning is already done. The transcription has value as an objective way of referring to what the learner has acquired. It may then become a useful tool for indicating the pronunciation of new words in class, or, more importantly, in a dictionary. The teacher will have to decide whether this is enough to justify teaching a system of transcription.

Diagrams of the organs in place for the production of certain sounds and detailed articulatory descriptions probably have limited value for all but the potential phonetician. Where an articulation involves contact between articulators at the front of the mouth, kinaesthetic awareness is strong and there is probably some value in directing the learner's attention to what his lips, teeth and tongue should do. Once it becomes a matter of tongue height, whether front, back or centre, or of contact between the tongue and anything further back than the teeth-ridge, there is less to be gained. At best, giving articulatory advice gives the pupil a better understanding of what he has to learn. It is not itself likely to play an important role in the learning process—the process whereby the feature of pronunciation passes into the learner's regular speech habits. It is a starting-point on which to build by means of other teaching techniques.

In the absence of any theory of pronunciation teaching we can use our linguistic knowledge to assess the adequacy of some teaching procedures. From what we have already seen of the nature of phonemic contrast and allophonic variation, we can conclude that the practice of sounds in isolation is of limited value. Learning a pronunciation system is learning to operate a set of contrasts, and this can only be done if the practice itself gives the pupil the opportunity to relate phonemes to one another. As an isolated unit a phoneme has no phonetic form. We can only know how it is realized phonetically when we know its position and phonetic environment. As we saw, difficulty for the learner may also stem not from the phonetics of the sound itself but from the need to produce it in an unaccustomed position in the syllable. A completely new sound might well be isolated to begin with, while muscles are brought into play together for the first time, but everything argues that practice must be, above all, of sounds integrated into syllables, words and sentences.

The most systematic approach to pronunciation teaching reflects the procedures of phonemic analysis very closely and is the product of them. It employs the technique of contrasting minimal pairs to teach pronunciation just as the linguist has used it to establish inventories of phonemes. The contrastive technique is used both to ensure that the pupil does not simply substitute the nearest mother-tongue segment for the one he is acquiring and to enable him to discriminate the phonemic contrasts of the foreign language when he hears them and to produce them when he speaks. Let us look at a typical example of such an approach.

2.3.1.1. *The teaching of Spanish* /e/. I will take as my example the teaching of Spanish /e/, although as we shall see this quickly enlarges itself into consideration of the diphthong /ej/ too. A glance at the phonetics of English—and any experience of teaching Spanish to English-speaking pupils—will reveal that English pupils will attempt to substitute for /e/ not a pure vowel, but the diphthong /eɪ/, as in *day*, the first element of which is the closest sound to the Spanish. Such a substitution would certainly cause confusion, since in Spanish there is also a diphthong /ej/ which, although not phonetically identical to the English diphthong, will cause difficulties of identification for the Spanish hearer. No doubt there is more than one solution to this problem, but here is a possible strategy.[12]

The probable substitution of English /eɪ/ for Spanish /e/ and /ej/ may well result in the Spanish hearer perceiving /ej/ wherever /e/ is intended and /e/ where /ej/ is intended. It seems likely therefore that an undiphthongized [e] is desirable and also a phonetically

[12] The examples given are adapted from J.D. Bowen and R.P. Stockwell, *Patterns of Spanish Pronunciation* (Chicago, University of Chicago Press, 1960).

accurate [ej], for fear that the hearer will identify the shorter English glide with /e/. Our first task then will be to establish distinctions between the Spanish and the English vowels. To enable us to do this we will establish lists of phonetically contrasting pairs like the following:

I	say	/seɪ/	se	/se/	
	bay		be		
	fay		fe		
	may		me		*etc.*

and

2	lay	/leɪ/	ley	/lej/	
	day		dey		
	base		veis		
	ray		rey		*etc.*

It is commonly argued that a speaker cannot logically be expected to produce distinctions which he cannot perceive, and therefore the first stage with this strategy of teaching involves practising the capacity to discriminate the differences between the vowels in the Spanish and English words. Pairs of words from (1), one Spanish, one English or two Spanish or two English (i.e. the same word twice) will be read aloud to the learner and he will be asked to say whether the two words are the same or different and, if different, which is the Spanish and which the English. Such practice would continue until the pupil can identify the vowels with complete reliability. The practice then moves to a productive stage during which the learner has to repeat and read the contrasting pairs until the teacher is satisfied that the distinction between the English diphthong and Spanish vowel is being made consistently. Precisely the same process will then be repeated with minimal pairs like those in (2) to discriminate between /eɪ/ and /ej/. When the learners can then readily produce three distinct vowel nuclei, /e/, /eɪ/ and /ej/, the teacher can move on to the next part of the strategy.

From here on the aim is to establish the contrasts that exist within the Spanish language. It is likely that the contrasts with English will have produced a Spanish /e/ that can be distinguished from the nearest pure vowels /i/ and /a/ and the diphthong /ej/. However, one is certainly not entitled to take this for granted and practice and testing along the lines above should be conducted with pairs like the following:

3	dé	/de/	di	/di/	
	sé		sí		
	vé		vi		
	mé		mí		*etc.*
4	queso	/keso/	caso	/kaso/	
	pesa		pasa		
	pera		para		
	beca		vaca		*etc.*
5	vente	/bente/	veinte	/bejnte/	
	reno		reino		
	ves		veis		
	re		rey		*etc.*

In view of the simplicity of the Spanish vowel system, it is unlikely that these distinctions will cause much difficulty. It might be thought that the features necessary for the hearer to identify the phonemic distinction have been adequately acquired by the learner. However, what has taken-place so far to some extent represents a simplification. Each of the Spanish vowels being practised occurs in a stressed syllable. But the vowels, including /e/, also occur in unstressed syllables whereas, in English, vowels in relatively unstressed syllables are often weakened to a central vowel, /ə/. Just as it is difficult for a foreigner learning English to weaken the unstressed vowels, it is difficult for the English speaker learning foreign languages to prevent himself from reducing them. The result would be that instead of /penár/ he will produce /pənár/, and the Spanish hearer will be faced with difficulties in determining the intended phoneme and indeed will face this problem on all unstressed syllables. Interpreting one syllable, given grammatical, lexical, phonological and situational context, would not prove difficult. But when the same thing occurs on every unstressed syllable, then serious interference with communication could take place. It is important therefore for the English speaker to have extensive practice to prevent vowel weakening on unstressed syllables.

6	menár	/menár/	manár	/manár/	
	besár		basár		
	apegár		apagár		
	méses		mésas		
	quíten		quítan		*etc.*
7	penár		pinár		
	pequé		piqué		

descánte   discánte
pesáda   pisáda   *etc.*

The practice of these pairs proceeds in the same way as I have outlined above, going from discrimination to production. When this has been done to the teacher's satisfaction, the phonemic contrasts in which /e/ operates will have been established. It should be consistently identifiable in the learner's speech.

It is still probable that complete accuracy has not been attained and that, although communication is not impaired, an 'English accent' remains at this point. Eventually the teacher will want to return to this to achieve greater phonetic accuracy. There is no sure way of enabling a learner to reach complete accuracy. The adult learner, for example, who attains a perfect pronunciation in a second language is very rare indeed. There is no easy way to determine how any phonetic problem is best approached. Here we are only concerned to show how contrast is employed, and this applies to less significant features as much as to phonologically distinctive features. In an open syllable /e/ is a high vowel—[e], whereas in a closed syllable, that is when followed by a consonant in the same syllable, it tends to be lower—[ɛ]. The following pairs, to be used in the manner already described, illustrate this:

8   mesa   [mesa]   mesta   [mɛsta]
     pesa   pesca
     vena   venta
     nive   nivel
     pasté   pastel

Through such practice non-significant, allophonic variations may be acquired.

Pronunciation is perhaps one of the least satisfactory aspects of language teaching, probably because little is understood of pronunciation *learning*. The approach that I have just outlined is not the only one that is possible, but it is cogent and systematic to a degree that others are not.[13] It also reflects the linguist's notions of how phonological structure operates. Objections to it, however, cannot be lightly dismissed. The first is an objection to all pronunciation drilling. What is achieved in the drill situation may not be transferred to other situations in which the language is used. It is all too familiar

[13] See P.R. Léon, *Laboratoire de Langues et Correction Phonétique* (Paris, Didier, 1962).

to get a pupil pronouncing a sound accurately while it is the specific object of the practice, but for him to lapse into error as soon as his attention is directed to some other part of the language. There is too little evidence of how learning may be transferred from a drill to a natural situation. Some methodologists, who feel that drilling is not an efficient procedure, prefer not to dissociate pronunciation practice from full situational use of language. It is a characteristic of some audio-visual teaching that dialogues are contrived to permit the recurrence of various pronunciation features. The repetition of sounds in a larger context is thought to provide the necessary practice. Practice in this form will be less intensive and it is not entirely clear what one can do about repeated error, except take the sound out of its larger context and drill it. On the other hand, at least it is the phonetics of connected speech that is being learned. The minimal pairs technique deals only in isolated words and word pronunciation can undergo considerable changes when the word is integrated into connected speech. Testing pronunciation through minimal pairs may have the disadvantage that the very juxtaposition of the contrasting phonemes may assist the pupil to identify them and may not be a true guide to his performance when the contrast is not being pointed in this way.

The task of the language learner is presented here as the acquisition of phonemic contrasts through the mastery of relevant allophonic variation. Although we can view it as our function as teachers to ensure that this learning takes place, we should not assume that phonemes are learned in succession one at a time. Every phoneme is made up of a number of phonetic features, and it is possible that it is features rather than phonemes that are learned. There is strong evidence that an English child learning his mother-tongue does not learn three separate distinctions /b/~/p/, /d/~/t/, /k/~/g/, but acquires the single distinction voiced ~ non-voiced (lenis ~ fortis), which enables him to learn the three phonemic distinctions simultaneously. We do not know whether the same thing happens in second language learning, but it seems perfectly feasible that it should. One wonders, for example, whether a French speaker who has learned to aspirate /p/ in English then has to repeat the practice with /t/ and /k/. If research were to prove that second-language learners acquire features like first-language learners, it would open up the possibility of a wholly new approach to explicit pronunciation teaching based on features. I do not know of any work that has been done on these lines yet.

2.4. Generative phonology

I have left till last a brief mention of recent developments in phonology. Generative phonology is a part of transformational generative linguistics. Although transformational theory is not discussed as a specific topic in this book, many of the innovations produced by this approach are reflected in a number of the discussions—for example, in the broader definition of *formal* (p. 87), in the notions of competence (p. 34) and deep structure (pp. 86–90), and in the mentalist theory of language (pp. 168–71). Generative phonology handles the sound system of language in highly abstract terms and it is for this reason that the details of a generative phonological description are likely to be of no more than academic interest to the language teacher.

A distinction is made between the phonetic forms in which morphemes,[14] words, phrases etc. are actually realized and the 'underlying forms' which they have. These underlying forms are more abstract in that they give less information about the actual phonetic shapes that units may take in a given utterance. Indeed it is not possible to state with any accuracy from looking at the underlying form of a word how it might be pronounced. For this we must know the rules, and the phonological component of a descriptive grammar is a set of rules for giving a phonetic form to an underlying unit. There is no place for the type of phonemes or the sort of phonemic level of analysis outlined above.

Why do linguists propose that there should be these underlying forms, often rather far removed from the 'surface' form words eventually have? If we take conventional phonemic transcriptions of *capacious, capacity, audacious, audacity, rapacious, rapacity*, they will look like this:

/kəpeɪʃəs/	/kəpæsɪtɪ/
/ɔ:deɪʃəs/	/ɔ:dæsɪtɪ/
/rəpeɪʃəs/	/rəpæsɪtɪ/

There is little indication of any relation between the noun and the adjective.[15] The linguist aims to make the widest and most significant generalizations about the language he is describing, and he must show *all* the relations that exist within the language. Relations of derivation such as hold between words like *capacious* and *capacity* are just as

---

[14] For discussion of the morpheme see p. 101.
[15] It was certainly not seen as the function of a phonemic transcription to show derivational relations. Each word would be treated as a form unrelated to any other.

significant as other types of relations in English. In the grammar of the language this should be clear. It would not be clear if we had only a phonemic transcription of such words.

This can be restated in mentalist terms, although not all linguists would accept this. It seems reasonable to suppose that when each speaker of English stores a word away in his mind, that word is not necessarily represented in a form that closely resembles its pronunciation, but in a form that makes the relations with other words most clear. It is hard to believe that as speakers of English we are not fully conscious that there is a relation between *capacious* and *capacity* and that this formal and semantic relation is the same as that of the other pairs above. In fact it may not be words that are stored but morphemes—roots and rules for adding derivational affixes.

Further evidence of the need for an underlying representation is found in those words which are pronounced in more than one way. We saw that *can* is pronounced /kæn/, /kən/ or /kn/. Are there then three different words? Surely not. But if there are not, which representation is the best candidate for a citation form? Probably /kæn/ because the other two can be derived by a general rule of English phonology from it. In making a language description we have to decide which is the best representation. In writing about English in conventional orthography, we have no difficulty. In writing the second sentence of this paragraph I was able to use the orthographic form for citation. I was using *can* as a fairly abstract representation, which enabled me to avoid using a phonemic transcription. The one representation permitted me to refer simultaneously to all possible actual pronunciations of the word.

As it happens the only detailed generative study of English phonology that we have to date sets up underlying forms that are often very close to the traditional orthographic forms.[16] We see the relation of *capacious* and *capacity* far more clearly from the orthographic forms than we could from the phonemic transcriptions. It was not the aim of Chomsky and Halle to justify English orthography, but it happens that their analysis has produced representations that demonstrate how much grammatical information there is in English orthography which would be lost if ever there was a major spelling reform.[17] In theory underlying forms need not resemble orthographic forms at all.

---

[16] N. Chomsky and M. Halle, *The Sound Pattern of English* (New York, Harper & Row, 1968).

[17] This probably explains why there have been few linguists among the spelling reformers.

In a generative grammar the underlying forms of words (or morphemes) are put into sequences by the application of grammatical rules and then a set of phonological rules is applied to them. In the case of English these rules assign stress patterns to morphemes, words and sentences, reduce vowels and produce vowel and consonant alternations, so that by the application of this explicit set of rules the underlying string of morphemes is converted into a sequence of phonetic elements which accurately represents our production of the sentence. It requires an extremely complex set of rules to do this, and in recent linguistic descriptions these rules are expressed in a form that makes them inaccessible to the non-linguist. The rules are applied to the underlying form in a predetermined sequence. Each rule changes the form of the word on which it operates and the next rule is then applied to the resulting form. A word passes through a succession of forms until the last rule has been applied. The result of this rule can be converted into a speech-form but none of the preceding forms can. They are all abstract.

A simplified example will illustrate how such rules operate.[18] The word *courageous* is seen to derive from the noun {kɒrage} and the suffix {-ɒs}.

Rule 1	places main stress on noun	$\overset{1}{\text{kɒrage}}$
Rule 2	softens *g* before *e*	$\overset{1}{\text{kɒradʒe}}$
Rule 3	changes position of stress when suffix is added	$\overset{2}{\text{kɒ}}\overset{1}{\text{radʒe}}+\text{ɒs}$
Rule 4	vowel in this position is diphthongized	$\overset{2}{\text{kɒ}}\overset{1}{\text{raɪdʒe}}+\text{ɒs}$
Rule 5	*e* is elided when in final position in a morpheme	$\overset{2}{\text{kɒ}}\overset{1}{\text{raɪdʒ}}+\text{ɒs}$
Rule 6	Vowel shift changes aɪ to eɪ	$\overset{2}{\text{kɒ}}\overset{1}{\text{reɪdz}}+\text{ɒs}$
Rule 7	Unstressed vowels are reduced to [ə]	$\overset{2}{\text{kə}}\overset{1}{\text{reɪdʒ}}\text{əs}$

Only the product of rule 7 resembles the phonetic realization that we normally give to *courageous*. Rules 1 and 2 also apply to the noun *courage* but thereafter the derivation would differ from the above, finally producing a phonetic representation [kʌrɪdʒ].

It should now be clear why I said that the details of the analysis

---

[18] This is based on Chomsky and Halle, *op. cit.*, but I have changed their transcription to bring it into line with that used in this book and to make the rules more immediately comprehensible to the reader.

cannot be of direct interest to the language teacher. Even if one accepts that the native speaker operates rules such as these in using his language—and Chomsky and others believe this—there can be no question of teaching the pronunciation of *courageous* by working through the derivation from the underlying form. The language teacher can only work through the phonetic form that words have in actual utterances. We might wish to believe that the foreigner must learn those rules as the native speaker does, but 'learning' means the internalization of the rules on the basis on inductions from contact with the language. It is not credible that anyone could learn to internalize these rules on the basis of a prior externalization of them. Explicit discussion of the rules, far from being the short-cut that it might arguably be for grammar learning, would prove a very long way round indeed.

Chomsky and Halle say that their underlying representations, close as they are to normal orthography, are perfectly adequate for native speakers of English. After all, the native speaker does not require information on pronunciation from an orthography. He already knows how his language is pronounced. It is perfectly reasonable therefore that a system of orthography should reveal relations at a deeper, 'psychologically more real' level. We have seen that these relations are more evident in Chomsky and Halle's phonological representations. However, although they say that 'there is, for the moment, little evidence that phonemic transcription is a "psychologically real" system', they agree that their own transcription 'is of little use for one who wishes to produce tolerable speech without knowing the language'. The student, learning English as a foreign language, is just such a person, at least until he has mastered a great deal of the language. 'For such purposes a phonetic alphabet, or the regularized phonetic representations called "phonemic" in modern linguistics, would be superior'.[19] The authors are in effect suggesting the inapplicability of their theory to language teaching.

If there is nothing to be gained by teaching these generative rules, that is not to say that one has to throw in the towel and say that nothing can be done to facilitate the development of the rules in the individual. Modern language teaching has not substituted simple random exposure for rule-teaching. Instead it has attempted to predigest the raw language data by organizing the exposure system-

[19] Chomsky and Halle, *op. cit.*, p. 49. Their example is of an actor speaking a language he does not understand. I have extended this to include the foreign language learner.

atically on lines which, it is assumed, ease the internalization of the language structure. There is no reason why one could not do the same with the phonology, presenting sequences of related forms to the learners in the belief, as yet unproved, but as least plausible, that this helps the learner to assimilate the rules. So, for the teaching of English, the learner might be required to repeat, with phonetic accuracy, sequences like these:

'alternate	al'ternative	alter'nation
'contemplate	con'templative	contem'plation
'demonstrate	de'monstrative	demon'stration
'indicate	in'dicative	indic'ation
'remonstrate	re'monstrative	remon'stration.

If we do not believe in the psychological reality of these or any other linguistic rules, but rather hold that the phonetic forms of units are learnt in isolation when the learner is exposed to the units, a view which it is not easy to defend, then, of course, there would be no advantage to be seen in the presentation of sequences like those above. But, really, few would try to suggest that no generalization are made by the learner, even though there are very deep differences of opinion on the manner in which they are made.

By emphasizing the relatedness of words, generative phonology brings to our attention something that has been neglected in language teaching in recent years. However, the teaching consists of no more than an arrangement of language data, and it does not require a generative description to enable the teacher to do this. The form and sequence of the linguist's rules do not influence the teaching, and therefore any subsequent changes in this kind of phonological description will be of little interest to the teacher. In the final chapter I shall attempt to assess the role of linguistics in language teaching. If at points we find that linguistic insights are helpful, we must not forget that there are areas of linguistic study which are of great interest to the linguist and central to his concern but which will remain at most marginal for the teaching of languages.

2.5. Summary

The science of phonetics provides the language teacher with precise descriptions of the articulations of the target language. Phonology helps the teacher establish the priorities of pronunciation teaching by enabling him to identify the most important features to be acquired.

It is not certain that the drilling of pronunciation effectively assists learning, but one of the more systematic approaches to teaching exploits the notion of contrast in much the same way as it has been used by linguists to establish the phonemes of a language. A more important influence on the learner is probably the teacher's own pronunciation. For this reason teachers should avoid all distortions in their speech. This applies as much to intonation as to the production of sounds. Intonation contributes directly to the interpretation of an utterance, and accuracy of intonation is therefore at least as important as accuracy of individual sound segments. Recent developments in phonology have produced radical, new approaches, but it is unlikely that they will prove very relevant to language teaching.

3
Grammar

3.1. Item and structure

It is axiomatic that language is systematized. If it were not so, we should not be able to understand one another. It is the aim of the linguist to reveal the system of language, the *langue*, and of the language teacher to enable people to learn it. Sometimes the extent of the systematicity goes unnoticed, perhaps because it is difficult to discover just how the system operates, perhaps because we take much of the system for granted. But behind everything that is shared by the members of a speech community there must be a system waiting to be discovered.

In traditional descriptions of the grammatical system there is usually a twofold division into *morphology* and *syntax*. Within morphology we find statements about the internal form of words—such matters as inflection for case, number or gender, tense forms, agreement, certain kinds of derivation and so on. Within syntax we find descriptions of the relations between words, including, for example, those shown by word-order. For the linguist the distinction between morphology and syntax is largely artificial. Both have the function of demonstrating relationships between items in a sentence. A relationship which in one language is expressed syntactically may in another be expressed morphologically. For example, because of the relative inflexibility of word-order in English a noun preceding a verb is more or less certain to be functioning as the subject of that verb. Nothing in the form of the noun itself indicates that it is the subject. German on the other hand permits greater freedom in the choice of word-order. A noun preceding a verb is not necessarily the subject of that verb. The relationship 'Subject of' has to be marked in some other way, and German uses for this purpose a morphological device—a nominative case as part of a case system, which operates not in the noun itself but in the determiner which precedes the noun. The differences between languages are not necessarily as great as they may appear to be, since it is often the means by which relations are expressed rather than the relations themselves which differ.

Although it is obviously essential to understand the meaning of the individual words in a sentence, if one is to understand the sentence itself, this alone is not enough. Grammatical devices like case, tense, word-order, concord and subordination express the relations between parts of the sentence, and an understanding of them is essential to the understanding of the sentences themselves. If the forms within a sentence are related to each other by the grammatical system, it follows that a change in any of the items changes the whole system of relationships and therefore the overall meaning of the sentence. It is this emphasis on the inter-relatedness of everything in language (not only in the grammar) that has led modern linguistics to consider itself *structuralist*.

Linguistics is structural in the sense that the linguist uses relational criteria in identifying or defining linguistic categories or units. He does not start by identifying a class of nouns and establishing its membership and then perhaps examine the way in which words of this class combine with others to form sentences. Instead he finds that by studying linguistic contexts it becomes possible to group items together because of the similar patterns of occurrence which they reveal. Any item has relations with other items along two axes. On the horizontal axis it is related to the other items in the particular sequence that is under examination. This is the case whether we are concerned with a fixed word-order language or not. A full understanding of the structural potential of any item can only be gained from the study of a variety of sentences. From our knowledge of the typical sentences of the language we can derive statements about the structures that sentences may have, the permutations that are possible within them and the word classes which can realize the particular structural functions. Relations along this axis are usually called *syntagmatic*, and it is to these that the term *structure* is most commonly applied.

However, relations also exist on a vertical axis. That is to say, any item in a sentence can usually be substituted by one or more other items that have similar grammatical characteristics in spite of some difference in grammatical and lexical meaning. For example, any one of a number of personal pronouns may occur as the subject of a sentence and the overall sentence structure remains the same. These pronouns are strictly limited in number and therefore form a closed system in which to say *he* is to say *not I, not you, not she, not it, not we, not they*. To some extent the meaning of *he* is defined by the other terms in the system, and in that we usually call it 3rd person singular, we might be inclined to say that it is much like its translation equivalent in most other languages. This would be a superficial conclusion, since non-Indo-European languages often have far more complex person systems, and in any case even within European languages choice of third person is not always made on the same basis. In English, choice is made generally though not exclusively on a basis of human (and animate) versus non-human (also animate) and inanimate. The first permits the selection of *he* and *she*, the latter of *it*. The choice of *he* and *she* is one of male v. female. In languages having gender systems, however, the features human and animate are irrelevant and the choice is made on a basis of masculine v. feminine v. neuter or, where there are only two genders, masculine v. feminine. Since gender and sex do not necessarily coincide we have the possibility, very bizarre to an English speaker, of referring to a female person by means of a neuter pronoun as in German when *es* substitutes for *Fraülein* and *Mädchen*. The structural relations exemplified here by choice of pronouns are often called *paradigmatic* and where the choice is limited to a finite number of alternatives as here, we are said to be dealing with *closed systems*.

As one would expect from a structural view, there is no rigid distinction between syntagmatic and paradigmatic considerations. Words in the paradigmatic class of nouns have to be sub-classified as *countable* or *uncountable* according to whether they may be preceded by words like *many* or words like *much*. Verb-words are sub-classified according to the type of structure which may follow them. *Transitive* verbs may be followed by a noun, *intransitive* verbs may not. *Ditransitive* verbs may be followed by two nouns (Objects). Some verbs may be followed by either a noun or an adjective. As we shall see later in this chapter, the interaction of verb word and complement structure is also most complex.[1]

For many years linguistics was dominated by the needs of field linguists who, faced with the task of analysing unknown languages, attempted to set up a fairly rigorous set of procedures for working out or discovering the structure of the language they were investigating. In such a situation the only evidence that the linguist himself could vouch for would be what he could record in his transcription. He could not trust an informant to provide him with any semantic insights and in any case, as we saw in the first chapter, he had considerable mistrust of semantic evidence whatever its source. The method he adopted was therefore formal. The analysis of sentence

[1] 3.2. *Deep structure and the study of syntax.*

structure would be largely a matter of recording the different number of elements that sentences could possibly contain and the sequence in which those elements occurred. Elements—morphemes, words, phrases—would be classed together if they could occupy the same positions in the structure of the sentence. Such an approach to linguistic description is sometimes called a 'slot-and-filler' approach. The assignment of words to a particular class (part of speech) would be decided by whether it would fit into the appropriate slot in one or more test sentences. Although this approach developed to meet the needs of the linguist in the field, it came to be applied to the study of the better known languages too.[2]

More recently linguists have been less occupied with *how* a linguist arrives at his analysis than with whether his analysis will successfully predict all the grammatical sentences of the language. The aim of this approach is to work out a complete set of rules for the language, which, if followed in the given sequence, would produce all of the sentences that the native speaker would recognize as grammatical and none of those that he would believe were ungrammatical.[3] If, in order to do this, the linguist finds that it is necessary to categorize some constructions as Noun Phrases, some words as Nouns, some Nouns as Common Nouns and some Common Nouns as Countable rather than Uncountable, he will do so. He does not attempt to relate his categorizations to particular places in particular sentences, but even though his criteria are not as directly explicit as they are for the field linguist, his categories are still in effect defined in terms of their structural function. A description of this type is a *generative* description.

One of the interesting consequences of the attempt to produce a generative description is the realization of the creative nature of our use of language—creative, not in the sense of literary creativity, but in the sense that most of the sentences we produce or hear are sentences that we have not produced or heard before. It is doubtful, for example, whether there is more than a handful of sentences in the whole of this book that the reader will have met before. In spite of this every sentence will, I hope, be understood. This is because,

---

[2] See for example C.C. Fries, *The Structure of English* (New York, Harcourt, 1952), and more recently, P. Christophersen and A.O. Sandved, *An Advanced English Grammar* (London, Macmillan, 1969).

[3] Actually the description relates to the actual usage of the people whose language is being described, not their opinion on the grammaticality of utterances, since this might be influenced by social acceptability.

although the sentences themselves are new, they are made up of elements that are familiar—or, as I would prefer to put it, they are the product of the application of familiar rules. These rules, which I as a speaker of English share with the reader, who is also a speaker of English, are limited in number, but can produce an infinity of sentences. There is no grammatical limit to the possibility of combining, re-combining and repeating the structural elements of a language. It is these rules, which underlie our production and comprehension of sentences, that the generative linguist tries to describe in a fully explicit way.

The structural view has certainly not been without influence on language teaching. For some years now the word 'structure' has been in some degree a vogue word. In many language text-books it is not uncommon to find sections which are headed 'structures' where formerly they were headed 'grammar'. In fact there is rarely a concomitant change in the contents to go with the radical implications of the label.[4] We also find the word used in such phrases as 'the structures of French' or 'the 100 (or 1,000 or 2,000) basic structures of English'. (The very range of figures here arouses one's suspicions.) In books on methodology we are often exhorted to begin by teaching 'the most simple structures of the language'.

Yet if we accept the generative view, the use of the word 'structures' in these different ways implies a somewhat erroneous view of language. It suggests that there exists a limited number of structures in each language—some admittedly more simple, more basic, more important than others—and that the learning of a language is the learning of these structures one by one. By learning a limited number of sentences, one would cover the possible range of sentence structures in the language. However, if language is 'rule-governed creativity', as Chomsky has called it, it is not that sentences in a language *are* structures, it is that they *have* structure. This structure is on each occasion created by applying the rules of the language. The same set of rules is capable of producing sentences as complex as those found in the writing of Proust and as simple as those found in Hemingway. Obviously language teaching cannot prepare the pupil for all the actual sentence structures he may meet. What we must do instead is familiarize the pupil with the elements of structures of a language and the rules governing the relationships between them.

---

[4] What is implied by use of *structures* is more a revolution in methodology than a revolution in content. 'Grammar' is more usually taught through explicit rules, while 'structures' are acquired more inductively.

Then he is able to construct and recognize sentences as occasion demands.

This can perhaps best be illustrated through an analogy. The raw materials that are used in building a house can be put together in an infinitely varied way, though naturally there are rules of sound construction that have to be followed. No two houses need be exactly the same. In practice we might not see much value in an infinitely long house, but it is not the characteristics of the materials used that would impose any limit on the length. The builder who knows the qualities of his materials is capable of constructing whatever type of house he or his client wants. He knows the rules that underlie house-construction. Another builder may have learned how to build ten or a hundred houses of different design, but he is not capable of building anything more than this limited number of structures. The builder who knows the rules knows far more about building than the one who has learned to construct ten basic kinds of house. A learner who knows the rules of sentence construction can say far more than the one who has learned a hundred basic structures.

3.1.1. The structural content of language teaching

It is not unusual to hear foreign learners and even teachers of English say that English grammar is relatively simple. When they say this, they are equating the learning of grammar with the learning of morphological variation. Compared with many other languages English may be fairly straightforward morphologically. There is no case system, no gender system and most verbs have no more than five forms. In fact, looked at overall, the grammar of English is probably no less complex than the grammar of any other language. However, learners do not often get an overall picture since the linguistic content of language teaching is usually cited as a list of items made up of morphological systems or parts of systems. Sections of a text-book may be devoted to the definite article, the indefinite article, prepositions, the past tense, the subjunctive and so on. There are types of language teaching in which learning is almost entirely the learning of morphological forms. A paradigm, for example, is often a set of morphological forms isolated from the structural relations which they are supposed to operate. How far a pupil learns the structural functions of items will depend on what kind of practice follows the learning of a paradigm. As soon as a complete sentence is introduced *some* structural information is being acquired. But the emphasis is very often on how well the pupil has mastered the internal form of an item. An error of morphological construction is commonly more severely punished than a fault of syntax or semantic choice. Viewing the content of language teaching in terms of morphology might be called an *item approach* to language teaching.

Its danger lies in the fact that once the form itself of the item has been mastered, pupil and teacher alike will be satisfied that learning is complete. At best one of the structural contexts that the item may have will also have been learned. From that point on, the item may never again be part of the explicit content of teaching, although there is much of the formal patterning of the item for which the learner will not be prepared. In due course new sentences of this type will occur. Their presence in the text will go unnoticed and confusions will arise as learners attempt to extend their existing knowledge to a new linguistic situation. If the confusions are serious enough they may even wash back and undermine the original learning that had been correct, if incomplete.

The inadequate recognition of the structural nature of language leads in teaching to a lack of specificity of the structural and semantic content of learning. There is an unsuspecting selectivity in such teaching, which causes error as the learner proceeds further in his language learning. There are even some aspects of language structure that are not easily classified under the heading of any one morphological form. We shall see this later in this chapter when I discuss some recent work in syntax.

To some extent the dangers are fewer in a European context, because the languages of Europe, being closely related, do express the same sort of relations, though not necessarily in the same way. Much of the structure of the language being learned does not have to be specifically taught, because it is the same in the mother-tongue as it is in the foreign language. Things that can be taken for granted in teaching English to a European cannot be taken for granted in teaching a speaker of a non-Indo-European language. Where the two languages are rather far apart, the controlled content of teaching will probably have to be much greater. Our unconscious assumptions about the universality of certain linguistic features, false though they sometimes are, do not always handicap language teaching in a purely European context.

It should be a part of the evaluation of teaching materials to see how adequately the linguistic content of learning is specified. In the case of a text-book this requires a very detailed analysis of the presentation and practice of new items and a careful comparison between this and a good linguistic description of the language being taught. In the case of a syllabus the analysis is rather more easily carried out, since a syllabus is usually no more than a list of what has to be taught, whereas a text-book is much more. I shall illustrate the consequences of an insufficiently specified syllabus and then examine how successful a text-book is in introducing an item of language in a controlled fashion; but before doing this I want to make a rapid outline of the English verbal system so that we can check the syllabus and the text-book against it.

3.1.1.1. *The verb in English.* The basic paradigm of the tense system in English has eight forms.[5] There are two tenses as such, *touches*, *touched*, respectively Present (Simple) Tense and Past (Simple) Tense, and a number of constructions which we might call 'tense-phrases', since they perform a similar function although they are not tenses in the strict sense of being inflected. These six tense-phrases are constructed by applying two modifications to the Present and Past Tenses. The addition of *be*+*-ing*, sometimes called an Aspect marker, gives *is touching*, the Present Progressive, and *was touching*, the Past Progressive. The addition of *have*+*-en* (*-ed* etc.) gives *has touched*, the Present Perfect, and *had touched*, the Past Perfect, The two together will produce *has been touching*, the Present Perfect Progressive, and *had been touching*, the Past Perfect Progressive.

The tense system, therefore, can be represented by the following forms:

touches	has touched
touched	had touched
is touching	has been touching
was touching	had been touching

From this it is clear that there is no future tense in English. There is a great variety of ways of referring to future time in English, but no one form whose essential function this is. The forms *shall/will touch*, commonly described as the future tense, are not part of the basic paradigm at all. They form part of a system of modal auxiliaries

---

[5] The treatment here follows W.F. Twaddell, *The English Verb Auxiliaries* (Providence, Brown University Press, 1965). For simplicity's sake I shall refer to all of the forms described as tenses.

including, among others, *can*, *may* and *must*, all of which by implication may refer to future time, but all of which express modality too.
The meaning of *will* is rarely purely temporal, and several of the
forms in the paradigm above are used at least as frequently to refer
to future time.

A complete account of the use of the tense system would require
each form to be discussed in detail, but it is enough here to say that
neither of the modifications is concerned with time as such. Aspect
is used to indicate relative duration, and the fact that events and
states referred to are not permanent. The 'perfect' modification
called 'Phase' by Joos,[6] has nothing to do with perfectivity, as its
usual label suggest, but is used to emphasize the significance of an
event at a point of time regardless of when it took place (linked to
the moment of speech by use of the present perfect, to a point in past
time by use of the past perfect).

To help in our analysis of syllabuses and text-books, we can look
at some of the salient features of the contrast between present simple
and present progressive. In most teaching grammars the progressive
is described as referring to events in progress at the moment of speech
and the simple form to habits or general truths. Neither is entirely
accurate, though they may serve their pedagogic function. As well as

> (1) Don't interrupt me! I'm working.

and

> (2) I come to work by car.

we have

> (3) I am working on a new project. (spoken while on holiday)

and

> (4) He lives a couple of miles away. (hardly definable as a
>   habit)

Regardless, however, of the over-simplification in the usual formulation, there are difficulties for the learner of English, since the progressive form is not incompatible with an habitual interpretation:

> (5) She's always making that mistake.

and the simple form is used for activities which apparently are
simultaneous with the utterance:

> (6) I (can) hear some music.

---

[6] M. Joos, *The English Verb* (Milwaukee, University of Wisconsin, 1964).

(7) I think it's going to rain.
(8) She feels ill.
(9) Mary resembles her brother.

The issue is complicated by the fact that although with sentences (6), (7) and (9) the progressive form would be wrong, the verbs are not simply exceptions to the general rule since in other instances progressive forms are possible:

(10) I am hearing you loud and clear.
(11) He's thinking about it all the time.
(12) Mary is resembling her brother more and more.

A progressive form of (8) is possible with little or no change of meaning.

It is also relevant that activities being demonstrated are described through the present simple and so too are events in a commentary:

(13) I connect the machine to the power supply and switch on.
(14) Laver serves to Rosewall.

There are other situations in which the present tense is typically used, but they are not important enough for the learner to delay us here. However, in view of the discussion of a future tense above, we can point out that both the present simple and the present progressive are frequently used with future reference, usually, although not always, with a future time adverbial in the sentence:

(15) I'm picking Jane up after work.
(16) They arrive at six and are taken straight to their hotel.

There need be no great learning problem with these uses, at least as far as potential confusion with the present time uses is concerned. As for the present uses, there is no way round the difficulties that face the learner who has learned sentences like (1) and (2) and is then faced with the apparent contractions implicit in (3)–(14). Any attempt to teach English must therefore provide for these difficulties, and syllabuses and text-books can be evaluated according to their success in acknowledging and preparing the teacher for the problems that the pupil will have.

3.1.1.2. *Syllabuses.*   No two syllabuses have quite the same purpose, but whether they are mandatory or advisory, they aim to make explicit the linguistic content of teaching in a particular situation.

If they do not have sufficient detail they cannot possibly do their job properly. Below is a sample of an actual syllabus listing what is to be taught during (part of) one year's teaching of English.[7]

Articles
   —normal use of definite and indefinite

Nouns
   —nouns and their plural
   —possessive form

Pronouns
   —personal as subject and object
   —possessive
   —demonstrative

Adjectives
   —position of adjectives
   —demonstrative
   —possessive
   —quantitatives or determinatives (*all, some, any,* etc.)

Adverbs
   —most common adverbs (time and place)
   —the *-ly* ending
   —position of adverbs of frequency and others

Prepositions
   —all common prepositions of time, place and direction (such as *in, out, to, from, of, at, on, with, without*)
   —omission of article in *at home, to school,* etc.

Verb Forms
   —use of *can* and *must*
   —irregular verbs (list)

Verb Tenses
   —present progressive
   —present simple
   —simple past
   —immediate future

---

[7] A book of this sort will always appear to be criticizing others. It is as well that I am able to include here for criticism this piece of work in the preparation of which I had a substantial hand, albeit some years ago. It was produced for use in secondary schools in the West African Republic of Guinea. Since French was the general language of instruction but not the mother-tongue, English was at least the third language.

Word Order
—affirmative (basic structure only)
—negative (statement and request only)
—interrogative:
   a with question words (*who, what, where, when, how much, how many*)
   b without question words
—requests (2nd person)
—question tags (such as *isn't it?, don't you?*)

This particular syllabus was prepared for a situation in which no text-books were available, but it is doubtful whether it could function very successfully since there are many points at which it is ambiguous. To take the very first heading, there is no indication as to what constitutes 'normal' use of the articles. It is still left to the teacher to decide which uses of the article he will actually teach, yet presumably the whole point of having a syllabus is to ensure that all teachers teach the same things. Which aspects of the functioning of the definite article system will a teacher decide to include? Will he include the *anaphoric* function?

I ran into a sailor yesterday . . .   Anyway, *the* sailor told me . . . Or the *cataphoric* use?

The horse has four legs.
Or the specifying function?

Shut *the* door, please.
Brazil won *the* World Cup in 1970.
It is also perfectly normal to use certain nouns without articles on some occasions:
The astronauts showed great courage.
but with a definite article on others:
The courage of the astronauts impressed the world.
There is the further complication of the use of the article with plural nouns. The use of the plural *without* an article can have the same cataphoric meaning as the use of the singular *with* an article.

Horses have four legs.
Any grammar will reveal much more about the use of articles, all of which is perfectly normal to the native speaker of English, Indeed, if there was anything abnormal about someone's usage, it would not be considered part of the language and therefore would not be included in the content of teaching.

One problem about situations like this where the whole of what has to be learned is not specified is that one has to be very alert to see that whatever one decides to omit at this stage of teaching does in fact get taught subsequently. In the case of this syllabus, in the second year the teacher is required to teach uncommon uses of the article system, but elsewhere in the syllabus this particular danger is well illustrated. In the section *Verb Tenses* we find *present progressive* and *present simple* listed. They do not appear again in this syllabus.

If we consider the complexities contained even in the simplified treatment of this contrast of tense above, it is inconceivable that everything that could be subsumed under these item headings could be taught in one year. In fact a teacher would not even attempt to cover everything. He would teach the use of the progressive as exemplified by (1) and the simple as exemplified by (2). He will do this because these are the uses most commonly taught in beginners' books. In practice such was certainly the intention of the authors of the syllabus. There is no admission that there is any difficulty in the complex interaction between these general uses and the lexical meaning of verbs that leads us to the simple form where the progressive form might be expected, as in (6)–(9). There is no preparation for the confusion of the learner who discovers that in sentences like (5) the progressive apparently has identical meaning to the simple, or that in the one common situation in which we actually talk about what we are simultaneously doing we use not the progressive as he will have been led to believe, but the simple tense as in 13. He will not be ready for the fact that the uttering of progressive forms need not be simultaneous with the event described, nor that simple forms are used not so much to describe habits as to make statements that characterize the subject. Eventually he will need to learn that the present forms of the verb can be used to refer not only to the present but also to the past, as in the so-called 'historical' use, and to the future as in (15) and (16).

Present progressive and present simple are mentioned only once in the syllabus. Once each form has been presented in one of these uses it is likely that teacher and pupil will conclude that each has been fully learned. The further uses will either not appear in the teaching at all, or, more probably, will appear in an uncontrolled fashion without proper provision for presentation and practice. It is an item approach which risks creating a situation in which I think I have taught 'the present progressive', when in reality I have taught only the form (*be* +-*ing*) of the verbal construction itself, together with a part of its semantics. This will lead to neglect of much of the semantic aspect of the verb and a great deal too of the structural relations that verb forms may enter into.

In this syllabus there is remarkably little attention given to the structural relations of the verb forms. We know that irregular (and presumably regular) verb forms are to be taught, and also four tenses. There is mention under 'word order' of the systems of affirmation, negation and interrogation, the emphasis here being presumably aimed at subject/verb inversion and use of the empty verb *do*. But verbs and tenses are not things which exist in isolation. They occur in sentences of the language. Affirmation, negation and interrogation similarly operate in all types of sentence. Yet there is no reference to the different kinds of sentence structure that are to be taught. We do not know whether both transitive and intransitive sentences should be taught; if transitive sentences are to be learned, should they be single or double object constructions; if double object, should it be direct and indirect object, or direct object and objective complement? Since the teaching of prepositions implies the use of prepositional phrases, should these appear in transitive or intransitive sentences? Are sentences with more than one prepositional phrase to be included? The verb *be* appears in the list of verbs, but there is no advice on which of the several types of complement that may follow the verb should be taught.

The specification of verbal structures to be taught is therefore imprecise in two ways. There is insufficient detail on the choices, and therefore the difficulties, that face the learner in the various forms of the verb paradigm. There is a complete absence of direction on the syntactic structures to be used and therefore the sub-categories of verb to be introduced.

It is by no means unusual for structural information of this and other kinds to be lacking from syllabuses. Any course will teach sentences which contain a subject, the verb *be* as copula and a complement. Once this has been done, with perhaps an article and a noun as subject and an adjective as complement, this type of structure is unlikely to be made the focus of explicit teaching. Yet, as the following sentences show, great variety is in fact possible within the same kind of sentence. In these sentences, what precedes the verb *be* in each case is in effect noun or noun phrase. No two of these noun phrases have the same structure and we could extend the examples indefinitely without repeating the same structure.

Ladies are beautiful.
He is a rich man.
Some are here.
John's is a new car.
That is an interesting point.
He who hesitates is lost.
Orange is an attractive colour.
The poor are deserving.
Ladies with blue eyes are attractive.
Ladies who have blue eyes are attractive.
Which way you go is up to you.
To arrive late is impolite.
His coming is of no importance.
His coming here is of no importance.
His coming here so often is of no importance.
What you want is a cup of tea.
That the manufacturers should advertise the product without
    first ensuring that adequate supplies would reach the shops
    in time to meet the demand was astonishing.

This exemplification of the variety of constructions that can operate
as the subject of a sentence permits us to see the extent to which
syllabuses may be under-specified and inexplicit. The information
that is brought together here is probably never brought together in
language teaching, although many of the forms are taught in isolation from one another. Most learners never appreciate the range of
expression that is open to them because the structural function of the
items taught is rarely fully presented. The learner would not be presented with these constructions simultaneously but there should be
a point in language learning, probably fairly late in the process, at
which some indication is given of how constructions that are intern-
ally very different can nonetheless function identically in the structure of the sentence as a whole.

3.1.1.3 *Text-books.* In the section above there are two criticisms
of syllabuses: first, that through being inexplicit and item-based
they are impossible to interpret accurately; secondly, that an item is
too easily equated with its morphological forms and that therefore
learning is directed at that form, or set of forms, functioning in one
kind of sentence structure only. To see whether a text-book consists
of a sequence of items we must look at the text itself for evidence

and not at the list of contents, which may well resemble the sample of a syllabus that we have been examining. An index does not have to be as explicit as a syllabus and the book should be judged by its actual contents and not by lack of clarity in its index. Spotting the faults of an item approach in a text-book requires a very careful study of the text indeed. In the lesson where, to continue with the example we have been discussing the present progressive is introduced, we may find that either, in a bad text-book, the complex of uses listed above is undifferentiated, or, in a better text-book, only one of the uses occurs. Even where we meet the latter situation, however, it is rare to find the other uses introduced in a similarly systematic manner. As we look through the book we may suddenly find non-progressive verbs being used without any warning as if they conformed to the general pattern of use of simple forms or as if the writer believed that their use is so obviously logical that no special teaching is required. This is far from the truth, as the many errors of foreign learners over this point testify.

We can examine one text-book to see how systematically forms are presented.[8] In Book One the *present progressive* is presented and practised in association with actions which are simultaneous with the speaking of the sentence. This is the orthodox approach in teaching English as a foreign language. Later the present simple is introduced. It is contrasted unambiguously with the present progressive by being demonstrated in association not with simultaneous events but with habitual actions, taken here to include not only personal habits, but also repetitive natural events such as the rising of the sun. Just after this the first complication occurs with the use of *want*, *like* and *see*. *Want* and *like* are arguably still within the habitual use of the present simple in the examples in this lesson. But since both are used also in the simple form even when they refer to simultaneous events, their presentation in the manner adopted here may lead to confusion later on if the point is not specifically taught. We may well find such forms as:

I am not liking this ice-cream*[9]

occurring in our pupils' work.

In the lesson in question, *see* is quite clearly not habitual. We find sentences like:

[8] A.S. Hornby, *Oxford Progressive English Course*, Book One (London, Oxford University Press, 1954).
[9] An asterisk denotes that the preceding sentence, phrase or word is ungrammatical.

Can you see him?
What do you see in the sixth picture?

Quite apart from the confusion that may be caused by the use of *can* and *do* here, there is no reference in the pupils' or the teacher's book to the fact that the form *are you seeing** would be wrong here, in spite of what has been previously taught about the use of the progressive form.

From the learner's point of view the distinction between the two forms at this stage is that habits are reported with use of the simple form, events concurrent with speech are reported with the progressive form. A few lessons later we find in a conversation the sentence:

Oh, you're always losing things.

This is entirely new to the learner. The progressive form is, after all, compatible with habitual events, yet the teacher's book makes no reference to it and there is no provision for practice. The previously firm basis for the distinction of use will be considerably eroded.

In the same conversation we find the two sentences:

Do you remember?
I don't remember where I left it.

The word *remember* is referred to in the teacher's handbook simply as a new vocabulary item, yet with its introduction the pupil comes into contact with a new sub-class of verbs which, like *see* and *like*, occur in the simple form, where the learner might expect the progressive. Verbs such as *remember, forget, think* and *believe* are not quite the same as *see* and *hear* and others, since the latter relate to perception while the former suggest mental activity of some kind. Formally, the verbs of perception are more likely to occur with *can* than in the simple form alone. This is not the case with verbs like *remember*. In this lesson there is no provision for practice nor for explicit teaching of the patterning of these verbs. When the word *forget* appears a few lessons later, the teacher's handbook does make a cross-reference to the previously introduced *remember*, but the object of the reference seems to be the contrast of vocabulary (lexical) meaning and not the similarity of formal/semantic patterning.[10]

[10] It must not be supposed that this analysis shows the text-book writer to have been at fault. To isolate every single rule, whether of general or very limited application, is not the only strategy that can be adopted in language teaching. Hornby may well have decided that there are some things, such as the use of *remember*-type verbs, which are best learned 'out of awareness' and that repetitive practice is best devoted to the most general rules of language. If the teacher

In the lesson after *remember* has first occurred, the author deals with a correct extension of the use of the present simple. The use is that of demonstrating some procedure as typical of the kind of actions one carries out in performing a task, as exemplified in (13). So, if one wants to show someone how to mend a tyre or use a washing-machine, one goes through the sequence of events, describing them as one does them. 'I plug into the wall-socket and switch on. I turn the control to "very hot". . .' and so on. Hornby points out that such a use is really 'no different from the habitual use that has already been taught, but that it requires specific practice since the physical situation has just those features of simultaneity of speech and action that have hitherto been taught as characterizing the use of the present progressive form.[11]

These examples, taken from a text-book that is generally very sound linguistically, show just how fully aware the writer and teacher need to be that the teaching of a form in one context, linguistic or situational, cannot be taken as all that is needed for the subsequent accurate use of that form in all contexts. If one is to specify precisely what is to be learned, one does not deal simply in terms of labels like 'present simple', 'comparative', 'negation' or 'definite article', since each of these is little more than a cover term for a whole structural system of relations and it is these that are the true aim of language teaching. This means that the content of any one teaching unit is probably best expressed for the teacher's benefit either as a very explicit rule or through a model sentence with the understanding that learning cannot go beyond what is strictly analogous to the model. Language teaching that neglects syntax and semantics is certain to be inadequate. By thinking of language learning as the mastering of structural relations rather than the acquisition of a set of forms, we can help ourselves to avoid this inadequacy.

---

approves this strategy, the text-book is not at fault. If the teacher's strategy is different, the text-book will require some supplementation with appropriate practice materials.

[11] This reflects the essential unnaturalness of the common procedure for teaching use of the progressive form in English, whereby a teacher performs an action and describes it at the same time: 'I am opening the door,' etc. In fact a person is most unlikely ever to need to do this where the hearer is present in the situation, precisely because it conveys nothing that the hearer cannot see for himself. It might occur where one is describing an event to someone who is not present, but that is a relatively rare situation anyway.

3.2. Deep structure and the study of syntax

Most foreign language teaching proceeds on the assumption that
linguistic structure has some psychological reality, and that learning
is made easier if similar pieces of language are taught together and
dissimilar pieces of language are separated. Almost all text-books,
old and new, attempt to reveal the structure of the foreign language
progressively, piece by piece, to the learner. The alternative, that of
exposing the pupils to the foreign language without control, may be
likened to teaching people to swim by throwing them into the deep
end. It has its advocates, but they are few and so far uninfluential.
If one is adopting the progressive approach, the linguist's descriptive
analysis of structure has considerable significance, since it will
identify the units to be taught, though not their sequence. The
teacher should base his teaching on that description which reveals most
satisfactorily the structural contrasts and relations of the language.

   To judge how satisfactory a description is may not be as easy as
one would expect. The structure of a sentence is not always what it
appears to be, and indeed linguists themselves do not necessarily
agree on how to interpret some pieces of language structurally.
Let us look at the following two sentences for example:

   (1) They gave John their vote.
   (2) They elected John their representative.

Most older grammars agree that the grammatical structure of these
two sentences is not the same, although their analyses of the second
sentence are not unanimous. (1) is usually described as an Indirect
Object + Direct Object construction. In (2), the second noun phrase
their representative is known by such names as predicative adjunct
or objective complement, with *John* quite simply as an Object.
Traditionally, therefore, these sentences are described as having
different structures.

   At least one linguist, however, argues that there is no formal
evidence for distinguishing these two sentence types.[12] He says:

   The presence of two complements is familiar under such names as
   indirect object and *direct object* for sentences of the type *I gave John a
   book*, and *object* and *objective complement* for *I called John a fool*. It
   should be emphasized that these names indicate semantic distinctions

[12] A.A. Hill, *Introduction to Linguistic Structures* (New York, Harcourt, Brace &
World, 1957), p. 296.

only and that nothing in the *formal* [my italics] structure distinguishes one relationship from the other. English signals both relationships in the same way, leaving the proper interpretation to the probabilities involved in the lexical sequences.

If we look at (1) and (2) we can see why Hill says this. Each sentence consists of an identical sequence, a pronominal subject, a verb, a proper noun and a noun phrase. If we look at this alone there are no grounds for saying that the sentences have different structures. Each unit within the sentences has the same internal structure and each stands in the same sequential relationship and therefore, it is argued, their functions must be identical. If we accept this description then, in teaching, such sentences as (1) and (2) would have to be classified and taught together. No special explanation would be required since understanding of the lexical meanings involved would be adequate for the pupil to comprehend the meaning of the whole sentence. Such an analysis contrasts strongly with the traditional analysis and this contrast would be reflected in any teaching that was based on Hill's description.

However, many linguists would find Hill's analysis unacceptable, since it rests upon taking as evidence only the sentences themselves as they might occur in speech. For linguists like Hill this is what was meant at that time by a formal analysis. Yet it can be argued that such an interpretation of what is required for formal analysis is excessively narrow; that since language is structured, no part exists in isolation, nor should it be studied in isolation. Each element has connections with other parts of the structure and to discover these we must look further than the immediately occurring pieces of language. The analysis which equates (1) and (2) deals only with what appears on the surface. Much more can be revealed about the structure of a language by investigating what underlies the sentences which we actually produce or receive or what inter-connections there are between them. The above analysis has been termed by a more recent linguistic school an analysis of the 'surface structure', and it has been held that such analysis is inferior to the analysis of the deeper regularities of a language—its 'deep structure'. Of (1) and (2) it would be said that the similarity in their surface structure is superficial and that an investigation of their deep structure would reveal that they are structurally distinct. Transformational generative linguists would say that the traditional grammarians were right in assigning a different structural description to these two sentences.

They would show by a set of explicit rules how two sentences which are derived quite differently come to resemble one another in their actual occurrence.

It would be irrelevant to give an example of how these linguists present their descriptions. But without going into the complex technicalities of transformational grammar it is possible to show how, by taking into account a larger linguistic context than the sentences immediately under consideration, one can demonstrate differences between them which argue strongly for the case that their structure is actually different.

The argument rests upon the fact that certain manipulations which can be applied to (1) cannot be applied to (2). We can say:

> John was given their vote.
> John was elected their representative.

and

> Their vote was given (to) John.

but not

> Their representative was elected (to) John.*

In other words, whereas in (1) the second complement can occur as the subject of a passive sentence, in (2) it cannot. Similarly we can say:

> It was their vote they gave John.

but not

> It was their representative they elected John.*

As a further point, the second complement in (2) can be deleted and a grammatical sentence remains:

> They elected John.

but not in (1):

> They gave John.*

It is considerations such as these, depending upon a wider interpretation of formal relations, that can lead us to accept that there is a structural distinction between these two sentences. The conditions under which such relationships are established in transformational grammars are very rigorous. The above illustration gives no indication of this.

The reader might think that linguistics has gone in a large circle to return to the same point. He always believed that these sentences had different structures and linguistics has told him nothing new. That can only be argued because the example chosen was a familiar one. Transformational analysis often returns to traditional analyses, but it is not the case that all its conclusions are found in earlier grammars. In the first place it fills in many of the gaps, making explicit what was left to the reader to supply. Secondly, the notion of deep structure may result in a distinction being found among sentences which were analysed identically by traditional grammarians. That is to say, for us as teachers, it may split into two or more teaching points what has always been one. The following two sentences provide an example of this:

(3) He was difficult to understand.
(4) He was slow to understand.

These two sentences are commonly analysed as having the same structure, with the infinitive being treated as the adjunct of a predicative adjective. Yet whereas *he* can be considered as the subject of *slow* and *understand* in (4), it is obviously not the subject of *understand* in (3). If we are to believe that separating different structures has any psychological validity for teaching, there are two types of sentence which must henceforth be kept apart. This is one way in which the notion of deep structure may influence the organization of teaching material.

This is probably the place to mention that a theory which recognizes deep structure would provide a different analysis of the morphology of the French adjective from the surface structure analysis which was given in the first chapter. That analysis would have faced one difficulty which I did not mention. If the feminine forms are taken as the base and the masculine forms are derived from them by deletion of the final consonant, how is it that in cases of liaison the masculine form ends in a consonant? One could say that the consonant is reintroduced if the following noun begins with a vowel, but this would seem unnecessarily complex, or one could say that the rule of deletion does not apply when a vowel follows. In either explanation we are making a special case of what is a widespread phenomenon in French—that a final consonant is heard when followed by a vowel, but not otherwise.[13] Bearing in mind the necessity of this last rule in a grammatical description of French anyway, we may choose to revert to the analysis of the adjectival forms which is based on the orthography. Taking *grand* as an example, we could say that the masculine form is the base and could be written in a

---

[13] This is, of course, an over-simplification, but the complexities are irrelevant to the general point being made here.

phonological transcription as /grãd/ and that the feminine form is derived from it by the addition of the schwa vowel, hence /grãdə/. In order to determine the exact pronunciation we simply apply the general morphophonological rule. A consonant preceding a vowel is pronounced. In *grand enfant* we would have [grãd]; in *grand garçon* we would have [grã]. The feminine does not have a final consonant anyway so the [d] is pronounced. The final schwa, [ə], is omitted as it is in normal French speech.

As teachers we are now faced with a dilemma. We have the choice of two kinds of analysis as the basis of teaching. One, the analysis of surface structure, is more immediately relatable to the actual forms of speech, but in a sense misrepresents the grammar of French. The other makes more significant generalizations about the grammar of French but requires the introduction of more abstract forms. If for the moment we assume that the latter is the 'best' analysis of the data, I do not think that we have equally to conclude that it is always the best for pedagogical purposes. If for methodological reasons we want to follow a purely oral approach, it would only create confusion if we were in effect to teach the feminine forms as derived from the masculine. We might prefer the approach outlined in the first chapter.[14] If the written language was to be introduced early—as might be the case with older learners—the organization of teaching could be based on the more abstract analysis above. Abstract phonological forms like /pətit/ and /pətitə/ are, of course, very close to the orthographic forms *petit* and *petite*. In this case early spoken practice would probably use the written forms as stimuli. The view has been expressed that in this and allied aspects of French grammar there are powerful arguments against a purely oral approach to the teaching of French. In particular, anyone who intends eventually to read and write the language has much to gain from meeting the orthography at the beginning and learning how to derive the spoken forms from it and much to lose from starting with speech and attempting to relate the written form to it afterwards.

3.2.1. Syntax

Language, we have seen, is structured, and the structure is not

---

[14] In theory it would be possible to satisfy the requirements of both surface and deep grammar by first presenting adjectives as modifiers of masculine nouns beginning with vowels. The final consonant would be known from the beginning and the learner could proceed to learn deletion of the consonant in non-pre-vocalic position and the retention of the consonant before feminine nouns.

necessarily revealed by the way in which the actual sentences of our speech are organized. The study of the rules governing relations between items of language is the study of syntax, and to it recent developments in linguistics have given a great impetus. It has now been realized that the structure of sentences is far more complex—and important—than early linguists recognized, and although traditional grammarians have often appreciated the significance of syntax, they have nonetheless failed to describe its complexities fully. These deficiencies in language description are very much reflected in language teaching where there is often little understanding of the difficulties presented by the syntax of a language. For this reason I should like to examine the notion of syntactic structure through a fairly detailed example.

Much recent work on syntax represents a rephrasing and formalization of existing knowledge of syntactic structure. It contains little that is very new. But sometimes a transformational generative description brings together syntactic information which was previously, at best, available only in widely separated places in the grammar; and the demonstration that hitherto unconnected parts of the grammatical system are in fact related is highly informative, not only in the description of that language, but also in developing an understanding of its acquisition.

3.2.1.1. *Predicate complement constructions in English.*[15] The name 'predicate complementation' is given by Rosenbaum to certain constructions involving use of *that*-clauses, the infinitive and the progressive, *-ing*, forms of verbs preceded by a nominal in the possessive case. The occurrence of these forms in conjunction with certain verbs, the manipulations that can be carried out on them by way, for example, of passivization are apparently highly unpredictable. Certainly, knowing the meaning of a verb-word would in no way assist a learner in deciding what syntactic functions that word might have. The situation is most complex and there is no possibility of finding a simple solution to its analysis. Rosenbaum in a full-scale study of this aspect of English grammar has still not been entirely successful in showing how many of these sentences are derived. The difficulties can best be shown by taking a number of examples.

---

[15] What follows owes much to P.S. Rosenbaum, *The Grammar of English Predicate Complement Constructions* (Cambridge, Massachusetts Institute of Technology Press, 1967).

Sentences (1)–(5) seem acceptable and analogous.

(1) I intend that he shall be a doctor.
(2) I regret that he is absent.
(3) They announced that he was an impostor.
(4) He remarked that John looked ill.
(5) I suspected that he was a charlatan.

The verbs *intend, regret, announce, remark*, and *suspect* therefore belong to a sub-class of verbs which can be followed by *that* constructions. There are alternative ways of expressing (1) which seem to be entirely synonymous with it.

(1a) I intend him to be a doctor.
(1b) I intend him being a doctor.

One might expect that the same kinds of manipulations can be applied to the other sentences, but when we attempt it a very untidy pattern emerges.

(2a) I regret him to be absent.*
(2b) I regret him (or *his*) being absent.
(3a) They announced him to be an impostor.
(3b) They announced him being an impostor.*
(4a) He remarked John to look ill.*
(4b) He remarked John's looking ill.*

In the case of *suspect*, we do have similar forms:

(5a) I suspect him to be a charlatan.
(5b) I suspect him being a charlatan.

However, (5b) would seem to have a different meaning from (5) and (5a), being paraphrasable as:

I suspect him when he is pretending to be a charlatan.

Synonymy would be retained if we inserted *of* before *being*.

(5c) I suspect him of being a charlatan.

So of these verbs, only *intend* participates in all three constructions. The others reveal different distributions including a fourth equivalent type with *of*.

If we look a little further afield, we shall discover that there are some verbs which may be followed by the a or b constructions but do not have the *that* constructions at all.

(6)   I like that he arrives on time.*

(6a) I like him to arrive on time.
(6b) I like him (his) arriving on time.
(7) I admire that John tries so hard.*
(7a) I admire John to try so hard.*
(7b) I admire John's trying so hard.

The similarity of *like* and *admire* to the earlier list becomes more apparent when we look at the following:

(1d) It is intended that he shall be a doctor.
(2d) It is suspected that he was a charlatan.

. . .

(6d) It is (much) liked that he arrives on time.
(7d) It is (much) admired that John tries so hard.

The presence of this *it* may be highly significant, because we find that by inserting it into (6) and (7) we obtain the acceptable sentences below:

(6e) I like it that he arrives on time.
(7e) I admire it that John tries so hard.

It appears therefore that these sentences with *it* are very closely related to (1)-(5) without *it*. It seems not impossible too that for some speakers the presence of *it* is acceptable after some verbs where for other speakers it is not. This is notoriously an area of grammar where even the native speaker is unsure of the boundaries of grammaticality and acceptability.[16]

However, the complications by no means stop there. There is another way of constructing these sentences, probably in order to express a different emphasis but not otherwise changing the meaning. This involves the application of what is called the pseudo-clefting transformation. It produces sentences like the following:

(1f) What I intend is that he shall be a doctor.
(2f) What I regret is that he is absent.

We notice that once again there is no apparent difference between these verbs and *like* and *admire*:

(6f) What I like is that he arrives on time.

A similar process seems to be possible with the (a) sentences too:

(1g) What I intend is *for* him to be a doctor.

---

[16] The Rosenbaum analysis by accepting forms present in some dialects but not in others in a sense avoids the difficulty.

But in this case we have to introduce the word *for* which was not present in (1a). The sentence (3g) appears to be derived in the same way from (3a):

(3g) What they announced was for him to be an impostor.

This is a correctly formed sentence but its meaning is clearly not the same as the meaning of (3a). With (5a) it does not even seem to be possible to construct a well-formed sentence.

(5g) What I suspect is for him to be a charlatan.*

Stranger still is the fact that while (7a) is not acceptable, (7g) perhaps is.

(7g) What I admire is for John to try so hard.

The production of the *-ing* forms seems rather more consistent.

(1h) What I intend is him being a doctor.
(5h) What I suspect is him being a charlatan.
      What I suspect him of is being a charlatan.
(7h) What I admire is John's trying so hard.

As with *suspect* there are many cases where there is another verb which is closely tied to a particle of some kind.

(8b) I approve building the new town hall.
(9b) I approve of building the new town hall.
(10b) I planned your staying at this hotel.
(11b) I planned on your staying at this hotel.

In each these cases we seem to have two distinct pairs of verbs: *approve* and *approve of*, *plan* and *plan on*. In order to convey our meaning we have to select the right one. With some other verbs whether or not the particle is expressed is optional and does not change the meaning. There does not appear to be any difference in meaning between *decide* and *decide on*, for example. The particle is obligatorily absent in (12) and present in (12b). In (12f) we have the option of including or excluding it.

(12) I decided that he would come for the week-end.
(12b) I decided on his coming for the week-end.
(12f) What I decided (on) was that he would come for the week-end.

One could go on for a long time exemplifying the difficulties which surround the forms under discussion. However, here I will content myself with just one further observation. In the sentences we have looked at so far, to choose between the infinitive and the

-ing construction, where both of these have been available, has not involved differentiating meanings. Sentences (13a) and (13b) show this:

(13a) He began to eat his lunch.
(13b) He began eating his lunch.

If we had chosen *remember* as our main verb we should have had a quite different result:

(14a) He remembered to eat his lunch.
(14b) He remembered eating his lunch.

As I have said, this by no means exhausts the apparent anomalies that exist in the use of these forms. I would not wish to suggest that no order can be established here. On the contrary, descriptive linguistics sets out to do just this and we can expect that increasingly satisfactory analyses will become available. But it is by presenting some of the virtually unanalysed data such as we have above that we can best comprehend the bewildering difficulties that face the learner of English. In practice we inform him on how to construct forms like *that*-clauses, infinitives and *-ing* verb forms, but we give him hardly any insight into how these can be used. In short we neglect the acquisition of syntax.

3.2.1.2. *Pedagogic implications.* I have suggested that areas of advanced syntax like predicate complementation are generally overlooked in foreign language teaching. Comparison and negation would be two other areas where language teaching rarely concerns itself with anything beyond the more obvious forms. By 'overlooked' I do not mean so much that examples of the sentences in question never appear in text-books, but that the presentation and practice of them is not specifically planned in the way that the form and use of tenses or cases is. The sentences may indeed occur, but not as a result of a conscious decision about the appropriate moment to introduce them. There is rather an assumption that a learner who has been given the opportunity to practise the negation of a verb can recognize and master the negation of any other element in a sentence without the aid of specially constructed practice materials. If he can make a simple comparison of two adjectives then he should be presented with no great difficulty in grasping the syntactic rules necessary for the comparison of nouns or, say, clauses functioning as nouns.

In a sense there are good reasons why such constructions do not constitute the subject-matter of elementary learning. Even without mastery of the rules underlying these sentences a learner can express a lot in a second language. So perhaps one is concerned here with the content of fairly advanced language learning. It is possible for a foreigner to be a very fluent and accurate speaker of English and yet not to attempt to produce many of the complementation structures that I have sketched above. It might be that it is in just such a matter as this that a very proficient speaker of a foreign language differs from a native speaker of that language. The difference may lie not in errors committed but in a deliberate avoidance of sentences whose structure is thought to present difficulty, perhaps because such sentences were inadequately taught originally. We sometimes have great difficulty in deciding just what it is about a non-native speaker that marks him off as not using his mother-tongue. It would require a thoroughgoing statistical analysis to show that there was a difference in the range of syntactic structures attempted. An informal check with my own students, some of whom were extremely competent speakers of English, elicited the admission that all of them consciously avoided even trying to produce some of the sentence structures we had been examining. There was surprise in some cases that such sentences could exist in English.

I may appear to have suggested that the step-by-step process by which language teaching commonly proceeds should be extended to include aspects of syntax which have rarely been deliberately taught. It does not follow, however, that because such points present very real difficulties for the learner they have to be tackled in this way, even supposing that in general it is a satisfactory approach to language teaching. In the case of the complementation structures above such an approach would present problems.

In both traditional and modern language teaching the learning-points which are isolated for presentation and practice are precisely those points which offer the largest return for the learner. They enable him to make the most significant generalizations. We show, and practise, certain nouns marked for plural, certain adjectives marked for gender, certain adverbs in a given position in the sentence *because* they are typical of a large number of other nouns, adjectives and adverbs. We suppose that the learner will be able to generalize the skill he has in producing these words in the correct forms to all other words. What the teacher presents is limited. What the pupil learns goes far beyond what he is taught.

The less significant the generalizations that can be made on the basis of a particular example, the less value there is in attempting to organize language learning in some kind of graded sequence of steps. The early stages of most language courses are devoted to the learning of the most general rules. Sometimes items seem to be included more because they are of general applicability than because they are especially significant for communication. The complement structures that we saw above might be nearer the other end of the scale. No two verbs from among those that I exemplified behaved in exactly the same way. It is true that there are many more verbs than I have shown here and some of them, no doubt, may occur in exactly the same contexts. It should be remembered though that there are syntactic constructions that I have not mentioned. The difficulty will lie in the fact that the numbers of verbs which can be put together into sub-classes because of their potentialities for co-occurrence with the different structures will be very small. Each of these sub-classes will include verbs which are of little importance for the learner of a foreign language, and by the time we have excluded these we may find that we have very small lists of verbs indeed. Ideally we should like to be able to say that there is quite a long list of verbs which behave in the same way. A learner who had learned the syntactic possibilities of one or two of them would then have learned the possibilities of all of them. Each largish class of verbs, together with the complement structures that can follow it, could then be the content of a learning unit. Unfortunately, as we have seen, in this instance the classes are not likely to be large enough for this approach to have much value.

An alternative would be to construct units not in terms of sub-classes of verbs, but to present and practise one particular type of complement structure. So a unit might be devoted to sentences with *that*-clause complements, and in this unit the learner would meet all those important verbs which could be followed by such a clause. This is what existing teaching materials probably come closest to doing, but it presents the difficulty that it might actually encourage false generalizations. Most learners of English, to take a very simple example, have no problems with:

> I want to go.

and

> I wish to go.

but because of this limited similarity, they presume identical privileges of co-occurrence with other complements and the possibility of

> I wish that I could go.

leads to the production of

I want that I could go.*

Since both of these ways of producing materials so that the learners, generalizing processes are assisted seem to have their drawbacks' are we to conclude that, after all, there is nothing better than the unexploited and unplanned exposure that is the actual state of affairs? It might be that a solution lies in not using specially *constructed* materials at all, that there is an alternative in the use of *unedited* samples of natural language. The teaching of languages at advanced levels might, among other things, concern itself with the detailed linguistic study of texts, literary and non-literary, which were not written with the needs of language learners in mind. A slightly different argument for the use of natural texts throughout the learning process has been made elsewhere,[17] but I would not wish to go as far as that. While I would not see the texts as being primarily literary in style, it seems to me that the literary tradition in language teaching had at least one thing to be said in its favour. It brings the pupil into contact with a range of linguistic forms which is not provided by the more controlled content of the early years of learning. It is true that what the pupil is brought into contact with remains haphazard, but it is not clear how one would establish priorities among these more complex constructions anyway. What is important is that, as sentences with unfamiliar structures occur in the texts, they should not pass unexploited.

The technique to be employed for exploitation of the linguistic content could closely resemble the traditional French *explication de texte*. Any text might contain a number of sentences with structures that were in some way new to the pupils. The teacher would draw the attention of the learners to the sentence. The extent to which he would discuss its grammar explicitly would depend upon the methodological convictions of the teacher. He would exemplify the structure with further sentences and demonstrate the transformational potentialities of the sentence. He would have prepared drills and other practice materials so that some opportunity is given to the pupils to develop a mastery of the structures under examination. In this way the occurrence of an unfamiliar linguistic form is used to expand the pupil's competence in the language.

We can look at the complement structures to see what kinds of

[17] D.A. Reibel, 'Language Learning Analysis' (*International Review of Applied Linguistics* 7/4, 1969).

sentences might be brought to the learner's attention and practised in this way. This sentence might appear in a text being read by students of English.

(15) The Prime Minister likes his ministers to attend meetings punctually.

The teacher has the choice of operating with this sentence or of substituting for it a slightly less cumbersome one. Let us assume that he adopts the latter solution and shows his class that

(16) John likes his wife to eat well.

is similar in the aspect of structure under consideration. He could then show that it was related in structure to any of the following sentences (though not necessarily in this order):

(16a) John likes his wife eating well.
(16b) John likes it that his wife eats well.[18]
(16c) What John likes is that his wife eats well.
(16d) What John likes is for his wife to eat well.
(16e) What John likes is his wife eating well.
      and/or
(16f) What John likes is his wife's eating well.
(16g) What is liked by John is that his wife eats well.
(16h) That his wife eats well is liked by John.
(16i) For his wife to eat well is liked by John.
(16j) His wife's eating well is liked by John.
(16k) It is liked by John that his wife eats well.
(16l) It is liked by John for his wife to eat well.

He could also point out that *for* in (16d) would be present in (16) if there was an adverb present after the verb:

(16m) John likes very much for his wife to eat well.

Probably he would wish to make sure that the learners were aware of the contrast between (16) and such sentences as

John likes to eat well.
John likes eating well.

Of course we do not have to assume that *all* of these sentences must be dealt with at the same time, but (16) to (16m) provide us with an inventory of contexts for demonstrating the syntactic features of the verb *like*. It is the use of this verb in certain syntactically related

[18] It is important to note that the semantic implications of 16b are not the same as those of 16.

sentences that is being taught, not its membership of a particular sub-class of verbs and not the general formation of any one sentence structure. To discourage any possibility of over-generalization, one would probably contrast its behaviour with one or more other verbs which show only limited or superficial similarity.

3.3. Units of language

I think that general considerations of the nature of grammatical structure, such as we have been discussing so far in this chapter, are of more interest to the language teacher than the details of the way in which a linguistic analysis is presented. Even where linguists would agree that two forms are in contrast, they will not necessarily agree on the way in which that contrast should be expressed in a description. The language teacher probably stands to gain less from the manner in which the contrast is analysed than from the knowledge that there quite simply *is* a contrast. However I do not want to leave the subject of grammar without some discussion of the framework within which linguists make their descriptions. I am limiting my attention to units of language, since language teaching has not been uninfluenced by developments in this area.

We can summarize what I have said about the aims of the linguist in the following way. When he is investigating a language, he looks for forms that contrast with one another or forms that, although apparently identical, are seen to be in contrast because they have different meanings. His final description of that language will consist of a complete statement of all the contrasts that he has been able to find. By *form* might be meant the actual shape of words, phrases and so on, but also differences of relationship which may not be signalled in the overt forms of utterances, but can be inferred from accepted differences of meanings. The linguist would probably see it as the aim of language teaching to produce a productive mastery of these contrasts. In this case the contrasts that he identifies assume a pedagogic as well as a purely descriptive significance. The points of contrast are points of acquisition.

In identifying the units of language the linguist follows the traditional grammarian in recognizing the word. The fact that the linguist normally studies speech does present him with some procedural problems since, in speech, unlike in writing, the word is not conveniently marked off by pauses on either side. In practice he bases his acceptance of the word principally on the fact that it is the smallest stretch of speech that can occur as a complete utterance. However, many words are divisible into component units which recur in other words of the language with regular meanings, sometimes grammatical, sometimes lexical. To these smaller units the name 'morpheme' has been given. The morpheme has sometimes been defined as the smallest meaningful unit of language. The word *walked* may be divided into a morpheme *walk*, also found in *walk, walks, walking* and a morpheme *-ed* also found in *talked, wrapped, raced* and so on. Whenever one adds *-ed* to a root morpheme, one modifies the meaning in the same way to signify 'took place in past time'. Instead of looking at words as entities which have different forms under certain conditions, one sees them as made up two or more smaller units. In our description we must find a place for these morphemes to be listed and the rules governing their combinations to be stated. In such an interpretation *walked* is a different word from *walking* or *walks* since it has a constituent which is in contrast with one constituent in each of the other two words.

In linguistics there was at one time considerable preoccupation with the problems that arose in the attempt to introduce this new level of description. The situation is a good deal more complex than the single example above would suggest. It is all very well to think of words being constructed by the addition of more and more morphemes to a root morpheme, each addition bringing a specific addition to the meaning, as happens in agglutinative languages. However, in some other cases the facts are not quite so easily handled. The *-ed* morpheme in English, for a start, has several different phonetic realizations. Furthermore there is sometimes no overt addition to the root morpheme at all, as in a verb like *cut*. There are also verbs like *rang* where the past form differs from the non-past form by an internal contrast that can only very clumsily be thought of as the addition of a morpheme. Most of the morphemes like *-ed* which carry grammatical information do not occur in isolation. They are often 'bound' forms which have to be attached to another morpheme in an utterance. It is true that there are in English some morphemes whose function is principally grammatical which are conventionally thought of as distinct words, articles, prepositions and auxiliary verbs, for example—but even these only occur alone as complete utterances under very exceptional circumstances. The question does not arise therefore of attempting to teach the morpheme as an isolated unit of language. It is irrelevant to the teacher which of the possible analyses of the *walk/walked, cut/cut, ring/rang* relationship is linguistically the best. He has to ensure that the learner can operate the contrast, and he can only do this by teaching the word forms, since to break them down into any smaller consti- tuents would introduce an unacceptable degree of artificiality into the language of the classroom.

The value of the morpheme in language teaching is not that it leads us to new facts of the language so much as that it brings us to view the known facts in a different way. If a grammar is based on a descriptive framework that takes the word as the smallest unit of language, the various forms that a word may have are brought together in a paradigm. In traditional grammars of highly inflected languages there are paradigms of noun declension and verb conjuga- tion. In language teaching, especially in the past, each paradigm has been seen, not simply as a descriptive technique, but as a learning unit. Whole paradigms have been taught at a time and the overall organization of teaching has been aimed at exposing the learner to a sequence of paradigms until the range of morphological variation in the language has been covered. At times this analysis of learning has been applied in the teaching of both dead languages like Latin and Greek and living languages like Russian and German.

By postulating the morpheme as a unit smaller than the word, and by applying a pedagogic principle of 'one thing at a time', each contrast is seen to reveal the presence of a different 'thing' and therefore a different point of language to be acquired. A paradigm is not now one learning point, but contains as many learning points as there are morphemes in the paradigm. If we imagine a paradigm established for a noun system which recognized three classes of noun and a four-case system, there would presumably be twelve different forms for the learner to acquire. Theoretically, at least, these could constitute the content of twelve different teaching units. This suggests that, looked at from the traditional point of view, such teaching materials would contain relatively little new language in each unit and would appear to teach the language very much more slowly. A comparison of older and newer text-books will reveal just such differences. An older book will often cover in half the time what is now expected from a whole year's language learning. The common rejection of paradigm learning as a means of achieving the aims of lan- guage teaching has its own methodological justifications, but evidence for change in the same direction could be found in linguistics too. Morphemes as such have not been taught, but the influence of a mor- phemic level of analysis has been felt indirectly, as we shall see below.

The morpheme, however, is not the only unit of language in which the linguist is interested and before we consider the influence of the morpheme on decision-making in language teaching, we must look at the *sentence*, since the linguist has not only added to the number of units in terms of which a language may be described, but also re-emphasized the largest unit of grammatical structure. We have already seen in this chapter why the sentence is important for the linguist. The structural significance of an item cannot be understood when it is viewed in isolation. The sentence is the only unit which can display all the structural relations that are possible in a language.[19] The classification of word-classes or parts of speech is based on the function that words have in the sentence and not on semantic criteria as was usually the case traditionally. If the linguist describes only units smaller than the sentence, he cannot hope to have accounted for all the grammatical structure of the language.

The language teacher may find another reason for attaching importance to the sentence. It stems not from the structural nature of language, but from its communicative function. The aims of foreign language learners may differ, but it is unlikely that any of them will be learning for any purpose other than some form of communication in the language. People want to acquire language because language is meaningful activity. In most of our day-to-day uses of language we are in contact with stretches of language which are made up of sentences—reading and dictating letters, reading the newspaper, listening to the news, discussing our work and so on. In very few of these activities do we produce anything smaller than a single sentence as a complete utterance. The only exception to this is conversation, where our utterances may quite often consist of no more than a word or phrase. However, even in conversation a single utterance is commonly made up of one or more sentences. If something less than a sentence—say a single word—is uttered and understood, it will be understood only when the hearer is fully aware of what has not been said. A single word utterance is only comprehensible by reference to a complete sentence which provides the necessary context. If the speaker knows that the hearer will be familiar with part of the sentence that he intends to utter, it is no longer necessary for him actually to utter the entire sentence. A word or phrase will suffice. The analysis of discourse has not yet proceeded far enough for one to know exactly what is meant by 'familiar' here,

[19] There are in fact some grammatical relations *between* different sentences, but no unit larger than the sentence can be at all easily identified.

but there can be little doubt that there are fairly clear rules under which one can delete part of an utterance. Anything less than a sentence, then, is not meaningful unless it is clearly related to a sentence.

The sentence therefore is the best candidate for that unit of language structure which carries enough information within it to be conceivable as a complete utterance. One could presumably converse in single sentences. One could not converse in anything less. As a unit of communication it is far more meaningful than the word or phrase, and its structure is far better understood than anything larger, such as the paragraph. It is perhaps this feeling that the sentence has a particular communicative status that underlay the traditional attempts to define it as the unit for expressing complete thoughts.

It seems to me that there is some value in the foreign language learner being taught by means of pieces of language which can easily be seen as potential utterances. The whole process is more meaningful, and while it does not follow that because language *use* is meaningful the process of language acquisition should be so too, there is a strong supposition that this is the case. A method of language teaching that requires a pupil to produce lists of isolated words or paradigms or involves sub-sentence level translation is meaningless in more than one sense. Yet all these things are to be found in many available language teaching courses. The sentence carries enough linguistic and semantic context within it to be interpretable by the pupil as a possible meaningful utterance. The whole process of language learning seems to have much more point when the learner can see the practical value of the language he is learning. Quite apart from the effect on the pupil's attitude to learning, it seems likely that fully meaningful and fully grammatical language is actually more easily learnt. It seems, therefore, much better to use the sentence as the basic unit of language teaching.

3.3.1. Pedagogic example: the definite article in German

When one turns to the practical business of interpreting these developments for language teaching, there is no necessary contradiction between the identification of each formal contrast, even at the morphemic level, as an acquisition point and the necessity of using sentences as units of teaching, because of their meaningfulness and completeness of structure. One simply presents and practises sets of sentences which illustrate the contrast in question and only that contrast. The sentences all have the same structure and only when the sentences displaying one form have been adequately practised does one move on to sentences which include another contrasting form.

In the case of the German article one is likely to begin with the nominative form, since while verbs may have no objects they cannot do without subjects except in the imperative.[20] Since there are three contrasting forms of the nominative singular— *der, die* and *das*— one has to decide which gender to introduce first. If one decides on the masculine we have to bear in mind that only with masculine nouns is there a formal contrast in the article between the nominative and the accusative forms. Applying a principle of presenting only one new form at a time, we cannot include both *der* and *den* within the same unit of presentation. We cannot therefore at this stage include sentences with a noun in object position. One possible way of avoiding these is to use sentences containing the verb *sein*. A noun either preceding or following *sein* would be in the nominative case. The same limitation could be achieved by restricting the sentences used to intransitive structures. The noun would then appear only in subject position. As a further alternative, there would be less need to control the types of sentence structure if, instead of introducing the definite article through masculine nouns, one chose to present feminine or neuter nouns, since there is no formal contrast between nominative and accusative forms. Some restriction would however still have to be imposed when masculine nouns were being taught.

Basing the presentation on *sein*-sentences, a possible sequence of teaching would be:

A. Masculine nouns

Der Tisch
Der Mann   ist   hier.
Der Lehrer   da drüben.
          etc.
and/or Das ist der Tisch   *etc.*

---

[20] An alternative approach, which would be well suited to a method which made great use of classroom activity by the pupils, might be to start with the accusative following an imperative. The learner would practise producing and responding to sentences like: *Nehmen Sie den Bleistift, öffnen Sie den Schrank*, etc.

B. Feminine nouns

Die Tafel
Die Tür   ist   hier.
Die Wand   da drüben.
      etc.
and/or Das ist die Tür   *etc.*

C. Neuter nouns

Das Fenster
Das Mädchen ist   hier.
Das Papier   da drüben.
      etc.
and/or Das ist das Fenster   *etc.*

Each of these would be thoroughly practised with different nouns. At first the practice would be closely controlled so that the pupil is not selecting the correct form, but merely repeating it. But once it is firmly established that there are three genders (this may of course have been met previously through the teaching of the indefinite article), practice will become a little less controlled, in that nouns of the three genders will occur in random order, requiring the learner to select the correct form of the article. As alternatives to *hier* and *da drüben*, adjectives such as *weiss, schwarz, rot*, etc., or *gross, klein, lang, kurz*, etc., could be used as complements of *sein*, provided that a suitable choice of nouns was made.

The learners would be brought into contact with accusative forms only when the nominative had been mastered. Once again the genders would first be presented and practised separately, and subsequently control would be relaxed so that the learner is forced both to select and to construct the correct form of the article. Since we shall now be using transitive sentences, the noun (or pronoun) in subject position will require an article in the nominative case. There should be no need to restrict the nouns in subject position according to gender. By using a technique of question and answer, the contrast between the nominative and accusative forms of the definite article can be neatly pointed. In this case the presentation sequence would be as follows, with much the greatest emphasis on the first part:

A. Masculine nouns

Wo ist der Roman?   Er

etc.   Sie

Der Junge

Die Frau   hat den Roman.

Das Mädchen   etc.

B. Feminine nouns

Wo ist die Zeitung?   Er

etc.   Sie

Der Junge

Die Frau   hat die Zeitung.

Das Mädchen   etc.

C. Neuter nouns

Wo ist das Heft?   Er

etc.   Sie

Der Junge

Die Frau   hat das Heft.

Das Mädchen   etc.

The intensive practice carried out at each of these stages should produce a thorough, practical mastery of these forms. Although the teaching is sequenced to expose the learner to the contrasts within the article one at a time, the use of sentences as the linguistic unit ensures that the learner's experience is structurally and semantically meaningful.

The question now arises of whether to proceed with the teaching of the other two sets of case forms within one complete teaching sequence. There is no pressing reason why one should, although from the linguistic point of view it might seem preferable to teach the whole system. But criteria for inclusion and exclusion or for determining particular sequences are by no means solely linguistic, and there may be perfectly good reasons for deciding not to follow the teaching of the first two cases by the teaching of the genitive and dative. Whenever they are taught, the same principles can be applied as have been applied to the nominative and accusative forms. It would be needlessly repetitious to illustrate them here.

No mention has been made of whether the paradigm has any value in this teaching sequence at all. The implication has clearly been that the paradigm cannot be the basis of language teaching, but that is not to say that it has no place at all. Some teachers might prefer to present the paradigm either before or after such a teaching sequence. Alternatively the paradigm could be elicited from the learners themselves when their practical mastery is complete. If it is presented at the beginning, I would feel that practice along the lines described above is still necessary if mastery of the language is to be produced. Learning a paradigm is a short-cut to knowledge of the language, but by itself it does not seem to result in high performance in the language. Paradoxically it may be that knowing the paradigm is most useful for the learning of those languages which have a very complex inflectional morphology, one reason being that to condition the learning of each individual morpheme would be a very lengthy process indeed.

3.4. Summary

In this chapter we have looked at three grammatical topics. In the first place we examined the structural view of language and interpreted its significance in evaluating the control of the linguistic content of syllabuses and text-books. Secondly, we saw the difficulties that syntax can provide for the learner of a foreign language and discussed how these might be handled in teaching. Thirdly, we noted some of the units employed in language description and saw that language teaching has been and can be influenced by the types of units identified in the language. Since grammar is the core of language, linguistics tends to be much more occupied with the grammatical level than any other. The discussion here in no way reflects the range of grammatical interests to be found in linguistic publications. Many of these interests are of no direct value to the language teacher and are too technical to be summarized briefly.

4
Vocabulary

4.1. Grammar and vocabulary: a matter of priorities

We saw in the last chapter that linguists characteristically view
language as a structured system, and their preoccupation has been
almost entirely with those aspects of language whose structure is
most susceptible to scientific analysis—phonology and grammar.
Linguists have had remarkably little to say about vocabulary and
one can find very few studies which could be of any practical interest
for language teachers. Reflecting the linguist's concern with grammar
and the related view that mastery of a foreign language depends
upon complete control of its grammatical rules, we find the method-
ologist's emphasis on the subordination of vocabulary teaching to
grammar teaching. The range of vocabulary, we are told, should be
deliberately restricted while grammar is still being acquired so that
the learner's powers of acquisition can be concentrated on what is
most important. To spend time at this stage learning vocabulary is
to be diverted from the true content of language acquisition. Once
the pupil knows the many grammatical frames, then to expand the
number of words which can operate in the frames is a relatively
simple task. It therefore comes later. In practice techniques for
vocabulary extension have scarcely been discussed explicitly. Of
course any methods of teaching which aim to make use of actual
sentences rather than abstract symbols must have a vocabulary
content. Commonly, then, the lexical content of the earlier stages of
language teaching is consciously limited to what is needed either to
service the techniques of presentation and practice or to motivate
the learners. I hope this is a fair representation of a *structural* view
of language teaching.

However we need not accept the neglect of vocabulary that this
has led to. In the first place we can question whether grammar must
always dominate vocabulary. Secondly we must acknowledge that
there is a tradition of vocabulary study, stemming from what might
be called pre-structural days, whose results and techniques have
continued to be used and which has not been found contradictory
by those who would wish to emphasize the structural aspects of

language learning. Thirdly, we can ask just what are the problems of learning vocabulary and attempt to discover any implications for the organization of language teaching. The latter two points are discussed in Sections 4.2 and 4.3. We can now return briefly to the first.

The belief that vocabulary acquisition can be delayed until a substantial proportion of the grammatical system has been learned is tenable only where the learner is not likely to have a pressing social need to use the language. The obvious fact is that to communicate at all seriously and adequately through the language a command of both grammar and vocabulary is necessary. Most writing on language teaching has a faintly polemical tone and in recent years has tended to emphasize grammar as a corrective to the idea that simply by building up a large vocabulary in a foreign language one will be able to use it. Experience shows that to learn numbers of words without learning to construct sentences is of little practical value. Not enough attention has been paid to the converse view—that there is not much value either in being able to produce grammatical sentences if one has not got the vocabulary that is needed to convey what one wishes to say. One is literally 'at a loss for words'.

To delay the teaching of an extensive vocabulary will not prove a serious defect as long as the aims of a course are to give a practical mastery of language *in the long term*. Any temporary imbalance between grammar and vocabulary may very well correct itself with time. Where language learning is done in full-time educational establishments—in schools for example—not only will there be no necessity for the pupil to use the language in social intercourse, there will often not even be any opportunity for him to do so. It is at least arguable that foreign language teaching need not aim to produce practical communication skill from the beginning, and that a vocabulary extensive enough for varied communication can be the target of later stages. A skilled user of the language would be the desired product of such a course, but his ability to communicate would not really develop until he approached the end of his course.

A methodology evolved with such a situation in mind—and it is possibly the most common language learning situation—must not be taken over and applied to situations which are critically different. It is easy to conceive other situations in which the learner will earnestly desire to put whatever he learns to immediate social use. He may hope in the long term to become a skilful user of the language, but he has a short term need for the language which cannot be subordinated to this. Anyone emigrating to a new speech community finds himself in just this position. However important it may be for him eventually to master the grammatical system, it is even more important that he should be able to communicate with those people with whom his daily life brings him into contact. He will have needs that can only be met by use of language and those needs will be there from the moment he arrives. He cannot be an effective member of his new community, and consequently will not be accepted by it, if he has no means of contact with it. The language to be learned by him must therefore have immediate practical value.

Slightly different from this case is the learner who has no long term aims at all. He is not concerned whether he can ever have a wide grasp of grammatical structure, nor whether he can range over a varied set of topics. He may need language for a clearly limited set of situations, and possibly even may expect to use it only over a limited period of time. He will certainly never hope to be mistaken for a native speaker, nor even to approach such skill. The acceptability of his speech to the native speaker may be less important than his ability to convey his social needs.

In either of these cases we could not accept that vocabulary would be initially less important than grammar. The fact is that while without grammar very little can be conveyed, without vocabulary *nothing* can be conveyed. What we normally think of as 'vocabulary items'—nouns, verbs and adjectives—do indeed contain more information[1] than is carried by grammatical elements. Telegrams often consist of no more than a sequence of lexical items with no grammatical information other than order of words, and yet we have no difficulty in understanding them, any more than we do ungrammatical headlines and advertisements. Communicating in a foreign language is not so very different. Provided one knows the appropriate vocabulary, then some form of interchange of language is possible. Without the vocabulary it is impossible. Admittedly this can be no more than a very rudimentary form of communication, which is restricted in what it can achieve and which depends on the willingness of the native speaker to make allowance for grammatical errors. However, it is more than could be achieved with a mastery of grammatical structure and only a partial knowledge of the vocabulary needed.

If we were to take the conventional organization of language teaching, with its early concentration on the step-by-step introduction of grammatical structures, realized through a vocabulary chosen

[1] The word *information* has a technical sense which I am using here without definition, since this would not be relevant to the discussion.

largely for its pedagogic usefulness, we would not be providing our pupils with what they need. Proper consideration will have to be given from the beginning to the appropriate vocabulary, and that appropriateness will in turn depend on the social needs of the learners. I am not suggesting that the learning of grammatical structures should be replaced by the learning of lists of lexical items, merely that a different balance between grammar and lexis will be required. One must not assume that the same organization of language content will meet all needs.

4.2. The selection of vocabulary

The research that has been done to assist the process of vocabulary selection is perhaps not what would usually be called linguistics. It does not add to our understanding of the lexical structure of the language under examination. Instead, by investigating their use of vocabulary, we learn about the native speaker's need for their language. The relative frequency of occurrence of vocabulary items is determined by the kind of thing we most frequently wish to say. Our range of expression is in no way constrained by the frequency with which the items happen to occur in the language. If the speech of an individual had a distribution of lexical items very different from the 'normal' distribution, this would mean no more than that he did not commonly express himself on the topics that most people talk about. This is precisely why the research, with its predominant interest in frequency, has been carried out. The results have little interest except in their potential application to foreign language teaching. The most frequent vocabulary is presumably that which individuals feel most need for. Once one accepts that some restriction on vocabulary content is desirable, information is needed on which items will have the greatest utility for the learner. Before I discuss frequency and the other criteria which are needed, however, there are one or two historical points that I should like to make.

The idea of exposing a learner to language in a progressive manner is one that has developed continuously over the last forty years or so. There is a large literature on the relative merits of different sequences, on the best place for a particular construction in a graded course. Manuals for teachers discuss the advantage of teaching the more simple before the more complex, the more useful before the more rare, the regular before the irregular and so on. The justifications are no longer much discussed. Historically it is a process that can be seen as a reaction against materials organized into chunks largely unconnected with one another, failing to discriminate between important and trivial and containing large vocabularies with no evident objective basis. The conviction grew among practising teachers that learning could be made easier if some order could be brought to the business of deciding what language items to include and in what sequence they should be placed.

That their attention turned first to vocabulary reflected the relative lack of influence of linguistics on language teaching. If anything the situation has been reversed in recent years. In any case, misguided choice of vocabulary for teaching is so striking that the urgency to correct it is strongly felt. At worst vocabulary may not be selected in any real sense at all. The words learned will be those that happen to occur in reading passages—which themselves are not written with the learners' needs in mind—those which are needed for grammatical purposes—these may include words that are extremely rare but are taught as examples of a rule or exception to a rule—those that are met in the study of literature, and finally, those that are learned as lists related to given topics of varying degrees of usefulness. In any lesson unit the number of new words is commonly very large, demanding as much of the pupil's time as the grammatical content. Modern text-books with their visual means of presentation do not necessarily avoid these faults. One that I have come across has a picture with each unit, in which every single object is labelled. There is no distinction between more and less useful words and the load in each lesson is between 30 and 40 words, which is far too large. The point about all this is not that nothing useful is acquired but that so much time is spent on committing to memory items which are never likely to be useful to the learner. Learning a foreign language is a difficult task for most people. There is no point in diverting the learner's energies on to fruitless labour. We all know the situation where a person who has been learning over a number of years is perhaps called upon for the first time to use the language in a natural context and finds that he lacks the very vocabulary that he most needs. The aim of vocabulary selection is to remedy this and to make the learning process a more efficient one.

Over the years the incorporation of vocabulary into teaching materials has come to depend on a number of criteria.[2] The aim has

[2] I know of no better discussion of the purposes and problems of vocabulary selection than the Interim Report on Vocabulary Selection of the Carnegie Committee (London, King, 1936).

been to introduce greater objectivity into decision making. By far the most important single criterion is that of *frequency*. Presumably the most useful items are those that occur most frequently in our language use. If we take a corpus of material and calculate the relative frequency of the vocabulary items we shall discover that some words occur with far greater frequency than others. We can then establish a list in which the different frequencies are stated. The higher on the list an item occurs the more necessary it is to ensure that it appears in any teaching materials that we construct. No one would suggest that the items should be taught in exactly the sequence in which they occur on the list. Rather one would work within broad bands of frequency—the first 500, 1,000, 2,000 items and so on. The attempt could be made to restrict the vocabulary of a first book to the 500 most frequent items, for example.

The aim of vocabulary counting is fairly simply stated. The practice is rather more involved, since there are a number of other factors to be taken into consideration. First, an extremely large corpus is needed if the frequencies are not merely to reflect the texts that happen to have been chosen. Indeed the claim to objectivity would not be justified unless the choice of texts was also on a sound basis. If the intention is to establish some kind of general frequency, then the texts need to be drawn from all possible varieties of English. The usefulness of the Thorndike-Lorge word-list for English, for example, is reduced in that it is based entirely on written English. Its value is diminished wherever the aim is to teach spoken English. Handling a corpus that was a representative sample of all varieties of written and spoken language would be a mammoth task, perhaps larger than would be justified by the usefulness of the results.

There might be more value in statistics, not about global use of a language, but about each different type of language text. Wherever it is possible to predict the uses a language may have for the learner, it should be possible to limit the language taught to that which has the highest practical return for him. In this case the figures obtained might be seen as contributing to the description of a language variety, a topic which is discussed in the next chapter.

Until now I have talked of counting 'words'. Even if a count was confined to written language, where words are conveniently identified by the presence of a space before and after, there would still be problems of knowing precisely what the units to be counted were. Not all words have quite the same function. This would actually be revealed by a vocabulary count. Dominating any English frequency list would be things like the articles, auxiliary verbs, prepositions, and negative and comparative particles. These are sometimes called grammatical or function words because we use them to establish grammatical relations. The grammar of the language could not operate for long without them and they should be seen as part of the grammatical content of teaching rather than the lexical content. In that case it is rather pointless to include them among the items to be counted. So the count requires a grammatical basis which will clearly identify those items which are principally grammatical in their function so that they can be excluded from the corpus.

Even when we have set these grammatical words aside, we shall still need to use our description of the language to help us in sorting out cases where orthographic word and lexical item are not the same thing. The best examples of this in English are found in two-word verbs. Look at the following sentences:

He put the milk on the table.
I always put some money by for a rainy day.
My French teacher is putting up for Parliament.
She puts off all her husband's friends.
The secretary put me through to the manager.

The orthographic form *put* occurs in each of these sentences, yet to suggest that these are five occurrences of the verb PUT would be exceedingly misleading. None of the meaning of *put* in the first sentence seems to be present in the other four. One can replace the first *put* by *place* but not any of the others. In fact it is common to think of these as five (or six) different verbs: *put, put by, put up, put off* (two meanings) and *put through*. In our counting we must be able to distinguish what from now on I will often call 'lexical items.'

When actually counting lexical items it is fairly easy to identify the difference between *put* and *put off*. It is much more difficult in the case of *polysemy*.[3] It is not only grammatical words which occupy a high place on frequency lists. We will also find words with multiple or general meanings. They are words which are not specific enough to be confined to one context of use. An example of this category is the verb *make*, which will occur very high on any frequency list. The

---

[3] The range of meaning distinctions expressed by a single form is dealt with more fully in the next section.

Oxford English Dictionary notes 97 different meanings.[4] Sometimes we are clearly faced with homonyms. The form *case* may
denote some kind of box or alternatively a set of circumstances.
But not all differences of meaning constitute homonyms. Should we,
for example, consider *book* in its common sense to be the same as
book in *book of stamps*? To be useful the statistics should deal with
meanings as well as forms. If we were to do this, we might find
occurring much higher on the list words of highly specific meaning, the use of which is tied to clearly defined situations. At
the moment such words are considered to be of low frequency.
Richards points out that *soap* does not appear in the first 2,000 words
of the Thorndike-Lorge list, yet one could hardly deny that it is a
useful word to know.[5] We have our hair cut, go to the opera, travel
on a plane, write a letter, read a notice and ask the way. A person
using a foreign language may need to do all of these things and yet
they will occupy so little of his language-using time that the relevant
lexical items would never appear on a frequency list.

Another difficulty that faces us in counting frequencies is that,
however large the corpus, the results may reveal certain oddities. If
we take a number of items that form a closed set, like the days of the
week or the months of the year, we find marked incongruities in
their frequencies of occurrence. If we find that *Thursday* is absent
from a straight high-frequency list, we would not conclude that it
must be less useful than the other days of the week. We would
use our subjective judgment to add *Thursday* to the list. This
particular anomaly is easily rectified, but it raises doubts about the
assumption that underlies all frequency studies. If frequency does
not reflect usefulness in this case, why should it be thought to do so
elsewhere? Where items do not belong to such a clearly defined
lexical set, their distribution may be equally anomalous. If we look
on page 142 of the Thorndike-Lorge list, we find that *post-office*—
presumably a very useful word—is less frequent than, among others,
poverty, power, prairie, prayer, preach, precede and *precious*. The
explanation for this is to be found in the types of text that make up
the corpus, but this in turn shows that even counts based on a very
large corpus may not reflect the usefulness that we would intuitively
expect items to have for us.

[4] C.C. Fries and A.E. Traver, *English Word Lists* (Washington, American
Council on Education, 1940). Quoted by J.C. Richards in 'A psycho-linguistic
measure of vocabulary selection' (*International Review of Applied Linguistics* 8/2,
1970).
[5] J. C. Richards, *op. cit.*, p. 88.

Other criteria have been suggested to correct the inadequacies of simple frequency scores. High frequencies can be caused by the influence of a single text in which a few items recur a large number of times. To counteract this, we can make statements about the *range* of an item. By this is meant the number of different texts in which it occurs. A very frequent item might be discounted if its range was small. In French research into the establishment of *le Français Fondamental*, it has been suggested that to frequency could be added data on ease of recall. Given 16 'centres of interest', more than 900 French schoolchildren were asked to write down the twenty words that they thought would be most useful to them. There was apparently a large measure of agreement as to what constituted the most *disponible* or *available* items and the results were used to supplement frequency scores in establishing a word list.[6] Similar in that it requires individuals to assess the value of items for themselves is the criterion of *familiarity*.[7] The procedure is to give a word-list to a sample of native speakers and ask them to rate their use of each word on a five-point scale from 'very often' to 'never'. It proves a reliable technique for distinguishing the relative familiarity of words which do not figure prominently in a general frequency list. It could be used to bring the less frequent words of specific meaning into a more prominent position in a selection of vocabulary.

How necessary is it when constructing materials for learning a foreign language to base the lexical content on the results of a statistical study of language use? In the first place there are non-statistical criteria which would need to operate alongside. There is the question of interference from the lexical structure of the mother-tongue, of the need to include items that are useful in the classroom if nowhere else, of choosing those words which fit most conveniently with the methodology and of excluding those that present particular methodological problems. There is further the problem of reconciling what is desirable for the teaching of vocabulary with what is desirable for grammar and pronunciation. As often as not the criteria conflict and there is no obvious or easy way of determining what weight shall be given to the different sets of criteria.

The original frequency data seem in danger of getting lost among these other considerations. No doubt those items that would appear on a list of the 2,000 most common words in a language are indeed useful words for a foreigner to acquire. But, as we have seen, learning

---

[6] *Le Français Fondamental* (1er *Degré*) (Institut National Pédagogique, Paris).
[7] J. C. Richards, *op. cit.*

could not possibly be confined to these items. The teacher himself does not normally choose what vocabulary items his pupils will learn. This is usually decided by the writer of the materials he uses. If one is going to construct texts from which people are to learn the language, rather than use 'natural' texts,[8] then it may be that for the writer simply to be *aware* of such notions as frequency, range, usefulness, language variety and teachability is enough to ensure that he avoids the mistakes of uncontrolled introduction of vocabulary. The more language teaching is oriented towards meeting the needs of the learners the more likely it is that the situations used for teaching will produce 'useful' language without it having been necessary to draw up an inventory of lexical items beforehand. A reasonable behavioural prediction may do the work that a vocabulary frequency count sets out to do.

4.3. Vocabulary and its acquisition

So far we have examined the relative importance of vocabulary and grammar and the selection of vocabulary according to criteria based on the value to the learner of different lexical items. We now turn to the nature of vocabulary itself and thereby to some of the difficulties that vocabulary acquisition presents. I suggested above that the non-linguist probably considers the acquisition of a foreign language to be a matter of little more than learning a new set of words together with their inflectional characteristics. He will expect the words of the foreign language to have different shapes from those of his mother tongue and he will see his major task in vocabulary learning to be that of remembering which of the forms in the new language to attach to the concepts which he already possesses. He sets out to learn to substitute new words for those which he knows. The assumption that all languages have vocabulary systems in which the words themselves differ but which 'refer to' reality in the same way is common. From it follows the belief that for every word in the mother tongue there is an exact equivalent in each foreign language. It is a belief which is reinforced by the smaller bilingual dictionaries where single word translations are often offered, and perhaps too by the practice of teaching vocabulary by setting pupils to learn bilingual lists. It is a belief that should be corrected by even a short exposure

[8] For the alternative view see D.A. Reibel, *op. cit.*

to a foreign language, yet as teachers know it persists into quite advanced stages of learning.

To describe the meaning of words it is necessary to look at them in two respects—in terms of their relations with the physical world, and in terms of their relations with one another. The study of semantics has traditionally been the former, but in recent years linguists have been more occupied with the latter. Since both are necessary to the full understanding of meaning, we shall look at them each in turn.

4.3.1. Denotation and connotation

It is clear that there is a relationship between words and concrete objects and activities in the physical world. It appears that we recognize classes of objects and that for each there is an appropriate word which we may use to refer to one or more members of that class or, indeed, to the class as a whole. This relationship is commonly described as the 'denotative' or 'referential' meaning. It is equally obvious that not all the words we use are relatable to physical entities in this way. It is said, therefore, that words like *belief*, *hopeful* or *insist* relate to 'concepts'. It is a small step to take from this to saying that whereas *table* denotes a class of objects (of which we may also have a concept), *belief* denotes a concept of 'belief', however unobservable that may be.

Even within such an approach to the study of semantics, which linguists and others have found unsatisfactory, it is possible to discuss a number of problems of second language acquisition. The difficulties that face the learner are those of language and culture contrast. In the first place, the naive view expressed in the first paragraph of this section is wrong. The physical world does not consist of classes of things, nor are there universal concepts for each of which every language has its own sets of labels. Language learning, therefore, cannot be just a matter of learning to substitute a new set of labels for the familiar ones of the mother tongue. It is not difficult to find a word of equivalent meaning in a given linguistic and social context. It is most unlikely that the same word would prove equivalent in all contexts. Every language classifies physical reality in its own way. There is nothing particularly natural about the fact that in English we use the word *foot* to denote the extremity of the leg. In Russian there is no equivalent for *foot*—simply the word *noga* to denote the whole leg including the foot. Not all languages identify the same number of colours, nor are the boundaries between colours necessarily drawn in the same places. In English we operate with only one word *sand*, where in Arabic there are several, each denoting a different type of sand. The same applies to words which do not have reference to external reality. In spite of their equivalence in many contexts *education* in English and *éducation* in French do not mean the same thing. The concepts involved, though they might overlap, are not co-extensive. It has been argued that our thought and our perception are deeply influenced by the particular segmentation of reality that our language makes. In this view we tend to be restricted in our perceptions to the categories imposed on us by our language. Our language determines how we see things.[9]

The fact that two different words may have the same form probably does not present any persisting problem to the learner. *Homonyms* like *order* (command) and *order* (sequence) clearly have different denotations and are unlikely to be misinterpreted. However, differences of meaning are by no means always so clear-cut. The same lexical item may be used to denote very different types of object and yet be considered by the native speaker to be obviously logical extensions of the 'basic' meaning. To an Englishman it is self-evident that we should be able to use the word *branch* not only of trees, but also of railway-lines and banks. W. F. Mackey gives the following example:[10]

	of a person	tête
	of a bed	chevet
	of a coin	face
	of a cane	pomme
head	of a match	bout
	of a table	haut bout
	of an organization	directeur
	on beer	mousse
	title	rubrique

The very real danger for the language learner here is that, having learned first, as he almost certainly will have, that *tête* is the French word which denotes a part of the body, he will assume that it can be used in all other cases where *head* is used in English. As the example shows this will lead him into frequent error.

[9] See J.B. Carroll, 'Linguistic relativity, contrastive linguistics and language learning' (*International Review of Applied Linguistics* 1/1, 1963).

[10] W.F. Mackey, *Language Teaching Analysis* (London, Longman, 1965).

It is the recognition that the learning of bilingual lists encourages the learner's natural tendency towards inter-lingual identification that has led teachers to look for other ways of teaching meaning than the giving of a mother-tongue equivalent. The procedures adopted are usually 'ostensive' procedures. The word is presented in association with a visual image of an object or activity. The choice of vocabulary is for a time largely confined to 'demonstrable' items. In the commonly taught languages of Europe and America, objective reality is not chopped up by language in radically different ways. The language and cultures derive from common sources and have remained in close contact with one another. Whether we live in Rio, Chicago, London, Belgrade or Paris, we are surrounded by the same kind of things and spend our time engaged in the same sort of activities. Where our vocabulary refers to this concrete world, we can expect fairly consistent similarities. The vocabulary items that can be taught through ostensive definitions may not therefore present many problems, other than the mastery of the form, to learners in these cultures. It is even possible that one could make one's way fairly well by learning single word translation equivalents for words having concrete reference. The aim would be a modest one and the communication would be strictly functional, but this may be no more than some learners hope for.

The similarities between these languages may at the same time constitute a danger to any ambition that we may have to use the foreign language with great accuracy. Whatever the method the teacher employs, the learner will tend to try and translate, and given the type of vocabulary being taught, he will probably find that he can identify the new words with words in his own language. He will therefore be unprepared for the difficulties that will face him when he meets these same words with extended denotations and when he has to handle more and more words which do not have external reference. In order to enter the lexical system of a foreign language one may need to assume that its structure is like that of the mother-tongue—and this is achieved where ostensive procedures are used—but from then on the most important thing is to learn that it is in fact different.

Where people are learning a language which is linguistically and culturally very distinct from their own, the position may be different. Not only will their linguistic view of the world be strikingly different. The actual contents of that world and the life that is led in it may be very different too. Such learners will have the difficulty that even at the beginning there is very little that can be transferred from their mother-tongue. They will have to learn to categorize familiar things in different ways and unfamiliar things without the benefit of any point of reference in their own culture. It may be that in the long run they will gain from the fact that it is hardly possible for them to entertain the idea that words in different languages are equivalent to one another.

So far we have been talking about that relation between words and external reality which is called denotation. However important denotation may be, our understanding of a word is not complete if we know only to what it may refer. In our mother-tongue what a word communicates to us is also partly the product of the associations, linguistic and non-linguistic, that have been built up through our previous experience of the word. This aspect of meaning is usually called 'connotation'. Connotative meaning is additional to denotative meaning and need be related to it only in an indirect way. It is altogether more concerned with the attitudes of the language user, his emotional reactions to the use of a word. The words *relinquish* and *abandon* in the two sentences below illustrate this. Although each is denotatively equivalent to *give up*, what we understand on hearing these two sentences is by no means identical.

He abandoned his post.
He relinquished his post.

The strong implication of blame which is present in the first sentence is completely absent from the second. Since we share the contexts in which language is used with other members of our culture, it is not surprising that much of the connotative meaning of words is also shared. However it is also true that words may have associations of a purely personal character and therefore meanings which are not shared with anybody. The very fact that such meanings are not shared makes them irrelevant to language teaching.

It is perfectly possible for words to have similar denotations and connotations cross-culturally, in which case a learner is not presented with any real problem. Difficulty will most often occur where items of similar denotation have different connotations. The language of politics provides some obvious examples. Both Russians and Americans may refer to the sole political party of the Soviet Union as *communist*, but for the one it will have connotations of approval, for the other of disapproval. The converse might be true of *capitalism*. While on the subject of politics one might mention what seems to be a rare case of 'equatable' words having similar connotations but dissimilar denotations. *Socialism* is a word used in many parts of the world by politicians to denote their political philosophies and practices. These philosophies and practices, and hence the denotations of the word *socialism*, differ, but the connotations are almost universally favourable. To some extent connotations are derived from the culture and are only properly understood when the culture itself is understood. *Bull* and *bull-fight* will hardly mean the same thing to a Spaniard as they do to a member of the Royal Society for the Prevention of Cruelty to Animals.

Studying the differences of connotational meaning objectively is obviously very hard, since the nuances are often slight and difficult to grasp. An attempt to establish and display these differences was developed by the psychologist, C. E. Osgood.[11] He set up a technique known as the 'semantic differential' which required his subjects to rate the meaning of a given word on a number of seven-point scales. The end-points of each scale were represented by a pair of opposed adjectives. In effect the subject was being asked to classify his response to the word as relatively *happier* or *sadder*, *slower* or *faster*, more *flexible* or more *rigid* and so on. In all there were fifty of these pairs of adjectives. The fifty responses of one subject would produce a profile representing the meaning of that word for him and the responses from a number of subjects would produce a semantic profile for the culture as a whole. The connotational element in this profile would be a large one. The comparison of responses by native speakers of different languages to denotationally 'equivalent' words revealed that they did have different profiles. This research provides confirmation of a strong intuitive belief about differences of meaning between languages and at the same time makes available a tool for research into the acquisition of vocabulary.

The learner of a foreign language can hardly expect that words will have the same connotations for him as they do for native speakers. His experience of the language can never be as extensive or as intensive as theirs. But from the first moment that he begins to experience the language in use, especially language not produced specifically for the learner but aimed at other native speakers, he will begin to acquire some of the connotations that it has for the native speaker.

[11] C.E. Osgood, G. Suci and P. Tannenbaum, *The Measurement of Meaning* (Urbana, Illinois, University of Illinois Press, 1957).

4.3.2. Lexical structure: paradigmatic relations

Until now the entire discussion has been in terms of individual words and their meanings, and the implication of this has been that each word 'has' a meaning, and that although no doubt one can discover relations between the meanings of different words, these relations derive from the meanings that the words have and do not contribute to the meanings. This approach is largely the traditional one. Looked at linguistically the situation may be seen as exactly the reverse. Words are not comprehensible solely in terms of their referents. It is more important to study the complex and varied types of relations that exist between words. These are the relationships that determine the semantic structure of a language, and acquiring a language means acquiring its semantic structure as much as anything else. We can examine this notion of semantic structure by looking at some of the possible relations suggested by Lyons.[12] The list is not exhaustive.

1. *Synonymy.* A 'weak' rather than a 'strong' definition is given to 'synonymy', in that there is no expectation that words will be substitutable for one another in all contexts without distinction of meaning. However, in a given context, it is possible that one item may be substituted for another with the overall meaning of the utterance remaining the same. For example *conception* is a synonym of *idea* in the context:

   My idea of a university is of a community of scholars

   where the substitution of *conception* does not seem to change what the sentence communicates. However, in the sentence:

   His new idea seems a good one

   no such substitution is possible, and therefore in this context *conception* is not a synonym of *idea*. For any one lexical item over a range of contexts a pattern of substitutability would emerge as we discovered where words could replace one another and where not.

2. *Hyponymy.* By 'hyponymy' is meant a relationship of inclusion. *Vehicle* includes *car*, *bus* and so on. Just as the meaning of *vehicle* depends upon what its hyponyms are, so the meaning of *car* depends on its being a hyponym of *vehicle* and its sharing this

---

[12] J. Lyons, *Structural Semantics* (Oxford, Blackwell, 1963), and *Introduction to Theoretical Linguistics* (Cambridge University Press, 1968).

status with a number of other words. If there is some change in the constitution of this set, inevitably the meaning of each of its members changes. More important from our point of view is that relations of hyponymy are never exactly the same from one language to another. We will readily identify *potato* with *Kartoffel* in German, but *vegetable* and *Gemüse* do not have equivalent lists of hyponyms.

3. *Incompatibility.* The relation of 'incompatibility' is in a sense the reverse of hyponymy, in that it is one of exclusion. The incompatibility is between items that are similar in meaning. To say *morning* is to say *not afternoon, not evening* and *not night.* A relation of incompatibility also exists between colour terms since the choice of *red*, for example, entails the exclusion of *black, blue, yellow* and so on. Not all colour terms are incompatible. *Scarlet* is a hyponym of *red*.

4. *Complementarity.* This is a relationship in which to predicate one term is to contradict another. It exists between pairs like *perfect* and *imperfect, single* and *married*, or *dead* and *alive*. If we were to falsify one by inserting *not* before it we would automatically assert the truth of the other.

5. *Antonymy.* Lyons reserves the term 'antonym' for relations like that between *young* and *old*. The difference between these and the previous category lies in the fact that to say *not young* is not necessarily to say *old*. There is a gradation from *young* to *old*. In fact terms like *young* and *old, big* and *small* or *few* and *many* do not represent absolute values as one is inclined to think. To use one of the terms is to imply a comparison with some norm—*young* means *relatively* young. By an apparent paradox, use of the comparative forms is not at all incompatible with simultaneous use of the antonym:

She is young but she is older than her sister.

To be *older* she does not have to be *old*. It is also usual for one of each pair to be *unmarked* in certain contexts. To ask:

How old is he?

implies nothing of the speaker's expectations, whereas:

How young is he?

anticipates that the individual referred to is to be classified as *young*. As with synonyms relations of antonymy need not apply in all contexts. There are a number of possible antonyms of *dry*, although probably none except *wet* has as wide a range of use. In contrast to *dry air* we would prefer *damp air* rather than *wet* or *moist air**. In contrast to *dry lips* we probably prefer *moist lips*.

6. *Converseness*. In this case the predication of one term inevitably implies the other. It is illustrated by pairs like *parent* and *child*. *buy* and *sell*, or *employee* and *employer*.

This structural approach to meaning, which provides an alternative to the more traditional analysis in terms of denotation and connotation, does not in any way deny that items of language may relate to concrete features of the real world, but it does suggest that the *meaning* of an item can only be satisfactorily defined in terms of its relations with other words. If intralinguistic relations are really as important as this suggests, it is unlikely that meaning can be adequately learned through associations of words with visual and physical context. These ostensive procedures, while they may be necessary, will not prove sufficient. The use of *realia* and visual aids is to exploit ostension as a way of introducing the meaning of words, but valuable as it is to build up the range of associations between words and objects, the extension of meaning can only be brought about by integrating words into a linguistic context so that the complex inter-relationships can be allowed to operate.

4.3.3. Lexical structure: syntagmatic relations

We have now discussed the relations between lexical items and external reality and the intralinguistic relations between lexical items on a paradigmatic axis. However there are also relations between words occurring in sequence, and to round off our discussion of vocabulary I want to deal briefly with these syntagmatic relations in lexical structure.

Syntagmatic relations between lexical items are interesting because in every language there are items which co-occur with high frequency, others which co-occur as the need arises, and still others whose co-occurrence seems impossible. If one could predict these facts from knowledge of the meanings of the words in isolation they would present no difficulty, but prediction is frequently difficult and often impossible. Where items tend to co-occur repeatedly, a 'collocation' is produced. Items are said to collocate with one another.

To illustrate the difficulties presented to the learner by the probabilities of lexical co-occurrence, let us have a look at some adjective + noun combinations in English taking *noise* as the noun and bearing in mind that co-occurrence restrictions may operate between any lexical items in a sentence—subject noun and verb, verb and object noun, subject noun and object noun, verb and prepositional phrase, verb and adverb, and so on. First, there are some combinations that we will simply not expect to occur—*tall noise, fast noise, painted noise.* We will not expect them because in each case the semantic features of the adjective and the noun seem incompatible. Our knowledge of the semantics of the individual words will enable us to predict that they will not co-occur. Since we do not meet tall or painted noises in the real world, there is no problem here for the learner of English as a foreign language. Nothing will lead him even to attempt to produce this combination of forms, nor will he hear anybody else producing it.[13] This is one reason why some current preoccupations of linguists are unlikely to be of interest to language teachers. The linguists are very much interested in discovering just what the semantic features are which make it impossible for us to collocate certain items. They are trying to bring the absence of tall noises within their linguistic description.

Secondly, there are items which are semantically compatible and which may co-occur, yet which are not associated habitually enough to be considered collocations. From under the bonnet of one's car there may come *new noises* and *old noises.* Presumably we could include here *rustling, rumbling* and *clanging noises* too. The borderline between co-occurrences of this sort and collocations will not be a hard and fast one. It is presumably only because we need to talk about *loud noises* more often than new or old noises that we may consider it a collocation. But before discussing collocations, we must look at the first of the difficulties of the language learner.

Each of the above co-occurrences (and some collocations, as we shall see) would be understood the first time it was heard, because the hearer would already know the meaning of the separate parts. Similarly, the learner himself might produce them without ever having heard them because he knows that the meanings of the parts are compatible; but unfortunately joining together semantically com-

[13] Unless, of course, conditions in the world changed so that something was produced which could be called *painted noise.* It is not impossible to conceive that in attempting to synthesize speech by machine, someone might invent a process which involved painting a profile the product of which could come to be known as *painted noise.*

patible parts does not always produce an acceptable co-occurrence, and the learner has no way of distinguishing the acceptable from the unacceptable.

The words *low* and *high* can both be used to refer to volume of sound. We could ask someone to *turn it down low* or to *turn it up high*. Opposed to a *loud noise* we may have a *low noise* (this can also mean low in pitch, of course). Since *low* can be opposed to *high* it seems entirely reasonable to expect the co-occurrence *high noise*. In fact the sequence is permissible, but never with *high* as a synonym of *loud*. Similarly, since in many contexts *quiet* seems opposed to *loud*, we might expect *quiet noise*, and yet this hardly serms acceptable. The unacceptability of this kind of co-occurrence is quite unlike that described above. There is no incompatibility in the semantics of the individual words. For this reason it is a frequent cause of error in non-native speakers.[14] A native speaker looking at something written by a foreigner will often be able to pick out pieces of language that he feels not to be correct although very often he has great difficulty in deciding what it is that is wrong. 'It's not ungrammatical, but a Frenchman (etc.) wouldn't say it,' he might say. It is just as easy for a learner to make a wrong generalization about the lexical structure of a language as it is for him to over-generalize grammatical patterns.

Some collocations are not different in kind from the acceptable co-occurrences that we have just been examining. There is just a much greater likelihood of their occurrence. If I am sitting alone in a house any noises I hear are more likely to be described as *strange noises* than *unusual, bizarre, peculiar* or *abnormal*. It seems that from among a number that will meet our needs quite well we regularly prefer one. Not that the possibility of using the others is excluded, of course.

This does not introduce any new difficulty for the language learner except in a situational sense. Even the extremely proficient foreign language speaker is still likely to be marked out as a non-native speaker if in his speech and writing he seems to avoid the collocations that would be characteristic of the native speaker. The choice of a non-collocational sequence will go unnoticed in one sentence, provided it is semantically acceptable. But over a whole passage the pattern of regularly choosing the unusual sequence begins to look unnatural.

---

[14] It seems logical to expect that children learning their mother-tongue will also make the same sort of mistake, but I do not know that the matter has ever been investigated.

It is when the meanings of collocations cannot be predicted from the meanings of individual elements in them that they become most interesting and most difficult. These are the sequences that are often called 'idioms'. Their meanings will not be readily apparent even to the native speaker when he first comes into contact with them. They have a tendency to fossilize as complete units even to the point on occasions of preserving forms which no longer occur outside the collocation. We find this in an expression like *kith and kin*. The variety and range of idiomatic collocations in any language is vast— *to take someone in, to know your onions, to lose your head, a smashing time, a dolly bird* or, to stick with occurrences of *noise*, *a big noise*. Idiomatic collocations are not a feature restricted to colloquial uses of language, although informal speech is often particularly rich in them. There are plenty which are acceptable in all styles of speech— *to look after, to give up, to make up, so as to, in order to, in point of fact*, for example.

Collocations, both idiomatic and non-idiomatic, have always been included in monolingual and bilingual dictionaries. I do not know that they have ever been studied in a systematic way on a large scale. This means that those which come to be cited, in bilingual dictionaries at least, are often only an intuitive selection from among those that might have been included. Valuable as such information is, how often has one found on referring to a dictionary that everything seemed to be there except the collocation one was looking for? A further problem lies in the transitoriness of some collocations. Nothing else seems to date quite as rapidly as yesterday's idioms. Familiarity with collocations is normally considered a mark of high proficiency in a foreign language. The appropriateness of idiom to situation is very difficult to master, and where a student has acquired idioms through the memorization of lists of them it is usually apparent through his inability to restrict their use only to the appropriate circumstancss.

While collocations are clearly suited to differing degrees of formality, they may be situationally restricted in other ways too. There are collocations in English which will not be known to quite a large proportion of mature native speakers. Thus *white noise* would be understood only by people with certain professional interests. There may also be collocations—not idiomatic this time—whose meaning will vary geographically. The collocation *green orange* appears to be made up of two incompatible elements. Of course this is not so. As we read it we will understand that it relates to a fruit that is orange when ripe, but green when unripe. *Green orange* is synonymous with *unripe orange.* What most of us will not know is that there are parts of the world, and, I suppose, varieties of orange, for which the implication of *green orange* would be *ripe orange.* The meaning of the collocation *green orange* therefore will vary according to the provenance of the speaker.

4.3.4. Implications for the teaching of meaning

The problems of learning vocabulary are caused by the lack of equivalence between the lexical items of different languages. All the preceding discussion would have been superfluous if this was not the case. Vocabulary learning is learning to discriminate progressively the meanings of words in the target language from the meanings of their nearest 'equivalents' in the mother-tongue. It is also learning to make the most appropriate lexical choices for particular linguistic and situational contexts. The contribution that our understanding of vocabulary acquisition makes to teaching is largely that it enables us to define the necessary conditions for learning. The evaluation of vocabulary teaching is then a question of whether or not it meets these conditions.

To begin with, it will help us to understand the place of translation. To offer a translation equivalent of an unfamiliar word is not to teach its meaning, though it probably helps the pupil to understand the new word in that particular context. If any meaning is associated with the L2 word, it will be the meaning of the L1 word.[15] As a technique of teaching meaning, translation is in the long run unsound. However, there may be occasions when the teacher does not wish to teach the meaning of a new word, although he does want the learner to understand it in the single context in which it has occurred. For this purpose the teacher may use interlingual synonymy quite legitimately. Such a situation could arise where the teacher is more concerned with the general content of a text than with the meaning of the individual items it contains. What the teacher must not then do is assume that because his pupils might be able to tell him the translation equivalent of the word *in that context,* they have learned the meaning of the word.

The learning of word-lists is faulty not only because each word is usually associated with its mother-tongue equivalent, but also because each word is linguistically and situationally isolated. However, words are not learnable as isolates. In the first place, words which are

---

[15] L1 and L2 are commonly used abbreviations for the mother tongue and second (or foreign) language respectively. Other abbreviations are FL for foreign language and TL for target language.

used for referential purposes and which are usually taught through ostensive techniques, must be àssociated with as wide a variety of visual stimuli as possible. The use of a single visual image will imply that the class of items that can be referred to in the foreign language is identical to the class to which the object belongs in the mother-tongue. The use of a variety of stimuli may help to correct this assumption and at the same time will exploit the fact that according to psychologists, people learn and retain better words which have been presented to them with a range of visual and other associations.[16]

We have seen too that simply to present words in association with the things they denote is not enough. It does not help the learner to know which are the items to which the word *cannot* refer. In other words, for learning to be complete, there must be contrast. The boundaries of denotation are defined only when a number of related words have been introduced and associated with relevant objects and images. The learning of meaning is not simply a process of aggregation. The meaning of one word is not built up in complete separation from the meaning of other words. Since it is through our language that we classify things in the universe and since languages provide us with different classifications, linguistic and visual contrasts are essential to the learning of referential meaning.

The question arises as to whether we should make explicit use of the significant linguistic relationships indicated by a structural approach to semantics. Whenever the learner is in contact with spoken and written utterances, he is exposed to these intralinguistic relations, but it might be possible to go further than simple exposure by constructing materials to exploit notions like synonymy, hyponymy and antonymy. Practice is divided. There are ardent advocates and equally ardent opponents of using L2 synonyms and antonyms as a way of teaching meaning. The counter-argument is usually that in the absence of 'true synonymns' it is misleading to use them at all. Yet the structural interpretation of meaning might lead us to precisely the opposite conclusion. In the restricted use of *synonym* given above, it is recognized that there may be a substitute for a word in a given context. The synonymy will be with one or more of the semantic features that the word has, but not with all of them. For each context in which the word is used there may be a different synonym, because it is a different set of features that is significant. A study of the

---

[16] J.B. Carroll, 'The contribution of psychological theory and educational research to the teaching of foreign languages', in *Trends in Language Teaching*, ed. A. Valdman (New York, McGraw-Hill, 1966), p. 105.

different synonyms, antonyms and hyponyms that a word has may well be the only way that the full meaningfulness of a word can be brought out. Extensive reading in a foreign language without directed study of vocabulary may often fail to reveal to the learner all that he could learn about the vocabulary. No doubt even close word study of the sort that I am suggesting will not necessarily turn into an active command of words and their semantic features. However, it is to be expected that lexical items will only slowly become meaningful to a learner in the same way that they are meaningful to a native speaker. Just as one can have text-based study for the acquisition of syntax, so one can make use of texts to show the whole network of relations that a word may have. The justification is not that the pupil will retain all the details of the network, merely that he will take in enough for the word to have become slightly more meaningful than it was before.

Probably the clearest conclusion that can be drawn from the study of meaning is that given the complexity of relations involved, the acquisition of meaning is neither a simple process nor one that is ever complete. It is naive to believe that any pupil at an early stage of language learning 'has learnt' the meaning of a word. So vast is the network of intralinguistic and extralinguistic relations involved that the acquisition of meaning can only be a gradual process of progressive discrimination following on the rather crude initial assumptions of equivalence between first and second language lexical items. To achieve this is impossible without massive exposure to the language, and this in turn can probably be achieved only through extensive reading in the foreign language. Through reading the learner is led to recognize the non-equivalence of L1 and L2 items. He is exposed to the lexical items embedded in natural linguistic contexts, and as a result they begin slowly to have the same meaningfulness for him that they have for the native speaker. His exposure to language written by native speakers, especially language written in a variety of styles for a variety of purposes, will also develop his sensitivity to the collocations that native speakers prefer. Without contact on a large scale his judgment of lexical appropriateness will remain unsure and unsound.

There is one important implication to this emphasis on the necessity of extensive exposure through reading. Much discussion of foreign language learning has been bedevilled by the over-simple conviction, first, that a form will not become a part of the pupil's productive repertoire unless he is given ample opportunity to practise it when it first occurs, and secondly, that the only valid aim of foreign language teaching is to set up this repertoire. This has led to a very widely accepted methodology in which every item, grammatical or lexical, at its first occurrence in a teaching sequence is made the object of practice material. It is held that a lesson should not contain new items unless the learner is going to be given the opportunity of practising those items. The content of a unit is therefore bound to be restricted to what it is feasible to practise in the time available. If one was to insist on maintaining this approach, extensive reading would scarcely be possible, since many items will be met which are not immediately practised and which do not become part of the learner's 'active' vocabulary.

In fact neither of these points need be seen as a serious drawback. First, learners do sometimes remember and subsequently use an item which they did not repeat at the time they first heard it; and secondly, it is a wholly undesirable restriction on the learner to require that he should be unable to understand any more than he is able to produce. This would put him at a considerable disadvantage in comparison with the native speaker who has a far larger 'passive' than 'active' vocabulary. It would be unnatural, therefore, to limit the foreign learner to a purely 'active' vocabulary. It is perfectly proper that we should use texts in which some of the lexical content is intended for comprehension only. It is no argument against extensive reading to say that the learner may misunderstand or even fail to place any meaning at all on some of the lexical items. It is in any case an experience for which he needs to be prepared, since he will meet it as soon as he is exposed to the language outside the teaching situation.

4.4. Summary

In most situations a large vocabulary load in the early stages of learning is usually a hindrance. It is more important to ensure the learning of the grammatical system. The criteria by which the vocabulary content of learning is selected are not strictly speaking linguistic. They relate to the eventual usefulness of lexical items to the learner or their value to the teacher and his techniques. Learning vocabulary is learning how words relate to external reality and how they relate to one another. Every language interprets the physical world in its own way and intralinguistic relations vary from language to language too. So complex is the semantic structure of a language that it can be acquired only through wide exposure and this in turn can probably only be provided by extensive reading.

5
The social function of language

When distinguishing earlier between *langue* and *parole*, we saw that language can be studied as a stable structural system or in terms of its relation to social features. Subsequently we have been preoccupied with aspects of the system of language. In this chapter we shall examine more closely the importance of being aware of the varied social functions of language in determining the content of language learning. We can do this in three ways: first, by looking at the individual in the speech community and asking for what social purposes he uses language and how social norms influence his choice of linguistic forms, secondly, by looking at how the individual chooses language to express his intention and achieve effects; thirdly, by looking at societies in which more than one language is used to see how the varied relationships between languages, as well as the status of each one, channels decisions about the objectives and methods of language teaching.

5.1. Social norms

Few of us are aware of the range and variety of our uses of language during even one typical day. Language will occur almost wherever we come into contact with other people and will be different according to the nature of the contact. Language also assails us even in situations in which no other people are present or when other people are present but are not producing language for our consumption. Even people whose jobs may not appear to demand extensive use of language are placed in numerous situations which will require characteristic pieces of language. The linguist can study the relations between language forms and social context to understand how the individual's choice of language enables him to perform his social functions. Let us look at some of the important social influences on language use.

5.1.1. Dialect

The first set of influences produce *dialect* features. These are the product of the individual's geographical and class origin. Educational experience is also significant, but this is partly dependent on class anyway. If two speakers differ in grammar, pronunciation and vocabulary, we will conclude that they speak different *dialects*. Variation in pronunciation, but not in grammar and vocabulary, would be considered difference of *accent*. There is no clear quantitative linguistic measure to indicate where difference of dialect becomes difference of language. The issue is political and social, not linguistic. Everybody speaks a dialect, which is not seen, as it is traditionally, as some kind of deviation from the norm of standard English. Nor would a linguist feel that there was any linguistic justification for saying that one dialect or accent is better than another. It is a social judgment that leads people to say that one English dialect is the 'correct' one.

Dialect is not an important type of language variation for teaching. Although the potential teacher and the advanced learner might be made sensitive to the fact that there *is* dialect variation in the target language just as there is in their mother-tongue, we rightly settle for the teaching of a single dialect to most learners. All language teaching, however, at least implies an assumption about the best dialect to teach.

If asked to justify the teaching of the metropolitan standard that is normally adopted as the model for foreign language teaching, we would presumably say that it is the form of language most acceptable to the native speaker and therefore the form that will enable the non-native speaker to be accepted by the host community. This seems a powerful justification. But, if this is valid, it cannot also be valid to teach the standard form to learners whose contact is likely to be speakers of a non-standard variety. Should not Americans learn Mexican rather than Castilian Spanish and Canadian rather than metropolitan French? Should not French-speaking Swiss learn a Swiss variety of German? Can we expect that before long Indonesians will be learning Australian rather than British English? If these varieties were to be accepted as the target languages, it would be because they were the forms of the language with which the learners were most likely to be in contact. A different situation arises when the language being learned will be used where there is no native speaker present. It is being acquired not primarily to provide for communication with native speakers but to facilitate communication between people who do not share their mother-tongue and for whom it is a foreign (second) language. This is true for example in many Commonwealth countries. People do not learn English because they expect to visit an English-speaking country. It might be unreasonable therefore to argue that they should learn the form of the language used in Britain or the United States. This is especially so since in many cases a distinct local variety of English has arisen where standard British English spoken with a Received (Standard Southern British) Pronunciation is socially decidedly unacceptable. In this case it can be argued that to set up the local variety of English as the target of school language teaching is only realistic. In Nigeria the English used in education would be Nigerian, in India Indian and so on.[1]

An alternative argument against a standard form of language as a model for learning is that in some cases the very choice of this form may create extra difficulties for the learner. Abercrombie, for example, has suggested that it might be easier for a foreigner to learn a Scottish accent than the traditional Received Pronunciation (R.P.) whose rather complicated vowel system with its extensive diphthongization presents problems to many foreign learners.[2] An educated Scottish accent makes greater use of pure vowels and would be easier for all those learners whose own languages have predominantly pure vowels. A possible counter-argument is that R.P. is not limited to any one geographical region and its use does not convey information about the provenance of the speaker. It might be more acceptable to the native speaker to hear from a foreigner this geographically neutral accent than one which suggests erroneously that the speaker comes from Scotland.

5.1.2. Register

Our daily lives take us through a succession of activities requiring the use of language. The activities are very diverse and, whatever dialect we speak, have specific features of language associated with them. Many activities are connected with our job. We may be an

---

[1] On the other hand the value of English as an international language should not be underestimated. To admit regional varieties as educational goals might result in such fragmentation that there will no longer be mutual comprehensibility between the accents.

[2] D. Abercrombie, 'English accents', in *Problems and Principles* (London, Longman, 1956), p. 55.

engineer giving instructions to a draughtsman, a lawyer advising a client, a trade-union official discussing fringe benefits, a bus-conductor collecting fares, a sergeant instructing a soldier or a scientist reading a technical report. Other activities are part of our leisure. We may be playing tennis, chess or bridge. Or relating to our home life, we may be acting as mother, father, husband, wife, son or daughter. Look at the life of any individual and we will find that every day he passes through a succession of such roles, and in each he will produce or hear features of language that are typical of the activity involved. A careful study of the activity should enable us to establish what the linguistic features are that mark that role.

For language teaching the roles with the most productive potential are the occupational roles. Although these have scarcely been investigated yet, it is supposed that there are distinct varieties of language associated with people's occupations and to these the name 'register' has been given. This is not a matter of subject-matter, but of the language used in the pursuance of one's job. These may be very different things. The language which I will use to talk about aeroplanes and flying will be quite unlike the language of people who work in and with aeroplanes. The fact that I am talking about flying, a question of subject-matter, will probably be indicated by vocabulary alone. A pilot's language will be marked by restrictions imposed on his range of grammar. It will also have a specialized vocabulary which will not have much resemblance to the vocabulary that I have been using.

One possible view of the aim of language teaching is that we are preparing the learner to perform a specific set of roles in a new language and new culture. In a general course such as schools usually provide, exact prediction of further roles is probably impossible. But we should not restrict our interest in language teaching to what goes on in schools. Registers are potentially important in language teaching because many people do have an occupational purpose in learning a foreign language. The older a learner is the more likely it is that he knows why he is learning and that the language is needed to help him in his job. Science students have long been expected to learn German or more recently Russian. Abroad the justification for the teaching of English has often been explicitly given as making scientific information more accessible.

To continue with the example of learning language for scientific purposes, we could hope that linguists might one day provide us with a complete description of the language used by scientists in all aspect of their work. It would contain information on the vocabulary and grammar used in popular and learned articles, in research proposals, abstracts and even in the actual conduct of research. Given such a description, we can apply it to the particular needs of any one group of scientific learners. They will not need uniformly to learn the entire sub-language. One group might consist of students being taught science in their mother-tongue, but needing access to work reported in one of the major languages used for scientific writing. They would concentrate on the language used in learned articles and abstracts. There might be some value in familiarity with popular articles too. Their knowledge would not need to be active at all. It would also be restricted to the written language. The vocabulary content may not need to be technical since the lexical items might be identifiable with cognate words in the mother-tongue. They would however need to be taught the 'operational' vocabulary.[3]

A second group consists of students having to acquire their knowledge of science through the medium of a foreign language, since material published in the mother-tongue is either inadequate or non-existent. Their major source of information will be text-books. They will need to conduct practical work in the second language and to write reports. Their ability will need to be productive and receptive, spoken and written. Technical vocabulary will be acquired through the learning of the subject itself and vocabulary teaching will need to concentrate on the operational items.

A third group might be fully qualified scientists, needing to add to their sources of information. They will be almost exclusively interested in reports of research and abstracts of them. The aim will therefore be a reading knowledge. While understanding of the grammar used in these texts will be very valuable, it seems possible that with their existing knowledge of their subject people in this group can get information they are seeking with a fairly rudimentary grammatical knowledge. In this case, effort is best concentrated again on the operational vocabulary. Their learning would need to be expanded considerably if it were to take into account the possibility of direct contact with other scholars who spoke only the foreign language in question. This might be necessitated by attendance at international congresses or visits to foreign universities or laboratories.

In practice, to make a thorough analysis of a real learning situation

[3] By 'operational' vocabulary is meant the non-technical items which link the scientific terms and which are derived from non-technical language.

would require many more distinctions than have been made here. It is by no means certain that there is a clear variety of scientific language. We would need to take into account different functions of language within texts and different types of text according to the precise scientific field. Our knowledge in these matters is still inadequate, but our awareness that choice of forms does vary according to the social function of the language is an important advance. It opens up the possibility of highly efficient language teaching in a situation where language needs are highly predictable. The language descriptions are and will be, for a long time, lacking. The amount of information that we are asking the linguist for is enormous. However, even though we shall have to use our intuitions as to what the valuable forms are for any one type of use, we can begin to base the priorities of our teaching on the content of the sub-variety of language in question instead of on the general grammatical system.

5.1.3. The medium of communication

Language contains fairly permanent features of dialect and more transitory features demanded by social roles. Just as we switch roles through the day, so we continually change the channel through which communication takes place. Choice of channel may sometimes be dependent on the previous choice of role, but this is not necessarily the case. For most of us, the auditory channel—speaking and hearing—is used much more than the visual—reading and writing. In one day we may use the visual medium to read newspapers, books, letters, advertisements, notices in the bus and at work, our car instruction manual or a football programme. Whether we do much writing depends on the nature of our job. The person who never has to write at work probably writes little more ever than the occasional letter. For many people, however, a good proportion of the working day is spent writing. As for speech, virtually all person-to-person contact involves use of speech. Our family relationships, our leisure interests and many occupational interactions are expressed in speech. Even when we are not producing language we are often hearing it—through radio, television, record-player or film.

We will find enough difference of linguistic form between the two media to justify establishing *medium* as an important social dimension. Ellipsis occurs commonly in speech, and in conversation the quantity of deletion can be so great that a listener may have great difficulty in understanding. Further, one cannot re-hear spoken language in the same way that one can re-read writing. Whereas in writing there will be no need to repeat statements, in speech repetition is often necessary to ensure comprehension. It also follows that in writing one can attempt greater complexity of language since one knows that a reader can always go over it a second time. Most speakers will intuitively keep their speech simpler, preferring a larger number of short uninvolved sentences to fewer sentences with a greater amount of subordination.

A simple distinction between speech on the one hand and writing on the other is not really fine enough. We may write something with the aim of reading it aloud, sometimes, but not always, with the intention of making it sound like speech. We may speak something that was originally written or, alternatively, so that what we say can be written down by somebody else.

A study of news reporting reveals the intricate interaction of the linguistic medium and the availability of the visual channel. A *newspaper* report is written so that it can be read. Everything has to be communicated through the grammatical and lexical content. What was originally speech can either be retold indirectly or quoted directly. The first will require use of the rules concerning indirect speech. The latter will almost certainly demand some normalization of the spoken forms to bring them into line with what is thought appropriate in writing. In both cases the reporter is going to have to make up for the absence of an extremely important component of the original speech—its intonation. He can only do this by attempting to find words which will convey the same general impressions that the intonation of the speech conveyed to its hearers. A *radio* report will be written so that it can be read aloud. In addition to a rather similar reportage of events, the radio report may also contain recorded extracts of the speech so that the hearer can draw his own conclusions about the intonation. Radio, however, can still tell us nothing of the paralinguistic features of a person's behaviour and it will have to make up for this, as may a newspaper, by such statements as 'U Thant looked anxious, confident . . .' and so on. Radio will also have more descriptive reporting since it does not have even the newspaper's limited possibility of using still pictures. *Televison* news reports are often made up partly of language originally written and therefore not much like natural speech, and partly of semi-spontaneous speech, as when a reporter works not from a script but simply from notes or even ad lib. In the latter case we will hear features of repetition, false starts, hesitation and broken structure that characterize speech.

Extensive use of film will give us direct access to earlier speech events, with all their linguistic and paralinguistic features, and will also obviate the need for descriptive reporting.

This type of language variation is not the product of the subject-matter and is not caused by change of speaker, since the participant in each of the above events could be the same person. It is the product of the media employed, the relation of speaker to audience, and the format adopted.[4] In language teaching generally one uniform style is taught, whether the aim is to teach speech or writing. Instead of speech we teach 'spoken prose', basing our uniform language on writing not speech.[5] Even dialogues on tape were evidently originally written, since they would never be mistaken for real speech. Oral drills need not always be perfect and complete samples of language. The demand for responses in complete sentences, though sometimes desirable, can make it difficult for the learner to operate with the extensive deletion of forms that he finds in natural speech. One would like all learners to be familiar with the more obvious differences between the forms of spoken and written language, and since most learners are frequently exposed to natural written texts, we might rectify the balance by making use of unscripted speech and dialogue. As for the more subtle stylistic variation reflected in the above discussion of news reporting, most learners will be consumers rather than producers. If included at all in language teaching, it would seem to have its place in the more advanced stages of a course when it could be associated with comprehension work and language analysis.

5.1.4. Status

In some of the previous discussion there has been implicit a further factor which can affect choice of language. The social relationships between participants in a language event are regularly marked by features of language. People are generally aware of their own *status* in relation to one another and will, especially in the more familiar situations, choose the appropriate language forms quite unconsciously. Our most intimate relationships are obviously with our own

---

[4] Format has not been discussed here, but would account for the difference of forms employed to describe, say, a house in small advertisements, in an estate agent's publicity or in an personal letter.

[5] D. Abercrombie, 'Conversation and spoken prose', in *Studies in Phonetics and Linguistics* (London, Oxford University Press, 1965).

families. With friends and colleagues we are still informal but not to the same degree. When we meet people we do not know, we probably feel the relationship to be more or less neutral. Where we are in a situation of social inferiority, as when we are talking to someone in a position of some authority over us, our language will become more formal. Some language uses have become so formalized as to be almost ritualistic.

Status interacts with other social dimensions. Written language is commonly, though not inevitably, formal. This is because most of the relationships that are expressed through writing are formal in character. But, of course, where the relationship is less formal, this will be reflected in a more casual style of writing. The language of the income-tax form is different in style as well as content from a letter to one's girl-friend. Status is not inflexible since relationships can change according to the exact situation. A works manager may be a member of a gardening club with some of the factory workers and if he is, we will not expect the same type of language as in the factory itself. Our working day is a succession of language contacts in each of which social relationships are marked by linguistic features.

Status may be marked at any level of language. If I write to my employer asking for an increase in my salary, I would be most unwise to use either the imperative or the interrogative form of the verb. 'Give me a pay-rise,' or 'Will you increase my pay next month?' would certainly be counterproductive. A circumlocutory approach would suggest an appropriate recognition of our relative status: 'I should therefore be grateful if you could give serious consideration to the possibility of increasing my salary. . . .' Of course if I knew myself to be a particularly highly valued employee, I would be more direct, but then my status would be different too.

The more formal sentence above also shows a change in vocabulary. For *pay* we now have *salary*. There is a very large vocabulary of items used for money received for work done: *pay, salary, wages, money, screw, remuneration, income, emolument, earnings, fee, commission, honorarium, retainer* and no doubt many more. The formality of an utterance is undoubtedly a factor in our choice from these alternatives. Slang is not incorrect vocabulary; it is vocabulary that is appropriate only to a casual or intimate style.

In a speech situation phonology may also be an indicator of relative status. Deference thought due to a superior or indifference to an inferior can be shown easily enough through intonation. Television advertisers apparently find it valuable in the selling of their products to suggest an intimate relationship with us by using a low, husky voice. Changes in the actual sounds of speech seem less likely.

Language learning is not complete when we have acquired a 'general' language system. We can, it is true, understand and make ourselves understood, but we will not yet be producing entirely acceptable forms of language. We cannot possible work out for ourselves which of the many grammatical modes of expression we should use in a given situation. There may be several semantically and grammatically acceptable ways of saying what we want to say, but only one that is stylistically acceptable. It is as true of the second as of the first language learner that he cannot master these features unless he experiences the forms of language in association with features of the non-linguistic situation.

Language teaching has been and still is much more occupied with instilling a general system of language than with enabling the pupil to modulate his language in accordance with features of the social situation. Even at the most advanced levels teaching scarcely wavers from what Joos has called a consultative style.[6] The study of literature may familiarize the learner with a more formal style, although this may not be of great practical value since it will not be related to situations in which he may find himself. If he converses with a native speaker, he will find that he is using a more formal style than the person he is talking to. Of all aspects of variety differentiation status seems to be the most important. On the assumption that we teach foreign languages in the expectation that our learners will be called upon to use those languages with native speakers, it is inescapable that they will have to base decisions about the forms that are appropriate on the dimension of status (and medium).

5.1.5. Situation

Another possible extralinguistic dimension is *situation*. I say 'possible' because the name 'situational' has been given to all the features we have been discussing in this chapter so far. In practice, when applied this widely the term becomes almost useless, since not all relevant social features are situational in the sense of being observable. We could however use it more narrowly and apply it to circumstances where observable features are recognizable even without reference to the language that is produced. If we then say that there are occa-

---

[6] M. Joos, *The Five Clocks* (Bloomington, Indiana University Press, 1962).

sions when language is related to the situation in which it occurs, we mean to observable characteristics of the situation. Whether or not there is any value in isolating situation as a variable in the *analysis* of the social function of language, it is worthwhile for its possible *application* to language teaching.

If, with this notion of situation in mind, we look at the possible range of man's language activities, we would come to the conclusion that in this repect language behaviour is a continuum. At one end of the scale the form and content of utterances is fairly predictable from a description of the situational context. Language occurs predictably in situations like buying a railway ticket, ordering a meal, or making introductions. It will be less predictable in a law court, where, although there may be quite a large number of recurrent forms, there will be almost no limit on the form and content of utterances that *can* accur. At the other end of the scale the situational context of utterance is almost totally unimportant and prediction would only be possible if one knew what in practice one cannot know—the learned and inherited characteristics of the participants. This would be the case with literature or indeed with most conversations between friends.

The interest for language teaching is in those cases where a high degree of predicability can be reached. If we discover that a given group of learners needs the language almost entirely for situations where the language content is under the control of observable stimuli, we can predict the language that he needs to be taught with considerable reliability. The limited aims of a tourist, a waiter or a telephone switchboard operator might be provided for entirely adequately in this way. In this case they would, by definition, be unprepared for anything 'out of the ordinary'. A situational syllabus would be an alternative to the conventional grammatical syllabus in cases where a situational analysis of needs seems profitable. It would not necessarily be a valuable alternative for the general language learner.

5.1.6. The pedagogic significance of language variety

The fact that our choice of linguistic forms varies according to social norms is significant for language teaching because it offers an alternative to the view that language is a stable and unified system. The latter view does not provide us with any means of establishing the relative importance of the different parts of the system. There is no reason to assume that any one part of the rule structure of the language has greater value than another, and the description itself does not take social factors into account. The study of language varieties is useful in aiding us to decide the priorities of language teaching.

Language teaching is usually the teaching of *langue*. The preceding three chapters have explored the manner in which linguists describe *langue*. We organize the process of teaching by taking the description and ordering the elements in it according to criteria of simplicity, frequency, difficulty, methodological convenience and pedagogic effectiveness. Our judgement in many of these matters is inevitably subjective. The starting-point is the language and our aim is to expose the learner to it systematically.

In the other view it is the learner himself who is the starting-point. We ask first 'What are the language activities in which he is going to participate?' Since linguists have begun to examine *parole*, we have been provided with a vocabulary which enables us to identify the significant social dimensions in a person's language experience. We can ask ourselves with which social groups he will have contact. From this we can decide the appropriate dialect(s). We can study the anticipated roles he will perform. In consequence we can provide him with the required register-features. We can determine the relative importance of written and spoken expression and prepare the pupil accordingly. We can examine the range of relationships and see that the learner masters the relevant stylistic features. Finally, and pro-bably combining aspects of all these dimensions, we can attempt to predict the situations in which the learner may find himself and we can ensure that he has the linguistic means to communicate acceptably in these situations.

The information that will be provided by an analysis of this kind will relate to all levels of language. Only rarely will the features be quite different from those of the standard language. We seem to have nothing quite comparable to the mother-in-law language of the Australian aborigines. The social norms in European languages are principally a matter of how we select from the forms of the *langue*. One variety of language may contain a predominance of passive verbs; another may lack adjectival modification of nouns; yet another may contain extensive ellipsis. In some types of text there may be an unusual distribution of comparative or conditional sentences. Indirect speech may be completely absent and so may some tenses.

The information provided by the linguist's study of language variety may be used in two ways. Either it can be incorporated into a more traditional language ordered course where its role will be to decide the priorities, or it can be employed more radically in the construction of a situational course. In this case the content of learning is described in behavioural terms, and linguistic considerations have little or no place. The learner is taken through related situations, not through related language. The exposure to language will inevitably be less methodical than we are used to. Any lesson unit might well contain several new linguistic structures. There could be no clear sequencing of items with the aim of facilitating the acquisition of the more difficult forms. In comparison with conventional materials situational courses will *appear* unorganized, and in a narrow linguistic sense they will be so. The linguistic diversity may make it difficult to provide adequate practice for the learner, but the obvious functional value of the language could make learning highly motivated. Whether we are prepared to adopt the more radical approach must depend on the reliability of the behavioural prediction and on one's judgment of how much easier it is to learn a language when it has been 'predigested' by segmentation into learning units, each of which has a clearly defined linguistic aim.

5.2. Individual intention and social function

In spite of the importance of the social factors we have just been describing, utterances are predictable only to a very limited degree. This is because the content of utterances is determined much more by the individual than by external factors. Since we do not have access to the workings of the mind, we cannot know what language the individual will choose to produce in any particular circumstances. Looking at it from the individual's point of view, the aim of any spoken or written utterance is to communicate something to the hearer or reader. The forms of utterances are important only because they enable the speaker to do this. Language forms are a means, and the forms of a second language are not learned for their own sake, but only to enable the learner to express himself to speakers of that language. However fluent one's mastery of a language—fluent in the sense of the ease with which grammatically acceptable sentences can be constructed and produced—it will serve as nothing if one cannot use it to achieve the desired communication effects. Language teaching therefore must be concerned with effective communication.

The significant thing about this is that language learning is not complete when one is proficient in producing grammatical forms and has assimilated the relations which they express. What we describe as the *grammatical* function of a sentence is not necessarily the same as its *utterance* function. Our usual grammatical labels often mislead us in this respect, as the example below shows. An *imperative* form of the verb is used, we believe, for giving orders and in language teaching we are usually satisfied that once the imperative has been learned, the pupil knows how orders should be given and also knows how the imperative is used in the language. But in the first place imperatives are used for many other purposes:

Find a seat and I'll get the drinks	(suggestion)
Do that and I'll knock your teeth in	(threat)
Connect the hose to the water supply	(instruction)
Turn left at the traffic-lights and take the third turning on the left	(direction)
Watch your glass	(warning)
Have a drink	(invitation)

It is arguable that each of these imperatives is derived from some other form of the verb, but the fact is that in each case the imperative in the actual utterance is in no way intended to act as a command to the hearer.

Conversely, it is equally possible to produce utterances containing no imperative forms, but which still have the effect of imposing the will of the speaker on the hearer:

If you don't shut the window, you'll get a good hiding
I insist that you do it
You pay the bill
You're not going out in that dress
My husband will carry your bag for you

In the last case the remark is superficially addressed to the beneficiary, but it is clearly the husband who is incurring the obligation.

The example of imperatives is not exceptional. There is plenty of other evidence that we should not insist too rigidly on a parallelism between grammatical function and function in actual acts of speech. Declaratives do not always express statements; interrogatives are not necessarily questions; conditionals are not always conditions. Putting it the other way round, comparatives are not the only means of making comparisons, nor in order to utter a warning is it necessary to use the verb *warn*.

The narrower view imposes limitations on the range of communicative effects that the non-native speaker has at his disposal. If there are many different ways of saying the same thing, albeit with differences of emphasis and nuance, an advanced learner will want to be able to select the one that suits the purpose of his utterance. At that level of learning it is not desirable that the speaker should have to modify *what* he wants to say to bring it within the linguistic *means* he has available. Our job as teachers is to enable him to acquire the means to achieve the maximum rhetorical effect for his spoken and written utterances. This will be difficult because there is no one-to-one relation between communication function and linguistic form. It means, too, beginning with the context and purpose of utterances and asking how these might be expressed, rather than taking a linguistic form and asking what may be communicated through it. It is therefore a notional not a formal approach to language teaching.

The notional choices which a speaker makes are almost certainly universals of communication. Languages will differ enormously in the ways they realize these universals, but it seems likely that people everywhere need to express the same kinds of notion. We need to display our emotions—surprise, pleasure, sorrow, anger, anxiety, hope, enthusiasm; our emotional reactions to others—sympathy, condolence, affection, admiration, trust, dislike, ridicule, insult; attitudes and obligations — praise, blame, apologies, regret, promises, prohibitions, tolerance, permission and obligation; modalities and dialectics—degrees of possibility, probability, necessity, likelihood, doubt, certainty, ability, agreement and disagreement, persuasion, suggestion, invitation, demands, orders, insistence, warnings, acceptance, caution, refusal, assertion, opposition, qualification, admission, emphasis, contrast, understatement, exaggeration, frankness and tact.[7]

The list, of course, is not complete, but it is long enough for us to recognize the importance of mastering the means of expressing these notions and to demonstrate how little provision is made at present for teaching them. I doubt whether a learner at the end of a conventional course would feel confident in his ability to express many of these communication functions, yet much of our language use is

---

[7] My examples are taken from a much more comprehensive list given by J.L.M. Trim, *The analysis of language contents:* paper given at Council of Europe Symposium: 'Linguistic content, means of evaluation and their interaction' (Rüschlikon, Switzerland, May 1971).

personally motivated, as these examples show. I do not think that the learner will without assistance develop this ability on the basis of his existing formal knowledge of the language. The exact meaning distinctions that can be made are not self-evident, and will only be mastered if adequate provision is made in the organization of language teaching.

As with the situational dimensions discussed in the first section of this chapter, it becomes possible to replace a conventional linguistic organization of teaching only if we have some way of knowing exactly what notions a learner will need to express. The reason why there are sometimes restrictions on the formal features of language that occur is that there are restrictions on *what* the language user needs to express. If we can define the types of content, the formal features will follow from it. A student of science needs to be familiar with the ways of expressing hypotheses, generalizations, exemplifications, inferences, definitions, laws, instructions, proofs, and disproofs. A possible approach to the teaching of a student of science is not to list a set of appropriate linguistic features, but to list the needed communication functions and to teach the student to produce them or recognize their occurrences. The range of linguistic features involved would be wide because each utterance function has many different realizations.

In the context of a more general language course, we might find it difficult to see any advantage in replacing the conventional systematic grammar-based approach by the formally haphazard approach implied by these notions. In this case notionalism offers a solution, perhaps in conjunction with the situationalism of the previous section, to the planning of advanced language learning. The pupil learns to exploit the formal ability he has acquired for effective communication. At present there is often no guiding principle to advanced learning. Perhaps these communication universals provide a means for the pupils to practise the application of their linguistic knowledge.

5.3. The social status of non-native languages

'Getting educated is a personal matter, in contrast, providing education is a social enterprise.'[8] So far I have been arguing that the individual is central to our concern, but, as Bull suggests, society's

[8] W.A. Bull 'The use of vernacular languages' in *Language in Culture and Society*, ed. D. Hymes (New York, Harper & Row, 1964).

interests in education cannot be ignored. Society has its own reason for providing for the education of its young and if it chooses to teach them foreign languages, it is because it feels that in some way society's needs require this. There does not have to be any conflict of interest here, but the reasoning will be different. Society creates the context of learning and within this we can try to meet the needs of the individual. We can best understand society's reasons for providing for the learning of foreign languages by examining the socio-linguistic status of the languages to be learned. We shall see that even the material of language teaching is influenced by such broad issues. The reasoning behind policies is not always made explicit although, so long as one does not restrict one's attention to one geographical area, it is surprising in how many countries politicians and educationists have publicly set out the purposes of foreign language teaching within their system of education.

In spite of the fact that the labels subsume some very different situations, we must start by drawing up some broad categories for the distinctions of status that target languages may have. It is common already to differentiate *foreign* languages and *second* languages. To these I should like to add a third, *alternate* languages.

5.3.1. Second language learning

The common element in those situations which are usually called *second* language situations is that the language being learned (L2) is not the mother-tongue (L1) of any group within the country, but that it does have some internal, social function. Almost by definition the countries where the L2 will be a second language are multilingual states. It may be that there is no one local language that is sufficiently dominant to become immediately a national language. Even where there is a candidate for this role it may happen that there is political resistance to its general acceptance or that it has not yet evolved into an entirely satisfactory instrument for the expression of man's needs in the twentieth century. Until another language is ready to take over, some of the functions of a national language will be performed by a language which has historical connections with the country. In practice this means English and French and the situation arises mostly, though not exclusively, in multilingual states that were formerly colonies of Britain or France. The scale and variety of use of the second language differs enormously. It can encompass part or all of government administration, politics, law, medicine, industry, internal trade, newspapers, general publishing, and education. As a result, in education it may become the medium of instruction at any level from the primary school upwards.

It is *because* the second language has these other, non-educational functions that it has a place in education at all. If the other activities could be carried out entirely in a local language, the arguments for using a second language as a medium of instruction would largely disappear. The greater the general use of the language in the country the earlier in the educational system it is likely to become the medium of instruction. In states where the L2 has a major function, those who have to develop an education policy are perpetually torn between the general desirability of educating children in their mother-tongue and the need to produce very high levels of proficiency in the second language so that learning at the higher stages is made more effective. In all such countries the second language will at the very least be taught as a subject in the primary school. The question is whether and when it should become the medium, and this question will not be resolved in terms of what is psychologically and physiologically the best age to learn a foreign language, as it tends to be in situations where the language is a *foreign* language. Much wider considerations have to be taken into account. Paradoxically, in the francophone African countries, where in colonial times all education was in French, there is a tendency to introduce the mother-tongue in primary education, whereas in the anglophone countries, where, under the British, local languages were used as the medium for the early years, there is now a move towards introducing English as the medium.[9]

In countries where the social role of English or French has been reduced as local languages have taken over, they have come to play an increasingly smaller part in the educational system too. India is a country in transition. English is losing its status as a second language and in some states has already become a foreign language. It is now felt that the regional languages can cope with all aspects of education except technical and scientific subjects at the university level. Consequently there is a steady reduction in the use of English as a medium. Only in southern India does English remain a second language, because it can serve as a more acceptable *lingua franca* than Hindi. With the change in status comes an almost inevitable drop in the standard of English proficiency. No longer does the entire school

[9] B.W. Tiffen, 'Language and education in commonwealth Africa' in *Language in Education* by J. Dakin, B. Tiffen and H.G. Widdowson (London, Oxford University Press, 1968), pp. 68–9.

curriculum contribute to the pupil's exposure to English; and the pupil's learning depends upon the effectiveness of the English teacher's *language* teaching techniques. Since in most second language situations the English (or French) teacher was primarily a teacher of literature, he may not prove to be an efficient teacher of language unless he has been retrained.

In Tanzania a slightly different situation has arisen, because the adoption of Swahili as a national language has not given rise to any of the controversy that India has seen. Swahili cannot yet perform all of the functions that English can, but one can anticipate that it will steadily replace English both socially and in the educational system until the only place for English will be in the teaching of scientific and technical subjects. At that point English would have acquired foreign language status.

While the extent to which the second language is used in the educational system generally seems to stem from the importance of its overall social role, this is not always the case. Not all Arabic-speaking countries assign the same role to the principal foreign language that is taught. Whereas Egypt and Libya can restrict the use of English as a medium to the university level, in Tunisia, Algeria and Morocco, French is still used extensively as a medium in secondary schools. There are perhaps two reasons for their not using Arabic as fully as appears to be possible. First, they see some value in maintaining their link with French culture and feel that this is best done by keeping it as a medium of instruction. Secondly, there may not be enough teachers trained to teach at secondary level through the medium of Arabic, and to make full use of the teachers available it is necessary to continue education in French.

Are there any special characteristics that we can expect of the materials and methods of second language teaching? The most striking difference from materials provided in the situations to be described below is that the cultural and situational context of learning is deliberately local. The characters in texts, the vocabulary and the context created through visual aids are all drawn from the children's own background and not from the culture internationally associated with the language being learned. There are two principal reasons for this. In the first place, since they are learning the language in order to be able to use it to carry out the functions it has in their own country, it is only right that the content of learning should be what those uses require. In any case the close association of the new language to features of their daily life that are familiar to them probably makes the language easier to learn. In the second place the countries where English and French are learned as second languages have become independent states only in recent years. While they would not deny that there is an educational value in familiarity with other cultures, they feel that their first task must be the creation of their own cultural unity. Some of them explicitly reject the suggestion that English or French is being taught for cultural reasons and attempt to reduce or exclude the cultural content of language learning. As far as possible the teaching of these languages has to make its contribution to the development of an awareness of their own culture, and as a result prominence is given, in Africa at least, to the growing body of African writing in French and English. The content of language teaching is designed to meet the internal rather than the external function of the language.

Wherever the second language occupies a position of great importance in the daily life of the community we are likely to find that it is introduced at the primary level of education. As I mentioned above, the reasoning here does not depend on arguments about what is psychologically the best time for a child to begin foreign languages. This is the line of argument that has dominated the movement in Europe and the U.S.A. towards foreign languages in the primary (elementary) school. Instead it is justified by the necessity for starting at an early age if the language is to become an efficient tool of learning at the higher levels. Almost all second language courses assume a beginning in the primary school. Text-books are designed to appeal to the younger child. The language is graded much less steeply and the methodology must not be in conflict with the approach that is adopted to the teaching of the rest of the primary curriculum. Although in the first three to four years there may be considerable similarities with foreign language teaching, in its later stages the teaching of second languages comes progressively to resemble the teaching of the mother-tongue. The aim will be to expand the pupil's experience through language, developing his personality and his sensibilities. It is doubtful whether this can ever be a major aim of *foreign* language teaching.

5.3.2. Foreign language learning

A *foreign* language learning situation is one in which the target language is not the mother-tongue of any group within the country where it is being learned and has no internal communication function either. The aim of teaching the language is to increase ease of contact with foreign language speakers outside the country. Sometimes there is a prediction of the kind of contact that is anticipated. We have already seen how this prediction operates for the individual, but language teaching needs to cater for wider social needs too, and we increasingly read as a justification for language teaching that it is a necessary condition for the expansion of overseas trade. The provision of an adequate number of foreign language speakers is now thought necessary for a country's economy. In spite of this and other functional requirements that can be put upon the language being learned, few would quarrel with the traditional view that the learning of a foreign language itself contributes to the education of the individual by giving him access to the culture of a group of people with whom he does not have daily contact.

Through much of the twentieth century at least the tradition of *foreign* language teaching has been that access to foreign cultures was only likely to be made through reading the language, and reading ability has always been more developed than any other. The newer emphasis on spoken language skill is entirely consistent with the overall educational aim of foreign language teaching. It is not that one is providing the learners with the means to survive as tourists on their holidays abroad. It is that only now is there any likelihood of large numbers of people coming into contact with foreign cultures at first hand. Their understanding will be much greater if they have the ability to participate in rather than observe uncomprehendingly the events they experience in other countries. Teaching them to use the foreign language helps to ensure that visits abroad, now within the reach of most people, are themselves part of the process of education.

Foreign language learning, therefore, is like second language learning in that the material and method is designed to give a practical command of the language. But whereas the second language learner needs the language for use within his own community, the foreign language learner needs it so that he can form contacts with a community other than his own. The context of his learning, therefore, should be not his own culture but that of the group whose culture has provided the justification for his language learning in the first place. A French context will deliberately be created for the English child learning French and any explicit cultural content will be drawn from and have reference to the culture of the French-speaking world, and in particular of France itself, since that is the country with which the child is most likely to have contact. The language teacher's attempt to turn the classroom into a little bit of France by use of audio and visual aids is entirely right where French is being taught as a foreign language.[10]

The other big difference from second language teaching is that foreign languages are usually taught in the secondary school. It is true that in recent years experimental and not entirely successful efforts have been made to teach languages in the primary school, but the practical difficulties alone are likely to restrict the bulk of language teaching to the secondary school. This means that foreign language teaching will be typically directed to an older age group. As with primary age learning, the language teacher cannot neglect general psychological factors that affect the acquisition of language as much as anything else. At this level the pupil is accustomed to an altogether more analytical approach to learning. He is expected to be conscious of exactly what it is he is learning and to be able to direct his efforts to assimilating new knowledge and new skill. Provided he is well motivated he has a far greater capacity for concentrated effort than a younger child and this can carry him through material that does not interest him intrinsically. On the other hand his own motivation for learning may not be strong and the teacher may find greater difficulty in creating motivation.

Most modern methodologists argue against methods which depend on the pupil acquiring an explicit knowledge of rules of language structure, and instead recommend a more inductive approach to learning. The pupil might therefore experience some conflict between his language learning and his learning of other subjects in the curriculum. Some of the common techniques seem closer to primary methods and might be the less acceptable to an adolescent learner for that reason. About the motivating power of foreign language materials it is impossible to generalize. Where some, audio-visual courses for example, seem to devote much energy to engaging the interest of the learner, others seem designed to exploit an interest that has been created by some other means. Once the novelty of a language laboratory has worn off, few will find repeated drill sessions

---

[10] An exception to this generalization about the cultural orientation of foreign language learning is a situation in which a second language is also being learned. In much of Africa, for example, English is being taught as a foreign language in francophone countries and French in anglophone countries. The aim is often expressly political—to assist the process of political unification in Africa—and cultural content is not really relevant to this. If any literature at all is included, it is African in origin.

in the laboratory motivating in themselves. However, one should not underestimate the value of explaining to the learner why this type of practice is valuable. By this age he is much better able to judge for himself the merits of different ways of learning.

Foreign language learning in many countries does not get beyond the stage of progressive accumulation of linguistic knowledge. The language teacher is the only person to provide exposure to the language, and when that exposure is sometimes for as little as one hour a week and rarely for more than five, it is evident that in few situations can foreign language teaching reach the point where techniques resemble those of mother tongue teaching. Practice will take place only in the language lesson and overall progress through the structure of the language will be slow. Where the number of hours is very low, even practice may have to be dispensed with, so that the learner's knowledge will be latent, to be developed into practical ability only if he finds himself in a more intensive contact situation.

5.3.3. Alternate language learning

The society in which second and foreign language learners live will not normally provide them with any contact with native speakers of that language. The second language learner will use the language in his own country, more often than not in conversation with another non-native speaker. Certainly for most there is little likelihood of extensive exposure to native speakers. The foreign language learner will not use the language at all in his own country, and only if he goes abroad will he have contact with native speakers. There is however a third situation, which by definition cannot arise in a monolingual state, where the target language is in fact the mother-tongue of another group in the same country. It is a situation that we find, for example, in Canada, where English and French are each the L1 of one group and the principal L2 of another. An 'alternate' language, as I have chosen to call it, is like a second language in that it has a social function within the country of the learner, but unlike it in that this function will be principally in contacts with native speakers. It is quite unlike a foreign language because not only is it spoken in the learner's own country, but it is spoken by native speakers.

There are many well-publicized alternate language situations: English and French in Canada, English and Welsh in Wales, Flemish and French in Belgium, Russian in the Soviet Union, Hindi in the non-Hindi speaking areas of India, and Swahili in Tanzania. Each of the languages mentioned is the native language of one group and a target language for other groups in the country concerned. The related status of the languages in these situations is not necessarily one of equality. There are questions of geography and of dominance. To take the former point first: in some cases the L2 is only really an 'alternate' language for those living close enough to the region where the language is spoken to come into contact with native speakers. If they are far removed from the target language group the situation becomes much closer to that of a foreign language. In Canada, for example, an English speaker resident in British Columbia faces quite a different situation, if he is learning French, from the English-speaking resident of Quebec.

The other point is of far wider importance. One of the language groups in the bilingual situation may well be more powerful than the other numerically, politically, economically and educationally. It is this situation, and the concomitant threat felt by members of the minority group to their cultural identity, that has made political issues out of language policies. There is not equal pressure on each group to learn the other's language. If the French speakers of Canada want to flourish economically they cannot avoid becoming fluent in English. The converse is not true. How much more likely it is that the Welsh speakers of Wales will become ambilingual than that the English speakers will do so. In the belief that this is an undesirable state of affairs some have insisted that Welsh should be taught as an alternate language to all for whom it is not the mother-tongue, and in some parts of Wales it is a policy that is already being implemented. It is likely to produce the desired change in the status of Welsh only if Welsh becomes simultaneously necessary economically.

The pedagogically significant thing about an alternate language situation is that the provision made for *teaching* the alternate language may not be the most important factor in determining the *learning* of the language. If one accepts that in many cases an alternate language is learned to an unusually high degree of proficiency, it is altogether more plausible to seek the explanation in the bilingual situation than to expect that language teaching itself is somehow so much better. Learning is a response to the enormous social pressures on the individual to be able to use the language. Provided the social pressure is there, people will learn the language. Personal motivation, simple quantity of exposure and language aptitude are in themselves probably less important. People may learn an alternate language in spite of hostility towards it, whereas others, in a superficially similar situation but with no pressure to learn, may fail to acquire the language in spite of favourable attitudes. Older immigrants, in spite of ample exposure to the host language, rarely acquire it to an advanced level. This is probably because many of their most intimate social contacts are maintained through the mother-tongue. In the multilingual states of Africa many children are already fluent in two or three languages—which they have never been taught—when they come to school and are expected to learn what is misleadingly called a second language. Since some children fail to learn the second language very well, their earlier learning of one or more alternate languages must be ascribed to some factor other than an innate aptitude for languages.

Concomitant with alternate and, to some extent, with second language learning are problems of social identity. Through one's language one is identified and identifies oneself with a particular social group. The acquisition of an alternate language, because of the proximity of the people who speak the language, offers an alternative to one's native group. The possibility of switching allegiance or of being believed to have switched allegiance is a real one. The mixture of values that a learner often acquires makes it impossible for him to feel a member of either group. In the process he may come to a somewhat painful point at which his original roots are no longer strong, but at which he does not wish to cut them completely in favour of a new allegiance to the values of the target language culture. Once he is through this stage, the learner may benefit from the personal enrichment created by his ability to participate in two cultures.

The advantages that the learner of an alternate language often has are so great that one wonders how far teaching needs to meet the conditions required for second or foreign language teaching. How important is it to arrange for extensive practice in the classroom when it is so easily available outside it? How far need one go in creating motivation if external conditions are such that learning will take place anyway? Should the content be directed towards the social uses of language that can be predicted for the learner, or will this not be necessary since it is these uses that he will acquire in his social contacts whether or not he has been taught them? In this case perhaps teaching should concentrate on aspects of language use that his anticipated social experience will not present him with.

As long as there really is going to be extensive language contact outside the classroom, language learning material can be more steeply graded than in second or foreign language teaching. The teacher might be less concerned about his pupil's errors, since he can expect that with use of the language, the errors will tend to disappear as they do in 'natural' language acquisition situations. Where the alternate language is the language of the host community being learned by immigrants, there will be different priorities. The aim will be to achieve, as rapidly as possible, educability in the alternate language. Ability to read will be far more important, and it will not be possible to delay the teaching of reading until a substantial oral skill has been built up. Emphasis must also be given to the ability to understand spoken classroom language, so that successful integration into ordinary classes is achieved as soon as possible.

5.4. Summary

Language is a social activity, and choice of language varies according to social function and personal intention. Language teaching must provide the learner with means to select language which is suitable for the circumstances in which it is used—involving command of features of dialect, register, medium and style—and which is appropriate to express his personal states and ideas—requiring mastery of a range of communication functions. These factors may contribute to the priorities of language teaching content and even, where situational use is highly predictable, offer an alternative to the conventional grammatical syllabus. The aims, methods and materials of language teaching vary according to the socio-linguistic status of the target language, which may be that of a second, foreign or alternate language.

6
The psychology of language

6.1. Introduction

For most linguists the main aim of their discipline is and has been to develop the means for the most effective description of natural languages. In the first four chapters we have caught a glimpse of the attitudes and expectations that the linguist brings to the task of providing a structural analysis of a body of language data. Very often he has felt that to be truly scientific in his approach he has to deal with the substance of language in isolation from any sociological or psychological factors that may affect its use. Naturally enough linguists have been interested in the processes involved in using language, but they have believed it to be the function of the psychologist and not the linguist to investigate these. They tend therefore to have adopted fairly uncritically whatever the psychologists have proposed in their attempts to describe language behaviour.

While many linguists still retain this point of view, in recent years a substantial and influential school of thought has developed which argues that the true task of the linguist should not be the description of individual languages but the explanation of our language use. This in turn demands research into the human capacity for language itself. By exploring the processes by which an individual acquires and uses language these linguists, far from rejecting psychology, are actually incorporating it into linguistics. Linguistics is a branch of psychology, or, some might say, since language is central to all human experience, psychology is a branch of linguistics.

The object of research of this kind, whether carried out by linguists or psychologists, is to establish general characteristics of human language. They are interested in discovering what is universal in language and what general laws govern our acquisition of language. The field of discussion is almost wholly the learning of the mother-tongue, but if there really are general language learning principles involved, this cannot be without interest for foreign language learning. We can for the moment reserve judgement on the question of whether or not language teaching procedures *should* be based on general theories of language acquisition. As we shall see, at least one widely adopted method has been developed as an application of such a general theory. In this case the theoretical basis of the method is explicitly acknowledged, but more often the theory has to be derived from the apparent assumptions of a proposed method.

Such theories inevitably imply that individuals are essentially 'the same' in their language learning capacities. Most language teachers are probably more conscious of the diversity of language learning abilities that their pupils display. There need not be any contradiction. It is perfectly reasonable to suppose that there are some characteristics that are shared by all learners and others where there is considerable personal variation. In this chapter I shall first discuss two highly-contrasting general accounts of language acquisition, and then examine some of the factors that are said to account for individual variation in language learning performance.

6.2. General theories of language acquisition

6.2.1. Behaviourism[1]

For behaviourists there is not a theory of language learning as such, but merely the application to language of general principles of learning.[2] In general terms there is no difference between the way one learns a language and the way one learns to do anything else. Beyond recognizing that only human beings possess the capacity for language there is no need to postulate any complex internal endowment that allows us to learn and use language. The behaviourist is committed to admitting as evidence only that which he can observe, so that his data are the utterances that people make and the conditions under

---

[1] No one can write on this topic without acknowledging their debt to Wilga M. Rivers, *The Psychologist and the Foreign Language Teacher* (Chicago, University of Chicago Press, 1964). This book examines critically and with great expertise the theoretical assumptions of audio-lingual methodology. The reader who finds this chapter of interest should certainly turn to Rivers for an altogether more authoritative account.

[2] This section is very simplified. I include only what serves my purpose in this book. There are of course many different views held by psychologists on the processes of language acquisition and use. Since the most fully articulated account of language behaviour is that of B.F. Skinner, *Verbal Behaviour* (New York, Appleton-Century-Crofts, 1957), the sketch here follows him more closely than anyone else. In many ways his views have already had a considerable influence on language teaching, and indeed on the teaching of other subjects too.

which they are made. In fact he would say that these limitations, which he feels to be necessary if he is to be properly scientific in his approach, do not prevent him arriving at an adequate description of language behaviour. It follows from this that learning is controlled by the conditions under which it takes place and that, as long as individuals are subjected to the same conditions, they will learn in the same way. What appears to be variation in learning ability is really no more than different learning experience. This would include previous as well as actual experience, but in practice much less emphasis is placed on the influences of past learning than on the factors operating directly in the situation in which the learning is going on.

Every utterance and every part of an utterance is produced as the result of the presence of some kind of 'stimulus'. The stimulus, to which the utterance forms a 'response', may be physically present in the situation; it may be verbal, since language can be produced as a response to other language, or it may be internal, in that a state of thirst may provide the stimulus for an utterance like 'I would like a glass of water'. For a child to learn to make such a response in the first place, his first attempts at producing the piece of language will have to be 'reinforced'. A child can be reinforced in a variety of ways. Parental approval acts as a powerful reinforcer. A physical need in the child may be met as a result of his utterance. His own language may act as a stimulus to action or language on the part of someone else. If such reinforcement does not take place, as when a child says something which is not understood by those around it, the piece of language, the response, is not learned. In this way correct pieces of language are acquired, but incorrect utterances are not.

A single emission of a response, even if it is reinforced, is by no means enough for learning to take place. Only if a response is repeated can it be fully learned. Indeed strength of learning is measured in terms of the number of times that a response has been made and reinforced. A word that has been uttered thirty times is better learned than one which has been said twenty times. The notion of *repetition* is therefore extremely important. More important still is the fact that a response that is not made cannot be repeated and reinforced and therefore cannot be learned. It is the making of the response that is the learning process. If there is no reinforcement, the learning is then extinguished. If an individual learns by making a response, it follows that he cannot learn from situations which do not demand a response from him. He does not learn to produce language by watching and hearing other people use it. Nor does he learn by having language use described or explained to him. If it is active language use that he is to learn, his responses must be active language responses. Hearing may be a response, but through repeated hearing one learns only to hear and not to speak. In short, one learns only what one practises doing.

As long as a child is making correct responses he can be reinforced and will learn. If he made only correct responses he would learn that much more rapidly. In practice he may well utter incorrect forms. He may not hear accurately a form which he is expected to imitate, or, more significantly, he may create an incorrect form by analogy with another form which he has learned correctly. Having learned that *filled* is the past tense of *fill* he may overgeneralize this response and apply it to *sell*, thereby producing the form *selled**. The ability to make analogies is taken as given by behaviourists and it applies to non-linguistic forms of behaviour too. If incorrect responses were never reinforced this might not be an important consideration. However, an incorrect form can easily appear in a generally correct utterance and if the whole thing is reinforced, the incorrect is being learned as thoroughly as the correct. In any case, as learning advances, the absence of an adverse reaction on the part of hearers may be sufficient to provide reinforcement and the learner then becomes the judge of his own speech. Error may then pass unnoticed, be repeated and thereby be learned.

Since in his description of language behaviour the psychologist is concerned with the mother-tongue, like the linguist he is bound to assign primacy to speech. In all but pathological cases language appears first in the form of speech. It is inevitable that speech should be far more significant for the psychologist than writing which only develops later as a secondary form, very largely derived from speech. Writing is not a necessary stage in the developmental process and indeed it is still absent from the behaviour of many human beings. The approach to writing, therefore, can only be through speech.

In this summary of behaviourist views there is one further, most important point to be mentioned and this concerns meaning. So far I have talked of correct and incorrect responses as if this was entirely a matter of correctness of form. But a response does not only have to be formally correct, it has to be the appropriate response to the stimulus. In learning a language one has to acquire both a 'formal' and a 'thematic' repertoire of responses. Most behaviourists eschew use of the word 'meaning' altogether. To think of the meaning of a word as something built up and stored inside the individual is to imply a mental structure of some kind which the behaviourist finds objectionable and unnecessary. What we might traditionally call meaning is simply the ability to produce an appropriate response to a stimulus. One does not need to use such terms as 'understanding'. As he learns his mother-tongue, the child comes to recognize not just individual stimuli but whole classes of stimuli to which a word or utterance is an appropriate response. He learns to draw the boundary between those situations in which the word may be properly used and those to which it would be an incorrect response. The individual does not control his use of words. Through his learning experience the words are automatically elicited from him by the presence of the appropriate stimulus. We can be satisfied with any language performance where the utterance of the child constitutes an adequate response to the stimuli that are present. We do not need to enquire into the 'meaning' of what has been said, or whether the child has 'understood' or 'meant' what he has said.

6.2.1.1. *Behaviourism in language teaching.*   Most developments in foreign language teaching since the second world war have been based on the assumption that language is a form of behaviour. Even where there is no explicit statement of the theoretical foundations of a method, the underlying attitude can be inferred from the use of such terms as 'skill' or 'habit'. To quote the title of the fifth chapter in Rivers, 'Foreign-language learning is basically a mechanical process of habit formation.'[3] More deeply committed to such a point of view is Nelson Brooks: 'The single paramount fact about language learning is that it concerns, not problem solving, but the formation and performance of habits.'[4] On the previous page he has also used the word 'skill'. Analogies between language and 'other skills' abound. Learning a language is like learning to type, to ride a bicycle or to carry out any of the other routines that we characterize as habits. They are forms of human activity which, once learned, can be carried out without the conscious use of one's cognitive processes. The belief is that conscious attention to the principles underlying the skill does not assist the *learning* of the skill.

It is only fair to point out that use of these two terms in writings on foreign language teaching does not necessarily imply a commitment to all the details of a behaviourist theory such as that outlined

[3] Rivers, *op. cit*, p. 31.
[4] N. Brooks, *Language and Language Learning* (New York, Harcourt, Brace & World, 1960), pp. 46-7.

above. As often as not they are used as a corrective to the view that a foreign language is just another subject to be learned in school, a set of facts together with some rules for solving problems. Even so, it is the function of applied linguistics to make the implications of such terms explicit and this is necessary if the study of language teaching is to be properly scientific. Useful as it may be to emphasize the notion of language as a skill in the polemics of language teaching, we must eventually decide just how accurate in fact such statements are.

Here I am concerned with cases where the terminology of behaviourism is openly applied to foreign language teaching. From what we have seen, a behaviourist method of language teaching should embody at least the following principles. It should be firmly anchored in spoken language. We might expect an even greater salience to be given to speech than the goals of the course might justify. The teaching of writing would follow the teaching of spoken language. Since one can only learn responses by responding oneself, we would expect a great deal of language activity by the pupils themselves. They would be given the opportunity to repeat numerous times each new piece of language that they encountered. By contrast, little of what they were learning would be explained to them. We would notice the absence of formal explanations and rules from the teacher's language.

We might be struck by how easy much of the work that the pupils were doing seemed to be. The teacher would appear to be giving a considerable amount of assistance to the learner to enable him to get his response right. Indeed, at first the class may be doing no more than imitate what the teacher was saying. In the practice that followed the pupils would be left with little or no choice about what to say or how to say it. The practice would proceed rapidly and correctly. The justification for making correct responding easy is that the pupil does not learn by making mistakes but by having correct responses properly reinforced. If we can arrange the practice in such a way that the learner utters only correct sentences, he will learn that much more quickly. It is this principle that lies behind language drilling in contrast to the more traditional exercises in which a correct response is possible only if one has already learned the point in question. Drills are a form of practice; exercises are often a form of test. As soon as the learner is given the opportunity to make his own choice of language he is likely to commit errors. In such teaching therefore there would probably be an absence of occasions for the learner to select his language. The language itself would be organized into a careful sequence so that the burden of new material would never be very large. Each unit would constitute only a small increment of language content over the last. This too would facilitate correct responding, since error is often caused by trying to teach a number of different points at the same time.

Reinforcement, to be effective, should follow the response as quickly as possible. In the classroom it might take the form of approval from the teacher or satisfaction by the pupil that he has got his response right. There might be discouragement of any technique which cannot provide for immediate reinforcement. One sometimes meets the argument that homework should not be set, since the teacher cannot see it until long after it was done and by the time it is returned to the learner any reinforcement is lost. The only benefit to be gained from such work is that it has provided some further opportunity for language practice. However, the language being practised is as likely to be incorrect as correct. If the errors could be pointed out immediately, no harm might be done. But the inevitable time interval means that correction by the teacher is less effective in extinguishing the wrong response than the original repetition of the response was in strengthening learning.

The notion of immediate reinforcement is employed most power-fully in language laboratory drilling. The tape is produced to provide a sequence of stimulus—response—reinforcement. It further meets the requirements of the behaviourist model by demanding from each pupil numerous repetitions of correct spoken responses. Whereas in the classroom the teacher is present to judge the appropriateness of a response and a certain amount of flexibility is permissible, in the laboratory the learner is alone with the material. He therefore has to evaluate his own performance and provide his own reinforce-ment. This takes the form of knowledge that his response is a correct one. To enable him to make this evaluation the correct response is pre-recorded on the tape so that the learner can compare his own response with it. His recognition that the two pieces of language are identical provides the reinforcement that ensures that learning takes place. Of course it is only possible to pre-record a response if there is only a single possible correct answer. If more than one response was possible, one would know neither which response to record, nor which response the learner might select. These considerations lead to the by now familiar type of drill in which a stimulus sentence is recorded on the tape, followed by a pause during which the learner makes his response according to some predetermined pattern, and then by the pre-recorded correct response to provide the reinforcement. If the drill is left at that stage it is called a three-phase drill. Sometimes, however, the reinforcement itself is used as the stimulus to a further imitative response (four-phase drill) with, possibly, further reinforcement (five-phase drill).

Whether in classroom or laboratory, behaviourist teaching relies more on analogy than on rules for teaching the structure of the language. Teaching which encourages the learner to construct sentences according to a previously learned set of rules is thought to hinder the instinctive production of language. It does not resemble the 'natural' learning process, in which the child attempts to construct new forms on the analogy of the forms of language that he has already met. By being exposed to the language the child comes to recognize and operate the structure of the language in an unconscious way. In language teaching this analogizing process can be facilitated, not by giving the rule to the child, but by arranging each drill repetition so that the pupil constructs his new response along exactly the same lines as his previous response. All the responses in any one drill will have exactly the same grammatical structure. With enough properly reinforced repetition of the structure, the 'rule' will be acquired in a way that is not only unconscious but also more conducive to spontaneous language use thereafter.

This leaves till last the question of meaning. If you base a teaching method narrowly on a theory of learning, the method will reflect the strengths and weaknesses of the theory. It is conceivable that a set of procedures like those I have outlined will produce a reasonable mastery of the forms of language. There are doubts as to how well the meaning of language will be acquired, since the original analysis of meaning itself seems very naive. If this is so, it is a serious deficiency, since the whole object of language is to communicate meaning. If we assume for a moment that learning the meaning of a language is indeed acquiring a thematic repertoire of responses, it would appear that such a method as I have been describing, with its numerous opportunities for the pupil to respond to language stimuli in drills, would indeed teach the meaning of language adequately. Yet if we look closely at the language which typically occurs in such drills, we find that the relationship between stimulus and response sentences is quite unlike any that might occur in natural language use. The drills require the learner to transform, substitute, replace, expand or otherwise manipulate the stimulus sentence in a totally artificial way. Although a student may succeed in mastering the forms of language by such devices, he is hardly learning to respond to stimuli in an acceptable fashion. The very structural similarity in a set of responses is itself highly unnatural. It is true that drills can be made to appear more naturalistic and that dialogues can be introduced to make more realistic exchanges of language, but, although this is probably an improvement, it still depends on the assumption that what precedes an utterance, or is physically present in the situation, is the actual determinant of that utterance. To make proper scientific use of the stimulus—response relationship for the teaching of meaning one would have to be capable of identifying the stimuli in any situation *before* the language was uttered, and in practice this is utterly impossible. There might be a useful non-technical use of the word stimulus, which permits us to say that a question provides the stimulus for an answering statement, but one could not argue that the question determines what the answer is going to be. The form and content of the answer depend on many factors, most of them unknowable to the observer of the situation.

It is interesting that this point about meaning is not a somewhat esoteric academic squabble. In practice the greatest deficiency of the audio-lingual method, the method which is most closely based on behaviourist principles, is its failure to prepare the learner to use his language for communication. The meaning of language needs to be much more carefully planned and taught than assigning it to a simple stimulus—response relationship permits. It is of course perfectly possible to teach meaning satisfactorily while retaining many of the features of behaviourist teaching that I have mentioned. In practice this is probably what often happens, but it does mean that the original theory is not being applied consistently.

6.2.2. Mentalism

For the behaviourists, learning can be the same for every individual because it is socially conditioned. In teaching we can ensure that everybody learns equally well by making sure that the conditions of learning are the same for each. An alternative view, which I will call 'mentalist', contradicts the behaviourists at almost every point. Everybody learns a language, not because they are subjected to a similar conditioning process, but because they possess an inborn capacity which permits them to acquire a language as a normal maturational process. This capacity is by definition universal. In a sense then, the mentalists too argue that language learning is the same for everybody, but the similarity ends there, because for the mentalists what the learners share is a capacity the existence of which the behaviourists would deny.

For the mentalists, language is far too complex a form of behaviour to be accounted for in terms of features external to the individual. In a review of Skinner's account of verbal behaviour, the linguist Noam Chomsky demonstrates that this brand of behaviourism at least is quite incapable of *explaining* our ability to learn and use our mother-tongue.[5] He attacks with particular vehemence the notion that language responses are under the control of external stimuli— that, as he puts it, the individual is merely the locus of behaviour and not its cause. He suggests that Skinner himself cannot maintain this view and that there is evidence in his book to contradict it. For him the most important thing of all is that human beings use language whereas other animals do not. It is no use applying principles of learning that have been derived from research with animals, as he says the behaviourists do, to explain a form of behaviour that animals are not capable of. Since all normal human beings learn their language successfully they must possess some internal capacity for language that other animals do not have. Since this capacity cannot have been acquired socially it must be innate. It is their willingness to admit the possible existence of unobservable, internal mechanisms that leads these linguists to be considered mentalistic. Such mentalism, however, need not be regarded as an escape from rigorous scientific procedures. They would argue that the nature of language is such that it is impossible to explain it without postulating an innate mechanism of a fairly well-defined kind.

To the innate mechanism which they propose the name 'language acquisition device' has been given. It is said to operate in the following way. A child, from birth, is exposed to language which acts as a trigger for the learning device. The device has the capacity to formulate hypotheses about the structure of the language to which it is exposed. The child is, of course, quite unconscious of this process. The hypotheses are tried out in the child's own language production and are regularly checked against the further data that his exposure to the language provides. As he finds that his hypothesis cannot account for all the data, he modifies the hypothesis and checks it again. The first hypotheses are very simple indeed. Most children pass through a stage of two-word utterances for example, in which

[5] N. Chomsky, Review of B.F. Skinner, *Verbal Behaviour* (*Language* 35, 1959).

they appear to operate on the hypothesis that there are two classes of words, one limited and the other more or less unrestricted in number, which occur in a fixed sequence. As the child gets older the hypotheses become more and more complex and, applying them to his own use of language, he brings his speech closer and closer to the adult model to which he is for the most part exposed. What the child is doing is constructing an internal grammar of the language. This grammar passes through successive modification until it becomes the complete grammar of the adult language. At this point it should be identical with the descriptive grammar that the linguist attempts to write.

The arguments in favour of this view are twofold. First, the nature of language structure is such that the child *must* have some such device. Any other attempts to explain language learning are at best incomplete because they cannot account for the learning of all structural relations. Secondly, there is some evidence from the observation of the language of young children which seems to support the mentalists' account of language learning. If their theory is correct, many of the rules that the child formulates will be incorrect or incomplete. If these are then applied to the child's own language production, the result should be error in the child's speech. This is just what happens. Here, for example are forms that have been observed in the speech of children:

> I breaked (or even 'broked') my lorry
> I better go to bed now, bettern't I?

The significant thing is not that these are mistakes. Anyone can make mistakes in speech. They are mistakes that could not be due to faulty hearing or imitation, since they quite unlike any utterance that the child will have heard from an adult. Something other than imitation of adult speech is going on. The child is operating two overgeneralized rules, the first saying that the past tense of *break* is formed by the regular process of inflection, the second that *better* is a modal auxiliary verb like *can* or *must* and can be repeated in question-tags like those verbs. The making of error is now seen as an inevitable part of the language learning process. It is possible that it is not only inevitable, but also necessary since it provides the only means that the child has of finding out the limits to the domain of the rules that he is formulating.

What is the role of the social factors to which the behaviourists attach so much importance? For Chomsky they have virtually no role at all. The nature of the language acquisition device and its mode of operation are inviolable. The belief is that with research a clear developmental sequence will emerge, implying that given the nature of the device and the language to which it is exposed, learning will follow a predictable path. The stages through which children pass will be very largely the same. They do not, however, necessarily learn at the same rate and it is here that the possible influence of schedules of reinforcement can be admitted. But from the linguist's point of view, rate of learning is far less significant than the nature of the learning mechanism itself.

Observation of children learning language also suggests that there are occasions on which pieces of language are learned simply through being heard. A word may be heard, perhaps once, perhaps more than once, but not produced by the child at the time it is heard. There is therefore no active responding and consequently no reinforcement and no repetition. In spite of this the child may suddenly produce the word quite correctly in a totally new context. However useful the behaviourist notions of reinforcement and repetition may be, then, they do not relate to conditions that are essential for learning to take place.

There is another way in which the behaviourists and the mentalists may differ, though it is possibly only a difference in the language that they prefer to use. Whereas behaviourists will talk of the child using 'analogy' in the construction of sentences, the mentalists prefer to think in terms of the production and application of 'rules'. It is not clear to me that there need be any difference between the two. Chomsky says that the behaviourists break their own principles in admitting the possibility that a child is endowed with an analogy-forming mechanism. If this is so, then perhaps there really is very little significance in the choice of term. For us, though, the choice is important because, as applied to language teaching, they can seem to imply totally different teaching procedures.

6.2.2.1. *Mentalism in language teaching.* It is a matter of fact that behaviourism has influenced foreign language teaching. Whether or not mentalist attitudes will be equally influential is a matter for conjecture. While criticizing behaviouristic practices, Chomsky has said that he cannot see any application of his theory of language in teaching and indeed does not see why anyone should think that it ought to have applications. In developing his views little could be further from his mind than the interests of language teachers. A language teaching methodology is not something to be derived directly from a linguistic theory.

However, it is possible to accept this opinion while at the same time arguing that nonetheless language teaching ignores linguistic theory at its peril, and that a methodology that runs counter to what linguists believe to be the nature of language needs careful investigation.[6] I shall therefore attempt to discover the possible implications of the mentalist account of language acquisition.

If we take this point of view, it should not surprise us to discover that it provides us principally with arguments against certain practices rather than a comprehensive and constructive picture of the way things ought to be done. In the first place there is the notion that the learning process is essentially uninfluenced by external factors. Carefully planned schedules of reinforcement are unnecessary, since learning will take place whether or not the individual is reinforced. There is no need for the amount of active participation in language production that the behaviourists and others require, since learning can take place without repetitious active responding. Learning involves the internal mastery of the rule, and making the response is not so much a step in the acquisition of the rule as a sign that the rule has or has not been learned.

The learning mechanism operates through its capacity to formulate rules about the language once the individual has been exposed to it. The essential condition is exposure to the language, and as long as this exposure continues the learning mechanism will operate. What is needed in language teaching, therefore, is adequate exposure to the target language. The greater the exposure to meaningful language the more effectively the learner can formulate and revise his hypotheses about the structure of the language. As we saw, he induces rules from the data and then attempts to use these rules in producing and interpreting more language. Since external conditions are irrelevant, the whole panoply of principles that have been enunciated for the selection and sequencing of language for teaching purposes are quite superfluous. The material of language teaching should be extensive samples of natural language, not language specially produced and limited to suit the apparent needs of learners. Up to a point there is implicit approval here of the literary tradition in language teaching, since this did expose the child to language produced by native speakers for consumption by native speakers. The linguistic range that the child would meet would be enormous. Its weakness lies in its

---

[6] For a fuller discussion of this point see the final chapter.

incompleteness as a sample of language use. Much that a child learning his mother-tongue would encounter is not to be found in the literature.

All of this casts doubt on the careful linguistic control that is characteristic of modern teaching materials. It also raises the question of the validity of language learning through drilling. Drilling is a technique for maximizing active language production by every pupil in a way that allows him to be reinforced immediately. But it is hard to see the value of this if there is doubt about the notions 'active response', 'repetition' and 'reinforcement'. If the pupil is not to learn the structure of the language by hearing and constructing large numbers of analogous sentences, how is he to do it? The temptation is clear to fall back on the traditional procedure of expounding a rule and then testing the learning of that rule through exercises. Foreign language learning would return to the realm of problem-solving subjects. The question of whether or not explicit rules have *any* place in language teaching is something to be resolved independently of this discussion, but it is difficult to find any justification in mentalist theory for the view that rule-learning should be the basis of language teaching. It is unfortunate that the word 'rule' should have to serve to refer both to the small child's hypotheses about the structure of his language and to the generalizations that the language teacher has often found it desirable to make to his pupils and elicit from them. In the former case it refers to a totally unconscious process; in the latter it is quite explicit. I know of no clear evidence that the best way to develop unconscious mastery of the rules of a language is through the initial conscious learning of those rules. It is the informally reported experience of many learners that rules of language learned in this way are rarely fully assimilated and continue to interfere with the spontaneous use of language. Linguistic theory cannot possibly help here. Even if one believes that every language learner has to acquire the rules of the target language, the question of *how* they are best acquired is still left open.

Another feature of the behaviourist approach, and again this view is shared by many who would not subscribe to behaviourist theory in detail, is the insistence on the advantages of ensuring that pupil's utterances are always correctly formed. If what they say is correct, what they learn will be correct. In contrast to this we must now consider the possibility that a correct response does not necessarily indicate that the person is learning, and that an incorrect response may be a satisfactory sign that learning is proceeding normally. A pupil might be able to construct English or French forms correctly under tightly controlled conditions where what is required may be little more than imitation, but as soon as he is put in a freer situation we may discover that he has not in fact mastered the rule. Alternatively there are some kinds of mistake resulting from over-generalization, as in the example of the child learning English as a mother-tongue, which could be considered to show a reasonable sensitivity to the rule-structure of the language. The correction of such errors may assist the learner to accurate use of the rule more rapidly than a system which expects him to repeat only correct forms. Whichever approach was adopted, one could be satisfied that a rule had been fully mastered only when the pupil was using it correctly under free conditions. Practice in the choice of forms is an essential stage in language learning and cannot take place under fully controlled conditions.[7]

Since I suggested above that the behaviourist attitude to meaning was not very satisfactory, I should perhaps conclude with a word about meaning in mentalist teaching. There is little to be said from the psychological point of view about how a child acquires the meaning of a language. The difference from the behaviourists lies not only in a rejection of the stimulus—response analysis, but in the importance that is attached to meaning. Not only is meaning the whole point of language; the structure of a language itself cannot be properly learned unless it is fully meaningful. Purely mechanical drilling, such as it is possible to find in many courses, would be rejected because it would not even be an effective way of learning the structural elements of the language. The learning of a foreign language should therefore be a meaningful activity throughout. There seem to be no implications as to how meaning should be taught, only the conclusion that it is a most important aspect of language teaching.

6.2.3. Mentalism or behaviourism?

One should not leave this discussion without asking whether one

---

[7] Both modern and traditional approaches to language teaching may have been excessively concerned to eliminate error—modern teaching by restricting the freedom of choice that the pupil can exercise, traditional teaching by permitting more freedom but penalizing linguistic error severely. Both tend to breed an undesirable caution in language performance through the attempt to avoid mistakes. Yet inhibition is probably a far greater handicap to effective communication, through speech at least, than the recurrence of linguistic errors in the individual's language.

can or should make a choice between the two theories. There is certainly some value in developing each point of view consistently and showing the contrast between them. The bases for decisions are more clearly identified in this way and the theoretical significance of any one proposal can be more fully understood. It may help decisions in language teaching not to be merely a succession of improvisations. Even if one decides to adopt methods that imply theoretical contradictions, at least the decision is not being made in ignorance.

However, to take the decision to base one's teaching exclusively on one or other of these theories would be quite unjustified in the present state of our knowledge. If we enquire into the empirical basis for either theory, we shall find that they are rather weak. The experimentation that lies behind the behaviourist view is with animals and obviously is not itself concerned with language behaviour. The extension to first language learning depends on the assumption that the same principles apply to language learning as to the learning by rats of how to find their way through a maze. This may not seem a particularly reasonable assumption, but it is possible that some of the principles do operate even if they cannot account for language learning entirely. Language teachers had arrived at not dissimilar ideas on the basis of their practical experience.

As for the mentalist theory, it at least is intended to account for human behaviour. The empirical evidence for it is very slender indeed. It rests on the kind of evidence about child language learning which I described above and which seems to be open to alternative explanations, and on universal characteristics of language which seem to require a particular kind of mental structure, which would have to be innate. Even if one accepted the existence of an innate language acquisition device, as language teachers we would require further evidence that this device was employed not only for the learning of the mother-tongue, but also for foreign languages. It is not unreasonable to ask whether the capacity for language acquisition remains once the first language has been learned, or whether completely different processes are used in the learning of further languages.

The controversy is pursued with some vigour. In this new formulation of the nature—nurture opposition the mentalists are in the ascendant, among linguists at least, and appear to have influenced a

---

We ought to find it more acceptable that our pupils use language spontaneously with error, than hesitantly without errors.

number of psychologists too. Language teachers need not feel obliged to adopt either position, since foreign language learning can be considered a matter of both nature and nurture. In view of the uncertain foundation of the theories this would seem a prudent attitude anyway. On the other hand there does not seem to be much point in picking and choosing what suits one from the theories, since in that case there hardly seems to be much value in looking at the theories at all. We have to try and evolve a coherent position on the basis of present knowledge, while admitting that this cannot be done in a completely satisfactory way until much more is known about the psychology of second language learning itself. Working on inferences from other kinds of learning is bound to be unsatisfactory.

It has been suggested by L. Jakobovits, who accepts the developmental nature of language acquisition, that external conditions may influence the rate of learning even if they do not affect the learning process itself.[8] As language teachers we cannot ignore factors that might speed the learning process. In any case the only things we *can* influence are the externals. What goes on inside the individual is beyond us. It is hardly surprising that most of our attention is given to consideration of how we can create the best conditions for language learning to proceed. We can accept that the learner brings enough to his task for our job not to be simply a conditioning process. Up to that point we can adhere to the 'nature' argument. We can agree too that in some sense the learner is producing his own internal grammar. But our experience suggests that the environment that we create for learning has a considerable affect on how well the children are able to use the language. It seems feasible that the rule-producing mechanism is assisted by our programming its exposure to the language. We would wish to retain the results of our efforts to grade language for teaching rather than leave the learner to sort out the rules from a random experience of language. We would also wish to have the learners actively responding in the language, since it seems impossible to deny that learning is not fully effective without 'doing'. But the active responding here must not be confined to analogous sentences. Using language requires choices all the time, and a belief in 'learning through doing' demands that practice in exercising those choices should be an important part of our language teaching. The answer to the question at the beginning of this section then is 'Mentalism *and* behaviourism'. And there need be no contradiction.

---

[8] L.A. Jakobovits, 'Implications of recent psycholinguistic developments for the teaching of a second language' (*Language Learning* 18, 1968).

6.3. Individual variation in language learning performance

However true it may be that learning a language requires the operation of an innate capacity possessed by all human beings and that this
capacity will function most effectively when certain external conditions are met, success in learning a foreign language through instruction will vary from individual to individual and from group to group,
no matter how achievement is measured and no matter how the
language is taught. Significant as any universals of language learning
might be, we need to discover other factors if we are to account for
the fact that in practice two learners exposed to identical learning
conditions do not achieve the same terminal behaviour or indeed
that one individual's performance in learning languages fluctuates
where one might expect it to be permanent and stable.

With varying degrees of conviction many explanations are offered
for the lack of success of a poor learner. Perhaps he is not 'gifted
for languages', or whereas he has a visual memory, the method of
teaching is purely oral. Possibly his 'musical ear' is poor so that he
cannot reproduce the sounds of the foreign language. Alternatively,
he may be better suited to learning 'analytically', while the teacher
eschews any analysis of what is being taught. His failure to use the
spoken language with any ease may be put down to the inhibiting
effect of an introverted personality. With a hint of disapproval we
may hear that he is not 'well motivated', the suggestion being that
his achievement is well short of his potential. The older he is the
more likely it is that his age will be put forward as the explanation
of his failure to learn.

The converse of any of these statements may account for the success
of the rapid learner. The explanations are offered from experience
and a subjective assessment of the relevant factors. They are not for
that reason wrong, although some of the explanations almost certainly
have no foundation. However we are concerned with the effort that
can be made through research to give our knowledge of language
learning a more objective basis. I say 'effort' because research into
the factors that influence the learning of foreign languages is in its
infancy and clear conclusions cannot yet be reached. As we shall see,
however, even the attempt to do this kind of research can show that
we are quite unclear about the nature of the factors that we, with too
little thought, offer as the determinants of an individual's performance.
To illustrate how far research takes us at the moment, I will look at
three of the factors which are thought to underlie individual

variation in language learning: language aptitude, motivation and age.

6.3.1. Language aptitude

To investigate the nature of language aptitude is to assume that people are not identical in their capacity for learning a foreign language. We expect some people to learn a language better than others. Whether their language learning potential is the product of innate abilities or the result of their previous learning experience does not matter. We suppose that neither influence can be reversed and that therefore each individual possesses a stable and permanent ability, to which we give the name 'language aptitude'.

Research into language aptitude has been carried out in the attempt to construct tests that provide a reliable prediction of a pupil's success in learning a language. It is not my intention to discuss the use of language aptitude tests here, but clearly there are situations in which it is valuable to have a sound predictor of a learner's performance. It would seem reasonable to expect that any test that succeeds in providing such a prediction would inevitably tell us what the psychological components of a language learning ability are. However, as we shall see, the development of an effective predictor depends upon more than purely linguistic capacities, and intending as he does to produce an efficient test, the researcher does not stop to investigate the exact nature of the language learning ability.

There are two existing aptitude tests, Carroll and Sapon's Modern Language Aptitude Test and Pimsleur's Language Aptitude Battery. Both have been developed in the United States.[9] The MLAT, the earlier of the two tests, has five elements: the learning of an artificial system of numbering; the ability to manipulate a phonetic script; a vocabulary test using words spelt strangely but not illogically; a test of the ability to identify words of similar grammatical function in different sentences; and finally the ease of learning and recalling a paired list of words in English and Kurdish. These five sub-tests are all that remain of an original set based on 25 variables that were thought to be of potential relevance to language aptitude. These variables were grouped into six factors: verbal knowledge, linguistic interest, associative memory, sound—symbol association, inductive

---

[9] J.B. Carroll, 'A factor analysis of two foreign language aptitude batteries' (*Journal of General Psychology* 59, 1958).

language learning ability, grammatical sensitivity or syntactical fluency, and speed of association.[10] Many of the variables proved to have little or no predictive value. The five that were retained were simply those that proved the best predictors. While each seems to test a different ability, it cannot be claimed that together they make up the components of language aptitude. It could be that success in solving a mathematical problem would provide a fair prediction of future success in learning a language, but one could not pretend that it is necessary to have an ability in mathematics to be able to learn a foreign language.

The point becomes clearer when we look at Pimsleur's test. The MLAT consists entirely of tests that require the manipulation of language. In its preparation the validity of its predictions has been extensively tried out against people's actual success in learning a foreign language. According to Pimsleur, over a large sample of junior and senior high school pupils the median[11] of the coefficients of correlation between the MLAT scores and their actual performance in class was .53. This indicates a fair degree of validity for the predictions of the MLAT. The LAB, in contrast, has both linguistic and non-linguistic elements. The four linguistic tests are of vocabulary in the mother-tongue, the ability to construct new sentences on the analogy of those in a given set of data, the ability to discriminate sounds of a new language, and a test of sound—symbol relationships. If scores on these sub-tests alone are taken, the median of the coefficients is much the same as on the MLAT. But the LAB becomes a better predictor when to it are added a score for motivation— measured by the pupil's declared interest in learning the foreign language, indicated on a scale of 1–5—and another based on the average mark obtained by the pupil in his other school subjects, what is called the 'grade-point average'. When this is done the median of the coefficients goes up to .71. Whatever determines success in learning other subjects is clearly also important in the learning of languages. Indeed the grade-point average and the language aptitude sub-tests taken alone and in isolation from each other prove equally good predictors, each having a correlation of .62. It is only when the two are taken together that the correlation with actual language performance improves to .72.

[10] For a brief review of work on aptitude see E. Halsall, 'Linguistic aptitude' (*Modern Languages* 50, 1969, pp. 18–22).

[11] The median is the score that is the mid-point between the highest and the lowest scores obtained.

It is not easy to see where the notion of a 'gift for languages' stands after this. If the grade-point average is already a fairly sound predictor is there any value to the notion of language aptitude at all? Yet the prediction is improved by the addition of the scores on the linguistic tests. It seems that although the ability to learn a foreign language is not something quite distinct from all other learning ability, it is possibly partially dependent on some specific language-learning skill. We are usually most convinced of the existence of such a thing as a gift for learning languages when we see either a pupil who is weak in other subjects but does unexpectedly well in his language class, or, conversely, a pupil who obtains excellent results in other subjects but seems quite unsuited to learning languages. Pimsleur offers a possible explanation for the latter, at least.[12] It appears that underachievers; that is those whose perform-ance is substantially less than the prediction would lead one to expect, are often found to have done poorly on those parts of the test which examine phonetic ability. If, as seems likely, people do vary in their ability to acquire a new pronunication system it is hardly surprising that those who are weak in this ability will not score well on any language achievement test that includes a test of pronunciation. But the suggestion, tentative as it is, goes further than this. It is the general language learning performance of the pupils that is lower than anticipated, not only their performance on auditory parts of the test. If there is any ability underlying a specific-ally linguistic aptitude, it seems that ability in auditory discrimination is a strong candidate.

6.3.2. Motivation

'Motivation', like 'language aptitude', is a term which occurs in discussion of second rather than first language learning. Since virtually everybody succeeds in learning their first language, albeit at slightly varying rates, notions of differing aptitude and motivation seem to have no place. Obviously if learning the mother-tongue is a maturational process as was suggested earlier, nothing is gained by looking for evidence of motivation for learning. However the Soviet analysis of the psychology of first language learning is not without significance for our understanding of motivation in second language learning. Psychologists like Luria and Vygotsky have suggested that

[12] P. Pimsleur, D.M. Sundland and R.D. McIntyre, 'Underachievement in foreign language learning (*International Review of Applied Linguistics* 2/2, 1964).

it is through speech that a child learns to organize his perception and to regulate his behaviour and mental activities. Faced with problems and needs, the child will in his early years merely look for outside assistance, and language will have the function for him of obtaining this assistance. Then will come a stage during which the child spends a lot of time talking to himself or to anyone who cares to listen in his first efforts to find solutions to his needs himself. Finally the external speech is internalized, so that the child's behaviour is no longer simply a response to external stimuli but has come under the control of his thought processes. It is the environment that is controlled by the child rather than the other way round.

The parallel between this and the situation in which the second language learner finds himself is limited. The learner does not need the language in order to regulate his behaviour and his mental processes or to organize his perception. When he comes to learn a new language his modes of behaviour are already set in the ways that are appropriate to his first language culture. It can hardly be the case that he *has* to change the manner in which he regulates his own behaviour to suit the ways of a second language culture, although, as we shall see below, the *desire* to do so may be an important factor in motivation. The parallel arises more in the way in which the command of language enables the individual to control not himself but his environment. Of the child learning his mother-tongue it could be said, metaphorically perhaps, that he has the best of all possible motives for learning the language. It enables him to get what he wants. With his increasing proficiency he can obtain more and more complex responses from the people about him. The responses may be verbal or they may be physical, but the important thing is that they are initiated by the language that was produced by the child. The child learns to influence the behaviour of others in ways that suit him. In this way his needs can be met.

The same conditions may arise in an alternate language learning situation; and where they do we find what is probably the most powerful motivation of all for learning a foreign language, and consequently the greatest success. This is where the only means available to exercise control over events and people outside ourselves is the foreign language. If, to satisfy our needs, to influence the actions and thoughts of others, to pursue our occupation and our recreation, it is necessary to use a foreign language, then we will learn that foreign language more rapidly and effectively than under any other conditions. Such circumstances will normally only arise if one is living in the country where the foreign language is spoken, as in one's own country the most basic functions of language will be met by the mother-tongue, If we may call this environmental pressure to learn a form of motivation, then we would expect it to operate mostly among immigrants. Not all new residents in a country will learn the language of the host community by any means. If they are members of a sizeable group still speaking the mother-tongue, they will learn the target language correspondingly less well. This will be because the mother-tongue will meet many of the needs that require the use of language. Those who work in the host community will generally learn better than those who stay in the home. The children will learn best of all because the language will have the greatest value for them. That there is a whole gamut of other factors at work is not to be denied. Age, amount of exposure, attitude of individuals and groups, these and other factors have their part to play. But even with many of these factors stable, learning will vary from person to person. It seems that it is the differing needs that people have to communicate in the language that determine the extent of their learning.

This kind of motivation is inevitably characteristic of language *learning* situations but not of language *teaching* situations. It is in 'natural' learning situations that the individual is under pressure to acquire the language to control the behaviour of others. Where a foreign language is being learned in the pupil's mother-tongue country, this pressure does not exist and achievement seems correspondingly low. Is such motivation, then, of no relevance to the teaching of languages? The answer is that if it really does make for effective language learning, one would like to be able to make it relevant; but it is hard to see how it can be done within the conventional language lesson. What such lessons lack is the necessity to express oneself in the foreign language as a part of normal social intercourse. Artificial social situations are contrived, but it is the very artificiality that excludes this kind of motivation. Techniques of teaching alone seem unlikely to create the conditions where such motivation operates.

The solution may lie in doing away with the language lesson altogether. The need to use the language may be created by directing the pupils' attention not at the language itself but at something else that is being learned through the language. Provided the pupils are well motivated to learn science, for example, then the science could be taught through the medium of the foreign language. The language then becomes the only means by which the learner can comprehend and express scientific subject-matter. For this limited range of inter-action with the teacher and with other pupils the learner has to use the foreign language. Because it is necessary to him, he will learn it. With modern methods of teaching science it should not be difficult to ensure that the learners were exposed to virtually all the gramma-tical system, although the vocabulary would remain somewhat restricted. No doubt it would be administratively impossible to have foreign languages taught entirely in this way, but one could envisage both the growth of schools using a foreign language as a medium of instruction and the application of this approach more widely in situations where the pupils have to receive their education in a second language. It could be used in primary schools in anglophone and francophone African countries, for example, or with Asian immigrants in Britain.

6.3.2.1. *Integrative and instrumental motivation.* I may appear to be implying that good motivation is absent from pupils who are being taught foreign languages in classroom and laboratory. This is not so. Faced with a class any teacher will before long come to the conclusion that some pupils are better motivated than others. There is of course a danger that the concept of motivation will be little more than a rationalization resulting from the observation that some are learning better than others. In the absence of any other obvious explanations one may resort to motivation even when there is no evidence other than success in learning. In fact the notion of motiva-tion has rather more substance than that.

We recognize that people have different motives for learning and that whereas one person is 'well motivated' another is 'poorly motivated'. One person may be studying a language 'because he wants to', another 'because he has to'. The former would probably be thought to be better motivated. Motivation has to do with the reasons for learning and with attitudes—attitudes towards the language, towards the group that speaks the language as a mother-tongue, and towards bilingualism itself. In much teaching, not only of languages, we anticipate that pupils' personal motivation is unlikely to be strong, so we set out to motivate them through the learning process itself. Teaching is planned so that learning becomes an interesting, even at times an entertaining, process. This would be particularly the case in primary school language learning, where personal reasons for learning hardly exist and attitudes have not yet had time to form.

It is not the teacher's efforts to motivate the pupils but the pupils' own motivation that interests us here. The reasons for learning a language may be extremely diverse—to pass an examination, to use in one's job, to use on holiday in the country, as a change from watching television, because the educational system requires it, because one wants to know more of the culture and values of the foreign language group, because one wishes to make contact with the speakers of the language, because one hopes to live in the country concerned, and so on. Out of this diversity a distinction has been made between two different types of motivation—'instrumental', as represented by the first five reasons, 'integrative', as represented by the last three. The instrumentally motivated learner requires the language as a means to some other end, whereas for the integrative learner the language and all that it brings by way of culture is an end in itself.

Attitudes are likely to be closely related to the reasons for learning. Integrative learners are likely to have very sympathetic attitudes towards the foreign culture and its speakers. They may be prepared to take over some of its values or even to transfer their allegiance to that group. They will probably see great value in being able to speak foreign languages and have access to different cultures. At the other end of the scale will be learners whose attitudes are highly ethno-centric. They will show hostility towards foreigners and towards their values. They will tend to be authoritarian and intolerant. A most significant point about attitudes is that there is evidence that the attitudes of children are almost always determined by the attitudes of their parents. Since, as we shall see, attitude correlates positively with success in learning, it could be said that it is the parents who determine how well a child will learn a foreign language.

If we now expand the notion of motivation to include both reasons for learning and attitude, we find that at the extremes we have instrumental motivation, where learning is strictly utilitarian and attitudes are intolerant, and integrative motivation, where the learner sees himself as a potential member of the second language group and has liberal attitudes. A number of pieces of research have been carried out to see which reasons and which attitudes correlate with successful language learning and therefore constitute 'good motivation'.[13] All

[13] R.C. Gardner and W.E. Lambert, 'Motivational variables in second-language acquisition', (*Canadian Journal of Psychology*, Vol. 13, No. 4, 1959). W.E. Lambert, 'Psychological approaches to the study of language' (*Modern Language Journal*, Vol. 47, 1963). W.E. Lambert, R.C. Gardner, H.C. Barik, and K. Tunstall, 'Atti-

the most recent research agrees that it is the integratively motivated learners who are the most successful. Spolsky investigated the attitudes of about 300 foreign students in the United States. Having indirectly discovered the attitudes and values of the students, he compared these with the values and attitudes that the students ascribed first to their own group and then to the target language group, Americans. A study of those whose values were closer to American values than to those of their own group showed that these integratively motivated learners were the most proficient in English. It is possible, of course, that integrative attitudes are the product rather than the cause of proficiency, but either way a high correlation between attitude and proficiency is shown.

Research has therefore justified the concept of motivation and has gone some way towards defining what in an adult learner constitutes good and bad motivation, even to the point where prior testing of pupils' orientation towards the language could be used as a component in a test designed to predict their language performance.

6.3.3. Age

Aptitude is a stable and permanent characteristic of a learner. Motivation for language learning is not necessarily unchanging, for although attitudes to other language groups, once acquired, may not alter greatly, the reasons for learning languages may differ even in the same person. If *age* is a relevant variable, it is different from either of the other two in that it suggests that with age comes a change in the potential for learning foreign languages. The change would affect all learners and the usual hypothesis is that the change is for the worse, that with increasing age there is a decreasing capacity for language learning. It is a view that is very widely held and that accounts for the amount of foreign language teaching that is now being done in primary schools.

The evidence that language learning is an easier process at an early age comes from a number of different sources. It is found most strikingly in any language contact situation, that is to say a situation in which groups speaking one language live in proximity to and interaction with speakers of another language. Cases that have been most

tudinal and cognitive aspects of intensive study of a second language' (*Journal of Abnormal and Social Psychology*, Vol. 66, No. 4, 1963). B. Spolsky, 'Attitudinal aspects of second language learning' (*Language Learning*, Vol. 19, Nos. 3 & 4, 1960).

widely observed and reported involve the language acquisition of new immigrants and of children brought up by bilingual parents. In such circumstances as these it has been found that whereas with adequate exposure children become completely ambilingual, being able to speak both languages with a fluency and accuracy that makes them undistinguishable from monolingual speakers, adults brought into contact with the second language for the first time never succeed in ridding their speech in the second language of traces of the mother-tongue. In fact it is probably only the most intelligent and industrious who get as far as having only traces of the mother-tongue. Many adult immigrants, for example, remain fixed at a fairly primitive level of communication in the second language. It is not known for sure that ambilingualism is created in all young children under such conditions, but so striking is the contrast between child and adult that it seems as if the child is still learning language as he learned his mother-tongue, while the adult has somehow lost this ability. If it is 'normal' for a child to learn his mother-tongue, then it is perhaps no less normal for a child to learn another language with which he is in contact.

Evidence that helps to place and justify a boundary between young child and adolescent and adult learner comes from neurophysiology. Penfield and Roberts have argued on the basis of their study of speech mechanisms that the neurological evidence is in favour of language instruction beginning at the primary age.[14] The brain's control of motor activities is located in the left hemisphere of the brain. If the brain should be damaged in this area and the control of motor activities lost, it is only children below the age of puberty who can transfer control of motor skills to the right hemisphere. The use of language clearly involves muscular activity, so that there is the possibility that new articulatory skills, for example, are less easily acquired once this watershed has been passed. Claiming, rather more contentiously, to have been successful in localizing speech function in the brain, they also argue that before puberty the brain has a plasticity which is subsequently lost and that with it the capacity for learning language is lost too. This evidence is the more powerful because it seems to confirm the observations made in bilingual situations.

Thirdly, teachers and others working with children have observed differences between younger and older children that suggest that the

[14] W. Penfield and L. Roberts, *Speech and Brain Mechanisms* (Princeton, Princeton University Press, 1959).

younger children might find the task of learning a foreign language easier than older children. To begin with, a new sound system seems to be far less of an obstacle. They seem able to reproduce sounds in imitation with little difficulty. Activities like imitation and repetition, which many feel to be an inevitable part of language teaching, are apparently often a source of pleasure to the young child, whereas in the older learner they may do little more than cause irritation. At a time, too, when the approved methods of language teaching are largely inductive, they would seem to fit more neatly into the primary than the secondary classroom. The other thing is that inhibition is a very severe handicap to language learning. The primary age child usually lacks all the self-consciousness of the older learner and is altogether more prepared to submit to the norms of a new language and to perform in it without feeling at risk of making a fool of himself. It has been argued too, though it is outside the scope of this book, that to teach foreign languages in the primary school is educationally desirable, since attitudes are usually formed at this age and the teaching of languages will help prevent any tendencies towards ethnocentricity.

There is then quite an impressive case for considering age a significant variable in language learning. What is surprising is that more research has not been done into whether children being taught a foreign language learn it better than teenagers or adults. What research there is, is rather dated and may therefore not be very reliable. It suggests very strongly that adults do learn better than adolescents. Carroll found that with a group of learners mainly in their thirties, learning did decrease slightly with age, but he reports that aptitude was a far more significant variable than age. If research did show that adults had the best scores on achievement tests, perhaps we need not be so surprised. For a start they are likely to be exceptionally well motivated. Not all abilities decrease with age anyway. Memory, for example, actually increases, at least up to the age of eighteen, and memory is likely to be a relevant factor. The adult's ability to apply himself is likely to be far superior to the child's. If learning a language is a more difficult thing for the adult, he has a far greater capacity for overcoming difficulties than the child.

Unfortunately we lack any comparative study involving primary school children. Reports on the success of teaching languages in the primary schools suggest that the results are not all that had been hoped. This need not be taken to contradict the evidence of research into learning. There may have been more willing of the end than of the means. For a start, very few primary teachers are well qualified to teach languages and an effective FLES[15] programme would need to begin with a large teacher training effort. Enough time must be taken from the rest of the child's school day for regular contact with the language. It is not worth even starting if one is not certain that adequate time can be found to ensure real progress and that the teaching will be regular and continuous. A large weakness at the moment is that, at the time of transfer from primary to secondary level, often no account is taken of the fact that the child has begun the language in primary school, so that he is expected to start again from the beginning. The initial advantage that such a child has can hardly be expected to survive long.

To make foreign languages a regular part of every child's primary education would require a major administrative undertaking. Anything less than this risks occupying valuable time for little achievement. To be held in the balance are the fact that from the younger child, under the right conditions, a higher level of proficiency can be expected. This might not be difficult for the child to achieve although, since the child cannot take in much at a time, it might take a long time. The older child, with his greater capacity for concentrated effort, might be able to achieve more in a short time without having the full potential of the eight or nine-year-old. We still do not know enough of what is feasible at either age for us to be able to resolve the problem. Whether or not we can expect a better overall achievement from the child who starts to learn a foreign language at primary school we do not know. What we can anticipate is that he will acquire a better pronunciation of that language than an older learner.

6.4. Summary

Psychologists and linguists have attempted to formulate general theories of language learning and language use. Some have argued that learning is entirely the product of experience and that our environment affects all of us in the same way. Others have suggested that everybody has an innate language learning mechanism which determines learning identically for each of us. Although either view may have implications for language teaching, it is only the environment that we can manipulate in teaching. Other factors are sometimes

---

[15] Foreign Language Teaching in Elementary Schools, the American term, the abbreviation for which is now widely used outside the United States.

proposed to account for individual variation in language learning. It is said that aptitude, motivation and age are important variables. The evidence from research is so far very inadequate and needs to be expanded before we can say with any confidence how important these factors are.

7
Error and the mother-tongue

7.1. The evidence of mother-tongue interference

If we were to wander into a classroom where pupils were learning a foreign language and if we listened to them speaking that language or observed their attempts to write it, we should notice before long that the same mistakes of pronunciation, spelling, grammar and vocabulary tended to recur in the language of different individuals. In time, too, we should probably be able to identify the mother-tongue of the pupils even if not a word of it had been spoken in the classroom.[1] We should be able to do this solely on the basis of the recurring mistakes that we had noticed. Our ability to recognize the provenance of somebody who speaks our language with an accent, for example, is used by entertainers the world over. Comedians can be sure of raising an easy laugh with a protrayal of the German speaking English, the Englishman speaking French or the American speaking Spanish.

If, therefore, we look at the speech and writing of the foreign language learner, there is little reason to doubt that we will find many mistakes which can be traced back to the mother tongue. The comedian probably gets most, though not all, of his effects by imitating the foreigner's pronunciation, but in fact evidence of the mother-tongue is found on a far wider scale than this, even if it is not always recognized. It might be useful to begin this discussion by demonstrating the extent to which a learner uses features of his native language in his attempts to speak and write in the foreign language. If we imagine the efforts of a learner to produce the English sentence:

> His wife wants him to pay her grandfather a visit in the old people's home

we should be able to see some of the substitutions from the mother-tongue that are made by different learners and that cause errors.

[1] Provided, of course, the mother-tongue was not a language that was utterly strange to us.

In pronunciation the French learner will tend to omit the /h/ of *his* and to use the vowel /i/ as in *vite* because it is the nearest vowel to /ɪ/ that he has in his own language. To the Englishman it will sound more like the vowel which occurs in *heat,* /hiːt/. For the English /r/ in *grandfather*, which is produced by a movement of the tongue towards the teeth-ridge, he is likely to substitute the French /r/, which is produced by trilling the uvula against the back of the tongue. Like many other learners of English he will have difficulty with the consonant /ð/ in *the*. This sound, with its voiceless counterpart /θ/, as in *thin*, usually appears late in the speech of native English children too, and seems to cause general learning difficulty. The French learner may attempt to use either /d/ or /z/ to replace it, while the speaker of Hindi, for example, will probably substitute an aspirated /tʰ/. A typical mistake of a German saying this sentence would be for *old*, /əʊld/, to be pronounced /əʊlt/. This is because in German there is no contrast between /d/ and /t/ in final position. Final plosives are always /p/, /t/ and /k/ and never /b/, /d/ and /g/.

This last example brings us to the point that in his efforts to make utterances in the foreign language the learner is influenced not only by the sounds that exist in his mother-tongue, but also by their distribution and phonological status. There is a /d/ in German. It just does not occur in final position in a syllable. A Spanish learner would also have some difficulty with this sentence because it requires him to produce a syllable in which three consonants follow the vowel. However, in Spanish a syllable may have no more than one consonant after a vowel, so that for *wants*, /wɒnts/, he will say /wɒn/. Interestingly, this characteristic of Spanish learners of English, which often strikes the English ear as 'slovenly' or 'slurred' speech, may lead us to interpret as grammatical mistakes what are in fact phonological mistakes. For *liked*, /laɪkt/, he will say /laɪk/ and we will come to the conclusion that he has not mastered the rule for the formation of past tense, whereas a comparative study of the two languages will reveal that the error is caused by differences of syllable structure.

In both English and Spanish there are sounds that may be transcribed as [d] and [ð] although they are not phonetically identical. The phonetic differences are minimal and we may consider the sounds to be 'the same' in the two languages. Their status, however, is not the same. Whereas in Spanish they are allophones of the same phoneme, usually transcribed /d/, in English they are distinct phonemes, /d/ and /ð/. Spanish /d/ is realized as [d] in initial position, but as [ð] when it is preceded and followed by a vowel. In speaking English the Spaniard can expect some difficulty where /ð/ occurs in initial position, as in *the* in this sentence, but no difficulty where it occurs intervocalically, as in *grandfather*. On the other hand, where English has /d/ occurring intervocalically, as in *ladder*, /lædə/, the Spanish learner is likely to use his Spanish [ð] allophone and produce English *lather*, /læðə/ instead.

The extent to which intonation will cause difficulties depends very much on the particular mother-tongue. Many languages will differ from English in ways which are obvious but not significant. The pitch movements on the nucleus may operate much as in English although the rest of the pitch contour may differ. Such a speaker would be easily understood, although it would be noticed that he had a foreign accent. If an identical nucleus has a completely different meaning real confusion will result and its source will not be recognized. A Norwegian speaking the Stavanger dialect will habitually use a fall-rise nucleus in a statement. What he intends as a firm statement in English will be interpreted as diffidence, doubt or even as a question.

It seems that learners very rarely borrow directly from the inflectional morphology of their mother-tongue. We would be most surprised if the Russian learner of English were to start inflecting English nouns with Russian case endings or if the French learner was to attempt to construct an English tense system using the endings of French verb forms. If it happens at all, it will be between languages that are closely related to one another, such as Spanish and Italian or Russian and Serbo-Croatian. This suggests that it is by no means the case, as is sometimes claimed, that the greater the differences between languages the greater the difficulties will be. In this case it is the very similarity that may cause error. Apart from this, examples of morphemes from the mother tongue being used in utterances in the foreign language usually turn out, on closer investigation, to be derived from some other source. If a learner produces a plural form of the adjective in English by the addition of an {s} morpheme, this can be explained as the overgeneralization of the rule for forming plurals of nouns in English, and does not have to be accounted for in terms of the use of a mother-tongue form. In fact the same mistake can be made by pupils who, in their mother tongue, pluralize an adjective by the affixation of something other than an -s. The most likely morphological error in the sentence we are studying is the occurrence of *want* instead of *wants*. There is no need to look to see whether in the mother-tongue the third person singular form of the verb lacks an -s. There is simply an over-generalization of the form that occurs with all other Subjects. The position is confused by the fact that there are two[2] distinct {-s} morphemes in English: the one that we affix to nouns to indicate *plural*, and the one that we affix to present tense verbs in concord with a *singular* (and third person) subject. With the frequency of occurrence of the plural noun morpheme it is clear that there is great danger of confusion here. It is not unusual for a non-native speaker to produce the form *wants*, not after a singular subject, but after a plural subject, presumably because of the strength of the association between -*s* and plural.

If the actual shapes of morphemes are rarely taken from the mother-tongue and incorporated into utterances in the foreign language, the morphological and syntactic systems often are. The rules governing choice of possessive adjective in English are different from those in French. In our sample sentence the forms *his* and *her* occur. The choice between them relates not to any feature of the noun that they are modifying but to the sex of the person referred to. In French there are also two forms, *sa* and *son* (ignoring the plural form *ses* in this discussion), but the choice between them depends solely on the gender of the noun that they are modifying. The sex of the person referred to is irrelevant and indeed cannot be indicated in the possessive adjective. At a certain stage in his acquisition of English, the French learner will be likely to commit error in his construction of a sentence such as this because of the occurrence of an animate noun, *wife*, referring to a *female* person, and another, *grandfather*, referring to a *male* person. The *sex* of the person referred to by the noun will be taken as the *gender* of the noun and following the pattern of choice in French, the speaker will choose *her* to go with the female/feminine noun and *his* to go with the male/ masculine noun. Instead of

His wife wants him to pay her grandfather a visit

he will say

Her wife wants him to pay his grandfather a visit.

In most contexts of use the error will be clear, but if the situation does not make the intended meaning apparent, confusion could occur because the sentence is correct in a purely formal sense.

Another source of difficulty in this sentence is the occurrence of the definite and the indefinite articles. This presents particular problems for speakers of most Slavonic languages. In Russian, for

[2] Three, when we include the marker for possessive, e.g. *John's*.

example, there are no articles and it is indeed a common characteristic of a Russian speaking English that, following the Russian pattern,
he uses no articles. Once he starts attempting to use articles in English
his difficulties are better understood by reference to the grammar
of English, since he will no longer be using a Russian system to
avoid his problems. One would expect his learning then to resemble
that of a child learning English as a mother-tongue. The difference
between Russian and English provides more problems for the
Russian learning English than it does for the English speaker learning Russian. It seems to be far more difficult to remember to put
things in than it does to leave them out. A different type of error
might occur in the speech of a learner in whose own language the
indefinite article and the numeral *one* have identical forms. The
assumption of identity is transferred to English, with the result that
one is used as the realization of the article.

In French it is not possible for the equivalent of *want* to be
followed by a pronoun like *him* which is both the object of *want*
and the subject of the following infinitive. An infinitive can follow
vouloir only if the main verb and the infinitive have the same subject.
The construction that has to be used involves the French equivalent
of *that*, so that in English we may find the French speaker saying

His wife wants that he pays her grandfather a visit . . .*

It is not certain that this type of error can be explained entirely by
reference to the mother-tongue, since much the same mistake could
be made through an overgeneralization of a rule that does apply to
some English verbs. If the verb had been *demand* or *request*, it would
have been perfectly correct for it to have been followed by a clause
introduced by *that*. As we saw in an earlier chapter, the choices that
can be made with different verbs are very complicated, and in this
area of grammar there is clearly plenty of scope for error regardless
of the mother-tongue of the learner.

In selecting verb tense, learners often make their choice according
to the way choices are usually made in the mother-tongue. Learning
a new tense system involves the acquisition of a new set of forms,
but, as we saw above, the learner does not normally borrow from the
mother-tongue as he does this. He may however equate the tenses of
the target language with tenses in his own language and then choose
between them as if he was using his mother-tongue. In English,
as we saw in Chapter 3, if one is making a statement that relates to
present time, the choice lies between two forms—the present simple

tense and the present progressive. Unlike many other languages Spanish has a similar choice—between, for example, *habla* and *está hablando*. However the basis for the choices is different in the two languages. As a rule in English only the *be +ing* form may refer to current activity. At least it is the form normally used for this purpose. In Spanish either form may be used for current activity, with the compound form being used to stress the durational aspect of the event. If the speaker does not wish to place any emphasis on duration he will use the simple form, and in Spanish this is the form that is normally used. This will be the usage that the Spanish speaker will normally transfer into English, and it will cause him to say *he plays tennis now** when he means, *he is playing tennis now*. Oddly, in the case of the sentence we are looking at, this will lead to a correct utterance because *want* is an exception to the general rule in English, in that it is very rarely used in the progressive form. It is one of the class of verbs that is used in the simple form even when a current happening is referred to. Had the verb in the sentence been *ask*

His wife is asking him . . .

error would have been much more likely. The difficulty with *want* will come later, when the learner, having begun to learn something of the distinction in English between the uses of the simple and the compound forms, overgeneralizes his learning by making *want* fit the general rule. This will lead him to produce

His wife is wanting him . . .*

The same mistake is made by virtually all learners of English.

English and French tense systems provide overlapping choices which present difficulties for both the English learner of French and the French learner of English. The sentences below illustrate this:

il travaille cinq jours par semaine	he works five days a week
il travaille ici depuis 1950	he has worked here since 1950
il a travaillé ici de temps en temps	he has worked here from time to time
il a travaillé ici il y a cinq ans	he worked here five years ago

Error of choice reflecting the mother-tongue is made by the French speaker who says:

he works here since 1950*
he has worked here five years ago*

or by the English speaker who says:

il a travaillé ici depuis 1950*

He may also borrow a form from written French as a past tense
equivalent:

il travailla ici il y a cinq ans*

The most likely errors of vocabulary in our sample sentence will
probably be caused by wrong collocation. Where English people
pay visits, many other language groups *make* visits, and they are
inclined to use this expression when speaking English. There is no
special reason why we should in English call the building in which
old people live together a *home*, rather than a *residence, house, hotel,
hall* or *hostel*, all of which may denote inhabited buildings. The fact
is that none of these alternatives would be acceptable in this sentence.
Given the apparent choice, the learner could well make a mistake by
simply selecting wrongly from among the alternatives that English
seems to offer. The actual error may or may not be related to the
mother-tongue. A French speaker would be more than likely to use
house because an equivalent French phrase is *maison de retraite*
and in most contexts *house* is indeed the translation of *maison*.

How far someone speaking a foreign language uses words with
the meanings that they have in that language and how far they use
them with meanings derived from mother-tongue equivalents may
not always be apparent. What a person means by a phrase like *old
people* when he comes from a society where life expectancy is no more
than forty-five is liable to be different from what is meant by such
an expression in a country where people work until they are sixty-
five and expect to live past seventy. The difference may not be
noticeable unless the situation makes it clear. If a French speaker
uses the English word *hotel* to refer to a large private house or a
public building, we know that he is using *hotel* with the denotative
meaning of the French word *hôtel*. Mother-language *connotations*
will be even more difficult to distinguish. A word like *wife* is bound
to carry connotations derived from the relative status of men and
women and from the nature of marriage. These of course may differ
widely from country to country. However well one may understand
these differences intellectually, it remains very difficult to use a
lexical item in the matrix of the second-language culture.

This is by no means an exhaustive set of examples of the ways in which a person's mother-tongue is visible in his foreign language performance. There are many more cases at the levels of language that I have already mentioned, and one could extend the discussion further by considering stylistic choices such as were discussed in Chapter 5, grammatical features of continuous writing, phonological and grammatical characteristics of conversation and the ways in which languages convey the same meanings, but do it by employing different levels of language. The observation of any language learning situation or any bilingual communication situation would provide a host of additional examples.

7.1.1. Contrastive analysis

This evidence is quite enough to show how widespread influence of the mother-tongue is. As evidence it is not new. Most of the examples I have cited will long have been familiar to practising teachers. What is new is the recognition of the extent of the phenomena and the effort that has been made to make systematic use of this information in language teaching. A significant proportion of language learning theory has been based upon evidence of the sort that I have presented. A whole field of interest, usually called 'contrastive analysis' has grown up and become a major preoccupation of linguists and applied linguists. For many people applied linguistics *is* contrastive analysis.[3] Large scale projects have been set up for the comparative study of languages with the justification that the results will prove significant and valuable for language teaching.

The stimulus to all this activity was provided in 1957 by the publication of Robert Lado's *Linguistics Across Cultures*.[4] It was this book that brought together a large quantity of evidence of the sort presented above, and on this basis developed a view of language learning that has dominated the linguistic study of language teaching for fifteen years. The importance of contrastive analysis as stated initially by Lado and subsequently taken up by others is as follows. The errors and difficulties that occur in our learning and use of a foreign language are caused by the interference of our mother-tongue. Wherever the structure of the foreign language differs from that of

[3] For others 'applied linguistics' is to be equated with 'language teaching'. Because of ambiguities such as this and because of the generally misleading nature of the term, I have preferred to avoid its use altogether.

[4] Ann Arbor, University of Michigan Press, 1957.

the mother-tongue we can expect both difficulty in learning and error in performance. Learning a foreign language is essentially learning to overcome these difficulties. Where the structures of the two languages are the same, no difficulty is anticipated and teaching is not necessary. Simple exposure to the language will be enough. Teaching will be directed at those points where there are structural differences. By and large, the bigger the differences between the languages, the greater the difficulties will be. It follows that the difficulties of various groups of people learning, say, English as a foreign language will vary according to their mother-tongue, and since teaching is to be directed at the differences between languages, the teaching itself will vary according to the mother-tongue of the learners. If a comparative study—a contrastive analysis—of the target language and the mother-tongue is carried out, the differences between the languages can be discovered and it becomes possible to predict the difficulties that the learners will have. This in turn determines what the learners have to learn and what the teacher has to teach. The results of the contrastive analysis are therefore built into language teaching materials, syllabuses, tests and research. Different text-books will have to be produced for each language group. In summary, the function of contrastive analysis is to predict the likely errors of a given group of learners and thereby to provide the linguistic input to language teaching materials.

Some of these notions can also be expressed in Lado's own words. He says that 'the fundamental assumption of this book' is 'that individuals tend to transfer the forms and meanings and the distribution of forms and meanings of their native language and culture to the foreign language and culture—both productively when attempting to speak the language and act in the culture, and receptively when attempting to grasp and understand the language and the culture as practised by natives.'[5] Elsewhere he says, 'Problems are those units and patterns that show structure differences between the first language and the second . . . The structurally analogous units between languages need not be taught: mere presentation in meaningful situations will suffice . . . Different emphases in teaching are required for the different language backgrounds,'[6] and 'A comparison tells us what we should test and what we should not test'.[7]

In the first quotation above the word *transfer* occurred. It is a

---

[5] *Linguistics Across Cultures*, p. 2.

[6] R. Lado, *Language Teaching* (New York, McGraw-Hill, 1964) p. 52.

[7] *Linguistics Across Cultures*, p. 6.

term used by psychologists in their account of the way in which present learning is affected by past learning. Faced with a new learning task, an organism will make use of what knowledge or skills it already possesses to ease the process of acquisition. It is a process which has a wider significance for language learning than the point under discussion here.[8] When learning a foreign language an individual already knows his mother-tongue, and it is this which he attempts to transfer. The transfer may prove to be justified because the structure of the two languages is similar—in that case we get 'positive transfer' or 'facilitation'—or it may prove unjustified because the structures of the two languages are different—in that case we get 'negative transfer' or interference'. In either case there must be some reason why the learner has been led to identify the forms of the two languages in the first place. Some element of similarity must exist. Presumably, for example, a learner will not try and use a preposition from his mother-tongue as a verb in the target language. They are grammatically so distinct that any transfer is most unlikely. This would be a case of 'nil transfer'.

7.2. Other sources of error

Bearing these points in mind, we can now begin to evaluate the contrastive analysis argument as a linguistic strategy for language teaching. I continue to accept the assumption, which is not usually stated but which underlies all discussions on this topic, that difficulty of learning is indicated by a greater frequency of error in performance. To determine whether the difficulties that face a learner are to be entirely equated with the differences between his own language and the language he is learning, we must investigate how satisfactorily errors can be traced back to the mother-tongue. We can resolve this by trying to answer a number of questions.

First, are all the errors to be anticipated from the above examples cases of transfer from the mother-tongue? No. The Russian speaking English is only transferring mother-tongue forms as long as he is omitting articles in English. His difficulties do not disappear when he is no longer doing that. He still has to wrestle with the complexities of article usage in English and he will commit systematic errors in doing this. To understand these errors we need look only at the gram-

[8] See W.M. Rivers, *op. cit.*, pp. 126–9.

mar of English.[9] At the grammatical level there was mention of errors that could equally well be made through over-generalization of another English rule. In vocabulary an incorrect choice of lexical item to fit the frame 'old people's ——' need not reflect the native language in any way.

Secondly, are there cases where transfer does not occur as predicted? Yes. Particularly at the grammatical level, it is not always the case that differences of form between the two languages lead to the attempt to use mother-tongue forms in foreign language performance. The actual realizations of inflectional morphemes are rarely transferred. It may be that in syntax too there are cases of language difference which ought to lead to error through transfer and learning difficulty, but where the error at least does not occur. Evidence is not very easy to find because in practice contrastive analysis is scarcely ever carried out as a wholly predictive procedure. It is usually based on a good knowledge of the errors that do occur. There may also be a difference of behaviour according to the linguistic level. Transfer of mother-tongue forms seems far more complete in pronunciation than in grammar.

Thirdly, are there cases where a comparison will predict positive transfer and therefore no error, but where error does in fact occur? Yes. Dusková mentions examples where the structures of English and Czech seem exactly parallel but where nonetheless errors occur systematically. Confusions arise between the infinitive and the past participle or between the present and past participles. There is lack of agreement between demonstrative adjectives and a plural noun. The most likely explanation of these errors is that although the two languages may not differ at the particular points being discussed, these points are only part of much bigger grammatical systems which, if studied in their entirety, will show considerable differences. The learner's difficulty therefore is in acquiring a system that is different overall—even though at certain points it may produce sentences of apparently identical structure in the two languages. He is no less likely to make mistakes at the places where they are similar than at those where they are different. As Dusková says, her students produce the incorrect form *this workers** because it is a general rule in English that the adjective is not marked for plural.

[9] This and many other points relevant to this discussion are brought out in an analysis of the errors of Czech students of English by L. Dusková in 'On sources of errors in foreign language learning' (*International Review of Applied Linguistics*, 7/1, 1969).

In the learning of a grammatical system, wrong generalizations of this sort seem inevitable. If a comparison has to take entire systems into account and not just the translation equivalent of the sentence being studied, is one ever going to be able to say that two languages are the same at some point? May not error occur at any point through the making of a false generalization about the rules of the target language?

These considerations suggest that it is not always true that differences between native and target language lead to error through transfer. Nor is it true that the native language is the sole source of error. It is therefore an over-simplification to say that differences cause error, while similarities do not. Unfortunately this means that exact predictions about the language learner's behaviour are very difficult, since there is no way of being sure how he will respond to these varying factors. By prediction here is meant prediction from comparison of the structures of the languages, without reference to evidence of the actual language behaviour of learners. Such prediction is also made difficult by the fact that, although a comparison may reveal learning difficulties, it cannot determine how the learner will use his mother-tongue to resolve the difficulty. Lado points out that a French learner of English, faced with two new sounds, /ð/ and /θ/, will substitute either /d/ and /t/ or /z/ and /s/.[10] Which substitutions an individual will choose cannot be known until his learning behaviour is observed. In this case a purely predictive analysis will not provide the teacher with all the information he needs for a teaching strategy.

Prediction is also complicated by the clear necessity of taking into account the entire systems of the target language and not just those parts where contrast with the mother-tongue is clearly shown. Most of the errors above that are not caused by transfer from the mother-tongue are usually called hypercorrection. Use of this term seems to imply that a form is produced correctly at first but that its use is subsequently influenced by other learning, so that it is incorporated into a rule which does not apply to it. This will be true of many but not all of the non-contrastive errors above. A neat example is given by Haugen, in which he describes the learning of English nasal consonants by Spanish learners.[11] In Spanish only /n/ occurs

---

[10] In conversation recently with French and French Canadian teachers, I have discovered that Canadian learners of English substitute /d/ and /t/ and French learners /z/ and /s/.

[11] E. Haugen, *Bilingualism in the Americas* (Alabama, University of Alabama Press, 1956), p. 44.

as a nasal consonant in final position. In English /n/, /m/ and /ŋ/ occur. Spanish learners will at first substitute /n/ for /m/ and /ŋ/, thereby making errors. Eventually the new forms will be learned, but then the learner may overcorrect by using /ŋ/ instead of /n/. In place of *sun*, /sʌn/, he will say *sung*, /sʌŋ/, in spite of the fact that final /n/ occurs in Spanish.

What this adds up to is that prediction is going to be an extraordinarily difficult thing. There is no sure way of assessing the influence of these different factors in determining the actual performance of a group of language learners. If error was just a case of transfer from the mother-tongue and if it always happened, prediction would be straightforward. As it is, we are bound to take learners' errors into account; and if we have to do that anyway, it seems more sensible to make errors the starting-point for contrastive analysis and not just a way of verifying hypothetical predictions. In practice most of the people who have done contrastive analyses have had the experience of teaching to show them where fruitful comparisons could be made. Evidence of actual errors in learning is easy to collect. Contrastive analysis should be carried out to provide a linguistic explanation for known errors, rather than as a predictive procedure.

Some people might wish to argue that even the errors that do not involve transfer of mother-tongue forms are caused by the fact that the mother-tongue and the target language are structurally different. Even if a learner, faced with the complexities of English past tense inflection, does not use the actual forms of his own language, he still has difficulties in learning that would not arise if past tense formation was identical in his mother-tongue. This is obviously true, but it is also trivial. No one has ever disputed that languages are different. That is why second languages have to be taught. The question is how far it is possible to identify parts of languages which are the same and parts which are different and whether it is the case, first, that errors occur only at the points of difference and, secondly, that these errors are all cases of transfer from the mother-tongue. The evidence from errors actually made by learners indicates that the answer to both those questions is: No.

One does not want to deny that a speaker regularly uses mother-tongue forms in foreign utterances. The difficulty is caused by the attempt to explain all errors in terms of differences between native and target languages, when such an explanation can only be sustained by admitting that the entire linguistic system of the target language is different from that of the mother-tongue. The attempt to explain learning difficulty and error by reference to interference cannot account for all the facts, and it might be better to abandon the idea of transfer altogether. It is not possible to replace the notion of transfer by an entirely satisfactory alternative, but it is possible to formulate a hypothesis which manages to reflect the differing sources of systematic error.

7.3. The significance of error: a restatement

We saw in the previous chapter that the mentalist view of language learning was of a process in which the learner makes successive hypotheses about the structure of the language to which he is exposed and then tests hypotheses in his actual language performance. The rules that he formulates are proved correct if the form he produces is an acceptable one in the target language, but need to be revised if the form is unacceptable. The latter appears as an error in his speech. If we apply this interpretation of the learning process to second language learning, we find that there is one substantial difference from the first language learning situation. The child learning his first language is exposed to one language only and can make his hypotheses about the rule structure on the basis of that language and whatever innate notions of language he may have. When a learner is faced with the task of acquiring a second language, he also has to attempt to establish the rules of the language. Like the native learner he can use the evidence provided by the target language itself, and this will lead to errors of performance which may be very like those made by the mother-tongue learner. But, unlike the first language learner, he also has an alternative source of hypotheses. His grammar-forming mechanism has already mastered the rules of one language, and what it knows about the structure of that language is readily available to assist in the formulation of hypotheses about the structure of the second language. The individual's knowledge of his mother-tongue becomes part of the evidence to be considered in trying to determine what the rules of the new language are. In using this knowledge he may make errors which indicate clearly the source of the hypothesis. These are the errors which were exemplified in the first part of this chapter.

In this way both the errors that are normally explained as transfer from the mother-tongue and those which reflect the structure of the target language itself are seen to be the product of the same overall learning process. While providing a framework within which all the evidence of error can be discussed, it does not contribute to our understanding of *why* the learner bases his hypotheses on the mother-tongue at times and on the target language at other times. Nothing like enough research has been done into second language learning for us to be able to understand the interaction between these two ways of applying a learning strategy.

In deciding what should be the linguistic input to language teaching materials, we should certainly examine and seek an explanation for the errors that are typically made by different groups of learners. From what we have seen it is clear that the explanations will prove to be partly contrastive and partly non-contrastive. The fact that error may be caused both by contrastive differences and by the structure of the target language itself means that it is impossible to base the content of language teaching entirely on the results of contrastive analysis. Even if it were possible to make wholly accurate predictions of contrastive difficulties, we should not have predicted all the difficulties that a learner faces. The structure of the second language itself has to provide much of the content of language teaching. It cannot be assumed that non-contrastive aspects of the language will look after themselves. It is this that probably accounts for the fact that anyone who has taught English to pupils from differing language backgrounds has found that there are many aspects of the structure of English which are almost universally difficult for learners of English as a second language. Without wishing to dispute that every language group will have its own particular difficulties, we might come to the conclusion that even when large numbers of teaching texts have been produced on the basis of contrastive studies, in their grammatical, lexical and sociolinguistic content, if not in their phonetic content, they may prove to be remarkably similar.

7.4. The application of contrastive information

There is one final matter to be considered. Even when relevant contrastive information has been made available, are we sure how this will influence the actual teaching of language? There are many people who write on contrastive analysis and who make the assumption, especially at the grammatical level, that the analysis is to be conveyed directly to the learners in explicit form. The teacher describes the contrast and explains the difficulty. But the theory of contrastive analysis contains nothing to justify this or any other teaching procedure. It is a matter to be decided in the light of the methodological convictions of the teacher. In that case it is likely to be determined by the teacher's general attitude towards the value of explicit grammar teaching, which in turn will be derived from his own experience as a language learner and language teacher. In any event, few teachers would be likely to use the information in the same way with all pupils. Whatever value there might be in explicit discussion of language structure with older learners, one doubts whether there would be much to be gained from adopting this procedure with primary age learners.

The contrast of mother-tongue and foreign language structure will be demonstrated to the learners in the classroom if the teacher believes that the learners' potential language performance is thereby improved. It is a belief that runs counter to the direction in which language teaching methods have been moving in recent years. The teacher will therefore ask what use contrastive information is to him if he does not want to pass it on directly to his pupils. In the first place it will tell him where to expect an unusual degree of learning difficulty. This is information that will be more useful to the teacher in training. It could be argued that all new teachers should be prepared for the situation in which they intend to teach, by an examination of the contrastive difficulties their pupils will have. The experienced teacher will already have learned from experience where the problems are, and for him the information will prove less useful. Secondly, the analysis may reveal effective ways of overcoming the difficulty. The teacher may be able to use techniques suggested by the analysis. This rarely proves to be the case. More often than not the only conclusion to be drawn is that the anticipated difficulty will require a more extended and careful presentation and practice of the new item. The manner in which it is presented and practised is not influenced by contrastive considerations. Sometimes the analysis assists in determining a teaching sequence, the other forms of language through which a new item should be introduced and with which it should be contrasted, or the structural and semantic emphases that should be made. To take one of the examples from the beginning of this chapter, if an Englishman learns French, account has to be taken in the teaching of the conceptual difference that the learner will see between the verbs in

il travaille cinq jours par semaine

and

il travaille ici depuis 1950

Viewed from the point of view of the structure of French alone there might seem no reason to make any distinction between the use of the present tense in these two sentences. In fact the learning of the form of the present tense would certainly best be based on sentences of the first type, and sentences of the second type should be treated separately so that the association between its meaning and the use of an auxiliary verb construction which the learner will bring from English can be eliminated. The teaching will require the creation of situations in which French demands the use of the present tense where English demands the present perfect. If the learner were a speaker, not of English, but of a language where usage is the same as in French, this separation of teaching units would not be necessary.

7.5. Summary

In summary, the conclusion to be drawn is that errors in learning are significant. They are not, however, entirely caused by differences between the native language of the learner and the language he is learning. There is some value in analysing the reasons for errors, since this will lead at least to a greater understanding of the difficulties that learners face, and will perhaps assist in the development of pedagogic strategies. The errors will reveal either where the mother tongue does influence learning or where learners are particularly likely to make incorrect generalizations about the target language. It is not necessary nor, in my view, desirable that this should be carried out as a purely predictive process. Instead it can be based on the known errors of learners. The errors are still explained in terms of contrast, but contrast on the one hand with the mother-tongue and on the other within the target language. The resulting analysis is predictive in the sense that the linguistic behaviour of second language learners in the future is expected to resemble closely the behaviour of language learners in the past. That is why it is worth analysing the errors that learners have made.

8
Linguistics and the scientific study of language teaching

8.1. Methodology as fashion

It is not uncommon for approaches to foreign language teaching to be contrasted as either 'modern' or 'traditional'. In practice either term may mislead, since there is little in modern approaches that is entirely novel, and the history of language teaching is filled with such diversity that it would be difficult to prove the existence of a continuing tradition of any kind. If there is any tradition at all, it seems to be of an alternation between two distinct views of the aims and content of language teaching. The one, which would currently be identified as 'modern', sees the aim as a practical mastery, especially of spoken language, and the method as one which demands maximum participation on the part of the learner. The other, which is at present labelled 'traditional', sees the aim as the acquisition of the rules that underlie actual performance and the method as the explicit discussion of these rules with exercises in the labelling of grammatical forms and the deductive application of the rules. Naturally there is room for enormous variation within either of these two approaches and the distinction between them may become blurred, especially in situations where the aims of teaching languages are confused or go undiscussed. However most teachers would have little difficulty in deciding with which approach they would prefer to be identified and most of the figures who are dominant in the history of language teaching can be placed with little difficulty.

From our point of view what is interesting is that the alternation between these two approaches has not only been theoretical but also historical. First one and then the other has dominated language teaching. Viewed from the present day there seem to have been periods of enlightenment, often associated with the names of particularly brilliant innovators and advocates. The Romans provided their sons with Greek tutors and thereby forced them into active use of the language so that they acquired it in much the same way as they had learned their mother-tongue. Montaigne's father made much the same provision for his son's learning of Latin, although it was doubtful whether educational practice at that time followed his belief in the benefits of wide exposure and practice, since when Montaigne went to school he promptly forgot all that he had previously gained by way of practical command. The attempt to apply this approach to the teaching of languages in schools really stems from Comenius in the 17th century, Gouin and Viëtor in the late 19th century and Palmer and others in the 20th century. Comenius, Gouin and many others wrote in part out of dissatisfaction with existing methods, and their writings produced great changes in the ways in which languages were being taught. But in time, with the discovery that the new methods themselves were not proving as satisfactory as had been claimed, methods reverted to what they had been before.

We do not know just how far general language teaching practice has followed the recommendations of the writers on language teaching. It is probable that most of those whose job it was to teach languages—originally Latin, but subsequently modern languages—never committed themselves wholly to the view of a modernist, such as Comenius, or a traditionalist, such as Plötz, the German teacher who, in the mid-19th century, was a strong and influential advocate of what might be labelled a grammar-translation approach. Nevertheless there can be no doubt that there has always been a strong tendency for one or other of these approaches to be the dominant one. Viewed historically, language teaching has always been subject to change, but the process of change has not resulted from the steady accumulation of knowledge about the most effective ways of teaching languages : it has been more the product of changing fashion. Viewed objectively, the process has resembled the swing of the pendulum. Viewed from a more committed standpoint there has been an alternation of progress and regression.

Whether one holds the view that teaching is an art or a science, I doubt whether anyone would dispute that it should be based on whatever knowledge can be established objectively about the content and method of teaching. By studying language and language teaching in as scientific a manner as possible we should be able to make change in language teaching a matter of cumulative improvement. If the establishment of relevant knowledge is a necessary precondition for progress, we can see why in the past change has been a matter of fashion. The techniques and resources for studying the learning and teaching of languages were lacking. The nature of language itself has often been imperfectly understood. It has not always been thought necessary to understand learning in order to know how to teach. There has been no way of *proving* the effectiveness of language teaching methods, although it has not been so difficult to *convince* people of the virtues of particular approaches—for a while at least. Indeed it is this last point that reveals the roots of change in the past. The appearance of gifted teachers who have combined original thinking with strong powers of persuasion has often led to the adoption of new methods which have survived until another teacher has appeared to argue a different view with equal conviction.

It seems to me that one cannot escape the conclusion that to base language teaching solely on the experience of teachers is to perpetuate the situation in which teaching will be at the mercy of fashion. History shows that attitudes can change and then change back again, and there is no guarantee that at any one time teachers of similar experience will be drawing similar conclusions from it. This is a human characteristic that is by no means confined to language teachers. As I shall argue below, it would be equally foolish to derive one's approach to language teaching solely from linguistics or psychology. Let me make it clear that I am discussing here only what should determine the course that language teaching will take. Conclusions drawn from experience cannot be demonstrated incontrovertibly. If one teacher claims that in his experience a particular procedure works and another states that, in his, it does not, there is no way of resolving the disagreement. There is an unavoidable subjectivity about all judgments based on personal experience, and that is why we have to look for more objective means of evaluation.[1]

8.2. The problems of conducting empirical research into language teaching

The most obvious way to establish knowledge of language teaching

[1] Let me add, although it is not strictly relevant, that I am profoundly suspicious of anyone engaged in the study of language teaching who has not himself had sound experience as a language teacher. I doubt whether research can be well constructed or its results properly interpreted except in the light of relevant practical experience. Similarly, teacher training must also be in the hands of practised teachers. Only they have the necessary mastery of techniques and only they can prepare the teacher for the actual classroom situation. No one can claim to be an expert in something that he has not practised.

objectively is through empirical research. If there are differing opinions about such things as the effectiveness of a particular technique, about the relevance of the age of a pupil, about the advantages of a particular sequence of language or about the whole approach to language teaching, why not try out the alternatives in an actual teaching situation, compare the results and thereby resolve the difference of opinion in a scientific way? Could one not in this way investigate such diverse factors as the relative merits of a deductive and an inductive approach; the need for pupil repetition and, if this was shown to be beneficial, the best amount of repetition; the use of the mother-tongue in teaching meaning; the need for language drills and the effectiveness of different types of drills; the advantages of explicit comparison with the mother-tongue; the benefits of more or less intensive teaching; the separation or integration of linguistic levels or skills; the comparison of different methods as represented by different published courses; the effect of differing sequences of language on learning; the teaching of pronunciation with and without phonetic training and with and without the use of transcription; the effectiveness of visual and auditory modes of presentation; the relation of age to method? The list could be extended to several times its present length without difficulty and even so one could not be sure that one had included all the factors that are relevant in language learning. Still, even if the list is incomplete, one would be very happy if it were possible to conduct research that would establish the significance of the factors one had identified.

However, it is the very multiplicity of factors involved in learning that makes it difficult for such research to be carried out. If we wish to study the effects of only one variable, it is necessary to hold all the others constant and in any real teaching situation this is difficult, if not impossible. If one attempts to take these problems into account and compares not isolated factors but groups of variables, it becomes impossible to decide which of the factors is responsible for the results one has obtained. In any case what might be called linguistic factors, such as those listed above, are by no means the only significant variables in the experimental situation. There are also, for example, pupil, teacher and situational variables. Ideally pupils should be controlled for intelligence, known language learning ability and previous language learning experience, motivation and age (where this is not the variable being tested). Personality will also be important, perhaps mostly in determining the relationship with the teacher. As for the teachers, fairly obviously some are better than others. This will not necessarily be entirely a matter of proficiency in the language and professional training, although these are of course very important. Where an experiement uses more than one teacher, there will always be a problem in knowing whether it was the teacher or the methodological variable that produced the result. Using the same teacher does not help either. It is unlikely that he will be able to adopt two different techniques with equal conviction or skill. He may be much more familiar with one that he is with the other and he may therefore do it much better. If ordinary class teachers are used for experimental work, the existing relationship of teacher and pupils becomes a relevant factor. If teachers are introduced into the situation, they will probably have varying degrees of success in creating a good relationship with the pupils and learning will be affected accordingly. The situation may affect results in that it is clear that some schools provide much better environments for learning than others. Furthermore, it is well known that novelty itself has a powerful effect on learning, and any experimental situation is by definition novel to the pupils and may very well be testing techniques that themselves are novel. The interpretation of results has to be made with proper allowance for this fact.

On research in language teaching a recent report said:

> While tackling smaller aspects of the same problem individually might be more profitable, results of research on teaching methods in all subjects generally showed that method was less important than the teacher's competence—which in turn depended very much on the teacher's belief and confidence in what he was doing. In any comparison there needed to be a sufficient number of teachers involved to neutralize the teacher variable.[2]

This suggests that the way to overcome teacher, pupil and situational variables in carrying out empirical research in real teaching situations is to do the research on such a large scale that it can be assumed that overall the variables cancel one another out. The problem then is that the more subjects there are in the research the more difficult it is to exercise proper control. A recent project in Pennsylvania involved 58 schools and 104 different classes.[3] Over a period of two years a comparison was made, principally between traditional and audio-

[2] *Aims and Techniques: CILT Reports and Papers No. 2* (London, Centre for Information on Language Teaching, 1969) p. 30.
[3] For a discussion of the problems involved in conducting large-scale research see 'Critique of the Pennsylvania Project' (*Modern Language Journal* 53/6, October 1969).

lingual methods, but also such matters as the efficacy of different language laboratory systems, of commercial courses and the influence of such things as teachers' proficiency and training. Clearly a study on such a scale can only investigate global characteristics of language teaching; but equally clearly it is not possible for the researchers to know just what is going on in each of the classes in the study. There can be no assurance that in spite of some preparation of the teachers for the experiment, the methods and techniques that they employed in practice are unambiguously identifiable with either of the methods. In this particular instance 25 per cent of the teaching personnel were replaced by new teachers in the course of the experiment. This was only one of many inroads into the controls, and one need not be surprised by the fact that the results were inconclusive. In fact this seems to be a characteristic of larger-scale research projects. The very size is likely to blur the distinctions that are being studied, and the results will not lead to any clear conclusions. If significant differences are shown, there will usually be some feature of the design or conduct of the research which will enable people to question the validity of the experiment.

Clearer results are likely from smaller-scale experiments, but, as pointed out above, teacher/pupil variables loom larger in this case. The difficulty then is of the degree to which the results can be generalized. Probably one would not be satisfied that something had been proved until similar research had been repeated a number of times and had consistently produced the same results. Unfortunately research has a tendency *not* to get repeated, but in the long run one might expect more to be learned from these more modest experiments than from the more ambitious and much more expensive research projects.

The only way to conduct research into language learning so that the influence of uncontrolled variables is considerably diminished is to remove it altogether from actual teaching situations. It should be possible to isolate many if not all of the factors that one would like to know about and devise experiments into their significance under laboratory conditions. This is to bring research into language learning within the sphere of experimental psychology. Some books and articles on language teaching already contain statements about learning that are taken from such sources. Something is known of the difference between auditory and visual memory, of the advantages of distributed as opposed to massed learning, of the ease with which meaningful as opposed to meaningless language is acquired. It should not be difficult to discover whether people remember better for having had to repeat orally an item that they have just encountered for the first time, whether the repetition of analogous sentences as in a language drill really does assist the assimilation of the underlying rule, or whether or not language performance is improved by the explicit formulation or elicitation of a rule.

Such research as has already been carried out in this way has scarcely ever been done in the context of second language learning. It has been an investigation into general characteristics of verbal learning and verbal behaviour. To the linguist or the language teacher the type of learning that has been measured has often seemed rather far removed from what he understands to be the nature of language learning. Psychologists have made their comparisons in terms of success in acquiring and retaining lists of words or isolated sentences. There is, no doubt, a memory factor in the learning of foreign languages, but for the linguist language learning is the acquisition of a competence as defined above. It is much more difficult to study this under laboratory conditions, since the development of the competence may by its very nature be a long-term process. We would have to judge therefore whether conclusions drawn about this type of learning under these conditions can be extended to language learning as a whole. Furthermore, does the elimination of all those factors other than the one being studied create a situation so unlike the circumstances under which learning normally takes place that no practical validity can be ascribed to the results? For the conclusions to have a fairly assured validity for language teaching, it seems that the experimental situation should share at least some of the characteristics of the learning situation, and this will mean that more of this research will have to be done with the explicit aim of developing our understanding of the significant variables in second language learning and teaching. Most recent research still leaves a problem of interpretation, and there will be doubt about the generalizability of conclusions drawn from any laboratory research, however carefully it was constructed.

A further problem that all language teaching research faces, especially research into the psychological variables involved in learning, is the inadequacy of our techniques for sampling people's real language proficiency. In investigating the influence of psychological or methodological variables on learning, some correlation has to be established with actual language learning achievement. The measures of this are available language proficiency tests or testing techniques.

With older research this means a correlation with people's ability to translate. More recently it means a correlation with performance on objective tests. Although most people would agree that modern testing techniques are a considerable advance, few would argue with any confidence that they are entirely valid guides to people's ability to communicate in the language. For a start they are weakest in their attempts to assess what is the central aim of most modern language teaching—the ability to produce the spoken language; and secondly they assume that the ability to avoid making errors (i.e. to complete an objective test successfully) is an adequate indication of the ability to participate in real-life language situations. It is possible that *facility* of language use is more important than being able to construct formally correct sentences. Certainly communication may be unhampered by the presence of errors in people's speech. In this case we may need to assess people's fluency and spontaneity of expression as much as their practical knowledge of language structure. In time more valid forms of assessment may be developed, possible too cumbersome for everyday classroom use, but at least permitting researchers to claim greater scientific reliability for the results than can be justified at present.

It is clear that there are serious difficulties in the way of finding empirical solutions to language teaching problems, and that these difficulties will not be quickly resolved. None of the types of research that I have discussed are to be rejected. It is simply that it will be a very long time before they will enable us to manipulate language teaching with a confident knowledge of the way in which an individual learns a foreign language. Our ignorance is increased by the fact that there are some important features of the situation that the language teacher and his materials create that are probably not susceptible to this kind of research at all. For example, in the discussion of how the content of language learning should be programmed, it should be possible to determine experimentally whether there is any advantage in exercising some kind of linguistic control, as has usually been thought to be the case, or whether a random exposure to language would be just as effective, as has recently been argued.[4] If we assume that such research would show, as I believe it would, that there was something to be gained by limiting and predigesting language for the learner, the question arises as to the optimum way of doing this. Since there would be literally an infinite number of

4 D. Reibel, *op. cit.*

ways of sequencing language, it would be fruitless to attempt to discover the best sequence through empirical research.

8.3. The place of linguistics

So far in this chapter I have asked only what there is to be learned by looking at language teaching itself. This does not seem to provide us with entirely satisfactory answers. However, it is of course false to assume that language teaching takes place in a vacuum and that there are not other fields of study which relate to it. In practice, language teaching has always made use of information drawn from other sources, even if it has not always done it in a systematic way. As we have seen in the earlier part of this book, language—the very substance of language teaching—has long been the object of the scholar's attention, and the study of languages and language as a human phenomenon is now an autonomous discipline to which we give the name linguistics. Although I have argued that there is a lot that we do not know about the learning of language, it is unlikely that it is entirely divorced from other forms of learning, and it is right that we should take into account what is known from general, educational and social psychology. Language learning, like any other kind of learning, will partly depend on characteristics of the learners, and for an understanding of this we will look to sociology and social anthropology. Fairly obviously, the context in which learning takes place will also be important. We cannot ignore the resources that are available to the teacher. We can see what assistance can be provided by technology and how far proper administrative arrangements can be made to facilitate learning. Language teaching is not to be considered in total isolation from other developments in education either. It would be surprising if what we attempted in language teaching ran counter to the general educational philosophy of our school system.

Because empirical research cannot provide us with firm answers, it becomes necessary to evaluate language teaching procedures in the light of what is known from these related disciplines. It would be cause for concern if the way we went about teaching languages seemed to indicate bad linguistics, bad psychology or bad sociology. Linguistics is the subject that we are concerned with and because it has the same subject-matter as language teaching, we are entitled to assume that it has a greater importance than the others. One could foresee the day when the variables of language learning are well enough understood for the study of general psychology to be less than essential. It is hard to imagine that languages can ever be taught without reference to the available language descriptions. In that case linguistics will always be a field of study relevant to language teaching. What this book aims to do is to examine the precise nature of this 'relevance'. The organization of the book has been intended to suggest the range of linguistic enquiry and to interpret the results of linguistic research for its pedagogic applications and implications. Now is the time to make explicit the various relationships that have been demonstrated; but before I do that, there are a number of cautions that must be expressed.

First, linguistics has different aims from language teaching. Linguists set out, variously, to study the human language faculty, to develop theories to explain language behaviour, to provide the most efficient means for describing languages and to make the most accurate and comprehensive descriptions of languages available. In none of these activities are they concerned to provide evidence about the most effective procedures for teaching languages. It is quite wrong to argue, therefore, that developments in linguistics should *cause* changes in language teaching. The relationship cannot be one of cause and effect. Although there is much in linguistics that can be made use of in language teaching, the language teacher is entitled to modify what he uses in the light of his different ends. Provided the language teacher does not act in ignorance, he can ignore the objections of linguists who do not understand his purpose.

Secondly, in making language teaching decisions it is wrong to refer only to evidence drawn from linguistics. Language teaching is a pragmatic business. We cannot ignore strongly-held beliefs about what constitute the most effective approaches to language teaching, even though these might not have a sound scientific basis. Because of the subjectivity of these opinions it is right that we should look at adjacent disciplines for further evidence. However linguistics, as we have seen, is not the only field that may provide important evidence, so we should not expect linguistic arguments to be conclusive. We would hope that all the evidence might lead to the same conclusions, but it will not necessarily do so. What seems good linguistics might turn out to be bad psychology. The teaching of reading could well be an instance of this. This is why the ultimate decision has to be the teacher's. He is the only person who has to take all the evidence into account. Talking in general terms like this obscures the fact that the importance to be attached to linguistic arguments will depend on the nature of the decision being taken. In matters of classroom technique one would hardly expect linguistic considerations to carry much weight. On the other hand, they will have an important place in determining the content of learning.

Thirdly, the fact that there is some evidence, here and elsewhere, that linguistics *has* influenced language teaching cannot be taken as proving that linguistics *should* influence language teaching. It is perfectly possible to argue that at times the application of linguistics to language teaching has been a misuse of linguistics. The very term 'applied linguistics' is open to an interpretation that suggests that language teaching is somehow derived from linguistics, and it is because this has been a prevalent view that I have avoided use of the term in this book. The two paragraphs above show I do not share this view. The teacher must retain his critical faculties in his use of linguistic notions. If he does not he will be applying the good with the bad. It is a simplistic application of post-Bloomfieldian linguistics that has led in some methods to a too rigid distinction between form and meaning in teaching, the neglect of meaning, the attempt to separate the learning of different linguistic levels and an over-dependence on a behaviourist interpretation of learning. Actually in linguistics itself there has now been a fairly sharp reaction against these views; but my point is not that this is now thought to be 'bad linguistics' (placed in a historical context the principles they followed can be considered well motivated), but that they were applied too unthinkingly to language teaching. The relationship of linguistics to language teaching must be studied afresh. Past practice cannot just be continued with a change in the points to be applied.

8.3.1. The relation of linguistics to language teaching

8.3.1.1. *Insights.* By 'insights' I mean linguistic notions that increase one's understanding of the nature of language and consequently of the nature of language learning. They do this without necessarily providing specific points of information that can be built into language teaching. Language teaching decisions have to be taken at many different levels—defining the goals of learning, determining the broad methodological approach, assessing the value of particular techniques, organizing the language content—and there can be few of these that are not more soundly made when one has a deep under-standing of what language is. For the language teacher the study of linguistics is probably more rewarding in this respect than in any other. We have seen a number of ways in which linguistics may help the language teacher to make more informed decisions, even though he will not always come to the same conclusions. Linguistics defines the relationship between speech and writing, and although a teacher might decide that a knowledge of written language is his objective, he cannot ignore the fact that writing is, to a large degree, derived from speech. In defining his aims, and to some extent in developing his methodology, he will find it informative to look at the linguists' discussion of the *langue/parole* distinction. He faces a decision not unlike that which faces the linguist, since he has to decide whether he should set out to teach the general system of the language or a more restricted variety, probably related to situational needs. He also has to decide how far the language he teaches should replicate the speech of actual utterances and how far it should be an idealized or standardized form of language, as linguistic descriptions almost always are. With a real understanding of such differences he is in a better position to judge whether the approach he has adopted is likely to produce the results he wants. The form/meaning distinction is useful not so much because the teacher will follow the attitude of any one group of linguists to this distinction, but because it brings out the need to teach both the formal and the semantic characteristics of language satisfactorily. There is danger in an approach to language teaching which concentrates on what meanings can be conveyed by language and neglects the benefits of exploiting the structural regularities. Equally it is foolish to equate language learning with the learning of forms and to suppose that the ability to construct grammatically correct sentences is the same as the ability to communicate through language. The distinction between form and meaning is therefore useful in the analysis of learning, but it is not a distinction that is maintained in the process of teaching.

The above are choices which face linguist and language teacher alike. There are other notions which linguists use and which enrich our understanding of language. We have looked at the idea of language as structure and seen how, for the linguist, everything in language is inter-related and mutually defining. We have noticed how misleading it can be to think of grammar as a number of distinct and separate grammatical forms, when in fact every item enters into a variety of structural relationships and can carry a number of semantic features. The notion of structure was discussed above with reference to grammar but it can be applied equally to phonology and semantics. We have seen too that the structure of a sentence is not always what it appears to be. Sentences that are apparently identical in their formation may have different meanings because the relationships between the elements in the sentences are not in fact the same. There may be nothing to mark the difference and this leads the linguist to say that the surface structure of the sentences is the same, although the deep structures are different. If language teaching materials are organized on grammatical lines, an awareness of possible differences and similarities in deep structure can be valuable. Sometimes the insights provided by linguists are not really novel. There are times when important notions remain unexpressed or are taken for granted, with the result that they come to be overlooked altogether. Then it is worthwhile having someone state the obvious. The centrality of grammatical structure in language learning is a case in point. There was a period when language teaching reacted strongly to the practical uselessness of much of the language taught in traditional courses. The solution was seen in the selection of a more useful vocabulary, and teaching materials were constructed to facilitate the systematic introduction of this vocabulary, with the consequent neglect of the problems caused by grammatical structure. This period of development represents a short break in the belief that language learning is essentially the learning of grammatical structure. This belief would unite both the traditional grammarian and all modern schools of linguistics. The equation of language learning with the learning of vocabulary is, from the linguistic point of view, a considerable naivety.

It is our learning of grammar that provides what Chomsky has called our 'rule-governed creativity'. This is every speaker's ability to understand and construct sentences that he has not previously met in the language. Again the notion is not a new one, but it had become somewhat obscured in language teaching as in linguistics. Our language competence consists of the ability to recognize and construct grammatically correct sentences which are appropriate both to the circumstances of utterance and the intention of the speaker. This is what we are capable of as mature speakers of our native language, and it is what we aim at in learning a foreign language. In the last but one sentence 'construct' is a key word. If we do not know the rules of language well enough to be able to make new sentences, we have not yet learned that language. Any other kind of language performance, involving the uttering of remembered phrases and sentences, however fluently the pieces of language are spoken or written, is not true language behaviour, but only 'language-like behaviour'. It is easy to be seduced by the immediate appeal of this spurious fluency. We need to evaluate our methods according to their success in producing real competence in language. Similarly it is a learner's creativity, in this sense, that we should investigate when we are testing his language ability.

Insights of these kinds may be provided by any aspect of linguistic science. The examples I have discussed above are a selection drawn from the earlier chapters, but there are other notions which can inform language teaching in the same way. There will also be fields of linguistic endeavour which do little or nothing to develop our understanding of language learning. One suspects that the greater the technicality of the issue, the less its likely relevance to language teaching. I have preferred to call the relation one of insight, because they are further removed from the process of decision-making than either implications or applications. These are clearly not notions that are *applied* to language teaching. The boundary with implications is less clearly defined. I have kept them separate largely on the grounds that, because he takes his decisions in particular circumstances, the language teacher may have to override the conclusions that the linguistic insights might suggest. Because their value may, in this case, seem to many rather ephemeral, I would claim no more for these insights than that they create a frame of mind which is conducive to the taking of sound decisions in language teaching.

8.3.1.2. *Implications.*   Every day in his classroom work the language teacher makes scores of decisions, some prepared, some off the cuff, about his methods and techniques. Many decisions have been taken for him by the people who have produced the teaching materials that he uses. The decisions about *teaching* all aim to improve the process of *learning*. Whether or not one is aware of it, every one of these decisions in teaching has implicit in it a view on learning—either on the general principles that govern language learning or on the way that learning is proceeding in that particular situation. Let us suppose that a new word or collocation occurs. There is a multitude of options open to the teacher. To teach the meaning of the item he may translate it: this implies a belief that learning a foreign language is learning to map it on to the mother-tongue, or that eventual use is aided by the mediation of the first language. Alternatively he may present the item together with one or more visual images: this implies that meaning is simply the product of recurring associations. He may exemplify in numerous sentences: this implies that learning is an inductive process. He may explain the item: this implies that learning is the application of cognitive skills. Having presented the meaning of the item in one or other of these ways, he may do no more: this implies that language learning does not require productive participation by the learner. He may ask for repetition of the word: this implies the active production of item is necessary to learning. He may ask for numerous repetitions: this implies that learning is strengthened in proportion to the number of times that an item is produced. He may ask the pupils to select an appropriate item from among a number of alternatives offered: this implies that learning language is learning to exercise choices, and that contrasting items enables them to be learned more effectively than just repeating them in appropriate contexts.

As this example suggests, relations of implication exist most obviously between language teaching and what is known of the psychology of language acquisition. In any real situation implications like those above are not the only ones that operate. We might on the basis of this decide that translation is generally a 'bad' thing for the teaching of meaning. This does not mean that one never presents an item in association with its mother tongue translation. There are occasions when it is more desirable to obtain a rapid and easy inter-pretation than to enter on to a more lengthy, if more desirable tech-nique. One might not want to interrupt a highly motivating narrative. At three o'clock on a Friday afternoon near the end of term the pupils' receptiveness might be so reduced that a technique requiring the voluntary application of their attention might be doomed to failure. But even if these other psychological conditions will on such occasions seem more important, the implications that translation has for the teaching of meaning still hold. One might plump for the efficacy of a quick translation, but the implication is that one has not taught the meaning of the item, and one should be aware of that implication.

Our theories of the psychology of language learning have implica-tional relations with language teaching largely because they are as yet very crude theories. I pointed out in Chapter 5 that we are attempt-ing to account for language learning and language use with theories that are far too simple. This is inevitable, given the newness of psychology as a science and the difficulty of investigating human behaviour. If one could imaging a time—a very, very long way off—when a theory of language behaviour that accounted for a large proportion of our language use had been set up and verified, we would not be discussing the implications of that theory, but its applications. We have to be content with studying the implications of the differing ways that we go about things, because it would be hopelessly premature to do anything else. Language teaching aims to be practically effective, not theoretically consistent, and in the present state of our knowledge it seems right that the language teacher should hedge his bets. The study of linguistics and especially theories of language acquisition helps to articulate the implications of many current and proposed practices in language teaching.

8.3.1.3. *Applications.*   The relation of application is the easiest to understand. These will be cases where notions and information drawn from linguistics act directly upon the process of language teaching. This is the relation that is implied in the term 'applied linguistics'. Most language teachers who study linguistics expect to derive applications from it. The product of the linguist's work has its most obvious application through the descriptions of languages that he makes. Language descriptions provide the input to the construction of teaching materials. In this linguistics is no different from traditional grammar which was also used to identify units of language learning.[5] What the teacher expects is that linguistics will offer him quite new and very different descriptions of the language that he teaches. He also expects that linguistic descriptions by looking into hitherto uninvestigated areas of language will extend the range of his knowledge of the language.

Let us take the first of these points—that very novel descriptions of language can be expected from linguistics. The teacher who comes to linguistics with a sound knowledge of traditional descriptions of his language is likely to be very disappointed by what is contained in linguistic descriptions. The fact is that, although the criteria that are employed in making language analyses and the forms in which the analyses are presented to the reader are very different from those of traditional grammar, the relations that they express are for the most part remarkably similar. The fact that linguists have usually preferred to adopt formal criteria for the classification of linguistic segments ultimately matters little to the teacher if the

[5] I would view traditional grammar as part of linguistics. Most teachers, however, come to linguistics expecting it to contrast strongly with earlier types of language study. They may judge linguistics by whether it offers them applications quite distinct from those provided by the traditional grammar with which they are already familiar. For this reason, in the discussion that follows linguistics and traditional grammar are treated as if they were alternatives to one another.

classes he establishes have the same membership as those established by the grammarian on notional grounds. Linguists have often travelled by different routes to arrive at similar conclusions. Of course, in these days when there is much less formal grammar teaching in schools, the new language teacher might learn a great deal from linguistic descriptions, but he would learn almost as much from traditional descriptions. When the teacher looks at the teaching content to be obtained through linguistic descriptions, he will find that it bears a remarkable resemblance to the teaching content previously derived from traditional grammars. It has been pointed out often enough before that *linguistics* has had less influence on the *content* of language teaching than *linguists* have on the *methods* of teaching.[6] How odd it is that in the one area where the linguist is entitled to expect that his work will influence language teaching, it has scarcely done so, but that in the field of methods where he cannot legitimately claim that he should be listened to, he has been responsible directly and indirectly for many developments in the last thirty years. The strangeness of linguistic descriptions referred to in the first sentence of this book is in fact very superficial. Linguists themselves must take some of the responsibility for raising the expectations of the language teacher too high. By implying that the preparation of a language teacher was incomplete if he had not studied linguistics, linguists have suggested that the content of language teaching would be changed more radically than could in fact be the case. Many of the facts of language are inescapable whatever one's theoretical viewpoint, and traditional grammarians were as capable of recognizing them as linguists have been. It is hardly surprising, therefore, that there should be very great similarities in the content of language descriptions produced by older and more recent scholars.

If the language teacher is likely to be disappointed by the fact that linguistics will leave much of the content of language teaching unaltered, can he expect that the content will be extended by the addition of 'new facts'? This will partly depend on the language that he teaches. The more common European languages were so extensively studied pre-linguistically that it is rare to find previously unexamined topics. We saw in the first chapter that new facts are occasionally established, and we also saw that the aim of description rather than prescription and the continual reference to real language data makes for more accurate statements. However, looked at from the language

[6] See for example S. Saporta, 'Applied linguistics and generative grammar', in A. Valdman (ed.) *op. cit.*, pp. 81–92.

teaching point of view, most of these issues are likely to appear some-what marginal and the central core of teaching content will continue largely unmodified. If the language is a less common one, clearly the teacher will gain much of value. This stems from the greater intensity of linguistic enquiry and not from the particular character-istics of linguistic science.

New facts are established in areas where the boundaries of linguis-itics are more widely flung than were the boundaries of traditional language study. Traditional grammarians restricted their study almost exclusively to the written language. Inevitably the linguist's concern with speech brings new language data within his field. A linguist's description will contain extensive information on the phonetics and phonology of the language concerned. Speech also differs from writing in its grammar, and although it is possible that the differences have been overemphasized, a linguistic description will reflect the grammar of speech, not the grammar of writing. As we have also seen earlier, the attempt is being made to describe intonation systematically. This will be new information to the traditionally trained teacher. The attempt to study language in its social relations, which we looked at in Chapter 6, is a fairly new development and promises to extend our descriptive knowledge.

Perhaps until we have comprehensive and accurate descriptions of socio-linguistic variation available we are not entitled to say that this is an area of application. At the moment we do not know enough about the operation of stylistic features in language to derive teaching material from their description. Our use of the notion of stylistic variation still has to be a fairly subjective one. In that case we should label our awareness of the possibility of language choice based on social relations an insight and not an application. It refines our understanding of language learning without adding scientifically to the information that we can put into language teaching materials. Some insights, like the implications we saw above, are facets of our knowledge of language that are on the way to becoming applications but are, as yet, some way off.

Language descriptions are used in the study of error in language learning—a study carried out explicitly to increase our understanding of language learning, and making no claim to be a contribution to linguistics itself. To do a contrastive analysis or a study of target language over-generalizations requires a mastery of the techniques of linguistic description including much that, as we shall see, otherwise does not relate to language teaching. It is one of the few investigations into language structure that has improved pedagogy as its aim and is therefore truly a field of applied language research. It seems doubtful whether basing such research on traditional rather than linguistic descriptions would make it noticeably less useful. In itself it does not argue strongly for the contribution that linguistics makes to language teaching.

The applications of linguistics, then, are to be expected through the information and analyses provided in language descriptions. Since linguistics generally studies language in its spoken and not in its written form, and since thereby some new data is brought within the field of investigation, linguistic descriptions can add somewhat to the content of language teaching. But if we judge the applications of linguistics by the extent to which, when compared to traditional descriptions, they provide a highly contrasting input to language teaching content, we shall have to come to the conclusion that by applying linguistics we achieve little that is new. For this reason the study of linguistics will often not meet the expectations of a practising language teacher.

8.3.1.4. *Non-applications.*   For obvious reasons I have not gone at length into examples of linguistic investigation that have no applications or implications and do not provide insights of significance for language teaching. The fact is, however, that a great deal of what occupies a linguist's time will be of little or no value to the language teacher in any of the relations that I have suggested exist. The section in Chapter 2 on generative phonology provides an example of this. Although there is some value in having restated the phonological relatedness of words having similar derivations, the expression of the relations has to be made in abstract terms and consequently cannot enter directly into language teaching. Language teaching can make use of the product of the rules, but not of the rules themselves. Wherever linguistic analysis contains (abstract) forms that have no direct realizations in utterances of the language, teaching cannot follow. It matters in teaching only that *take* contrasts with *took*, not whether the past from is analysed as /tuk/ +-*ed*, where -*ed* is realized as ø (zero), or as /teik/ +-*ed*, where -*ed* is realized as an alternation between /ei/ and /u/. That *took* stands in the same relation to *take* as *walked* does to *walk* is obviously very important in language teaching. This is what the morphological analysis is attempting to express. It would seem absurd to follow the analysis to the point of getting learners to produce a form *taked** and subsequently to change it to *took*.

In current transformational generative descriptions of English, the verbal phrase has as its constituents: tense, modal auxiliary, *have* + *-en*, *be* + *-ing*, and the Verb word. The verbal form *he has taken* therefore consists of: present tense + *have* + *-en* + *take*, or, *-s* + *have* + *-en* + *take*. In any actual sentence of the language, of course, the sequence of elements is: *have* + *-s* + *take* + *-en*, giving *has taken*. In this form of language description there are good reasons why the constituents are first produced in an 'incorrect' sequence and subsequently re-ordered. In language teaching we do indeed recognize that the verbal phrase has these constituents, but since in teaching we operate only through potential utterance of the language, the original sequence of morphemes that the description sets up is irrelevant to us.

Irrelevant too are the particular order in which the rules of a generative description occur and the criteria which determine that order. It is a characteristic of generative description that the rules of language are expressed in a highly explicit form and are applied in a fixed order.[7] It is of no concern here just how these rules are presented and applied. The point is that it is sometimes suggested that these rules have pedagogic significance.[8] A sequence of teaching might reflect the sequence of rules in a grammatical description.

This raises the whole question of the relationship between the form of linguistic description and the ordering of language in teaching material. I have said a number of times that language descriptions serve as the input to language teaching materials. Whether—according to the theoretical basis of our description—we think in terms of rules, items or structures of language, we use the description to make an inventory which is systematically worked through in our teaching. For reasons which I have pointed out, the contents of this inventory have not changed much over the years. The description sets out for us what we might call the 'acquisition points' in the target language— what the learner has to acquire to become generally proficient in the language. What *use* is made of that inventory in teaching is a pedagogic matter, and there is no reason to suppose that the organization of teaching should necessarily reflect the organization of the language description. Descriptive sequence is not the same thing as pedagogic

[7] An early example of a partial transformational generative description of English is given in N. Chomsky, *Syntatic Structures* (The Hague, Mouton, 1957) pp. 111–14.
[8] See for example B. Banathy, E. C. Trager and C. D. Waddle, 'The use of contrastive data in foreign language course development', in A. Valdman (ed.), *op. cit.*, pp. 40–41.

sequence. As we saw, the aims of language teaching and linguistics are different. The linguist does not aim to facilitate the acquisition of a language when he describes it. I do not know of any criteria derived from linguistic science which can be applied scientifically to matters of selection and grading in language teaching. They are processes which remain heavily dependent on the linguistic intuitions of the teacher.

The notion that teaching should reflect the form of description is one that recurs and from time to time is applied with varying degrees of rigidity. In the forms of language description being proposed in the 1940s and 1950s, there was to be no difference between the manner in which the linguist proceeded in analysing a language and the analysis that he finally produced. He was to start with the phonetics of the language, proceed to the phonology, then to the morphology and eventually to the syntax. The analysis would be carried out with as little reference to meaning as possible and the study of semantics, if it had a place at all, would follow the analysis of forms. The equation of analysis and so-called 'discovery procedures', and the evaluation of the analysis in terms of how rigorously the procedures have been followed, is now very much in question, but at that time it was widely accepted. So too was the belief that language teaching should reflect this new approach to language description. We saw its most extreme application in the work of Rand Morton, who attempted to follow exactly the above sequence in his experimental teaching materials. But to a lesser degree it is a course that is followed wherever the teaching of the formal aspects of language is divorced from the teaching of meaning. It may be that in this and any other areas where language teaching resembles the form of linguistic description, the procedures are in fact perfectly good ones. However, this is something that has to be shown empirically. It must not be taken for granted that, as a matter of principle, the organization of linguistic description *should* be imposable on the practice of language teaching. There is much in linguistic research that contributes neither applications nor implications nor insights to language teaching.

8.4. Conclusion: the value of linguistics

The aim of this book has been to discover, by looking at the relationship between linguistics and language teaching, what the teacher can gain from the study of linguistics. We can now see that the procedure followed in this book of taking issues in linguistics and seeing how they affect language teaching is not the procedure that one would wish to follow in making decisions about language teaching. We do not take developments in linguistics and look for ways of applying them to teaching. Instead, we face problems in language teaching and in trying to solve them we look at the evidence from linguistics. The weight that we will place on linguistic arguments will depend on the type of problem we have to solve. In places where the relationship has been described as applicational, where we are making use of language descriptions, we should probably listen more closely to what the linguist says than to evidence gathered from elsewhere. Where linguistics has insights and implications to offer, we must expect that linguistic arguments will rarely be conclusive. Perhaps the point can best be expressed this way. In our approach to the teaching of foreign languages we should beware of contradicting linguistic principles. If some of our practices seem quite contrary to what the linguist believes to be the nature of language, then those practices should be subjected to the closest scrutiny. This holds for our definition of the aims of teaching, for the methods and techniques that we adopt and for our treatment of the linguistic content of learning. It may happen quite often that what is good for teaching is bad for linguistics. The important thing is that if that is our conclusion, it should be reached after consideration of all the possibly relevant information, including information drawn from linguistics.

We refer to linguistics in an attempt to make the process of change in language teaching less subject to fashion and more dependent on the cumulative increase in our knowledge of language learning and teaching. It is necessary to refer to linguistics for more than a description of the language we are teaching, because, although language teaching is a pragmatic matter, it is not at all easy to investigate it by means of empirical research. Linguistics shares this function with other fields of study, and for this reason linguistic arguments have to be properly placed in relation to psychological and general educational arguments.

What does the language teacher as an individual stand to gain from the study of linguistics? He will be disappointed if he expects to acquire a large body of information about the language he teaches which contrasts strongly with the information that he would be able to get from one of the more conventional grammars without any more linguistic training than he already possesses. Measured in terms of the specific points of information that can be fed into the teaching process, linguistics as a new science does not have as much to offer as people have perhaps been led to expect. The real contribution of linguistics is to increase one's understanding of the nature of language. Anyone who has studied linguistics is sensitized to language and thereby to the complexity of language learning. They will be better able to exercise critical judgment of attractive innovations in language teaching, including those that may claim to be supported by linguistic research. Language teaching still depends very heavily on the intuitive interpretations that the teacher constantly has to make—interpretations of learning and of language. The study of linguistics roots those intuitions in a more complete understanding of language and in doing so refines them. This is why, in my judgment, the insights provided by linguistics, however insubstantial they may appear, may ultimately be more significant than the 'new facts' that it offers. There may be no operational definition of grammatical complexity and simplicity, but through his knowledge of the types of structure that language have, the linguistically sophisticated teacher's judgment is better informed though still subjective. The *idea* of teaching the most suitable vocabulary for a given group of learners may be just as effective in correcting bad vocabulary content as the rigorous application of a set of selectional criteria. The awareness that appropriateness of language choice is also a stylistic matter and that error is not to be identified solely with grammar, vocabulary or spelling will prove as valuable to the teacher as any actual description of stylistic features that is yet available.

It is worth repeating something that was quoted earlier in this chapter. 'Results of research on teaching methods in all subjects generally showed that method was less important than the teacher's competence—which in turn depended very much on the teacher's belief and confidence in what he was doing.' It would be absurd to pretend that no one can be a good language teacher unless he has a knowledge of linguistics. It is possible that linguistics is not even one of the most important elements in the preparation of a language teacher. The value of linguistics is that by increasing his awareness of language, it makes him more competent and therefore a better language teacher.

KEY TO TRANSCRIPTIONS USED

English

Vowels

iː	beat	ɜ	bird
ɪ	bit	ə	*a*bout
e	bet	eɪ	bait
æ	bat	aɪ	die
ʌ	but	ɔɪ	boy
ɑː	f*a*ther	əʊ	so
ɒ	cot	aʊ	bough
ɔː	caught	ɪə	beer
ʊ	put	ɛə	bare
uː	boot	ʊə	pure

Consonants

p	pin	f	fin
b	bin	v	vine
t	tin	θ	thin
d	din	ð	this
k	kin	s	sin
g	game	z	zinc
tʃ	chin	ʃ	shin
dʒ	gin	ʒ	mea*s*ure
m	miss	h	him
n	nip	l	lip
ŋ	sing	r	rip

Semi-vowels

j	yes	w	win

French[1]

Vowels

i	vive	y	mu
e	thé	ø	eux
ɛ	aise	œ	seul
a	table	ə	p*e*ser
ɑ	âme	ɛ̃	bain
ɔ	homme	ɑ̃	banc
o	tôt	ɔ̃	bon
u	boue	œ̃	brun

[1] From L.E. Armstrong, *The Phonetics of French* (London, Bell, 1932).

Consonants

p	paix	l	livre
b	bas	r	rare
t	tout	f	faux
d	dos	v	vive
k	cas	s	si
g	gai	z	zéro
m	mais	ʃ	chanter
n	non	ʒ	jupe
ɲ	ga*gn*er		

Semi-vowels

w	oui	j	envo*y*er
ɥ	huit		

Spanish

Vowels

i	sí	o	lo
e	sé	u	su
a	sala		

Consonants

p	por	f	fin
b	baca	s	se
t	tú	θ	*c*inco
d	de	x	*j*ulio
k	con	n	nos
g	guia	m	me
l	la	ɲ	ni*ñ*o
ʎ	ella	tʃ	*ch*eque
r	rico[2]		

Semi-vowels

j	yo	w	*hu*evo

Diphthongs are produced by the combination of vowels and semi-vowels. Not all combinations are possible. See R.P. Stockwell and J.D. Bowen, *The Sounds of English and Spanish* (Chicago, Chicago University Press, 1965), chapter 7: The Vowel Systems.

---

[2] This analysis postulates only one /r/ sound (phoneme) in Spanish, which is doubled to produce the rolled /r/.

Recommended further reading

This select bibliography follows as far as possible the organization of this book. The titles that I have chosen are not necessarily those of the most significant publications in linguistics in recent years. They are books and articles which, in my view, the reader of this book is likely to find informative and interesting. Those in the first five sections will take the reader further in the field of linguistics than has been possible here. None of these publications has been written for language teachers. Most of the references in the last three sections are of more direct relevance to the language teacher.

A. General and introductory

D. Bolinger, *Aspects of Language* (New York, Harcourt, Brace, Jovanovich, 2nd edn., 1975). A general, relatively non-technical introduction to language, catholic in approach and containing a profusion of examples.

R. Quirk, *The Use of English* (London, Longmans, 1962). Intended for the non-specialist. Mostly concerned with attitudes to language and variety within language.

R.H. Robins, *A Short History of Linguistics* (London, Longmans, 1967). Puts modern linguistics in the context of a tradition of language study starting with the Greeks. A useful corrective to the view that nothing interesting happened before the twentieth century. For those with a special interest in the historical development of language study.

B. Phonetics and phonology

G. Brown, *Listening to Spoken English* (London, Longman, 1977). Demonstrates for the practising EFL teacher the characteristics of natural fluent speech and considers the significance of this for teaching purposes.

A.C. Gimson, *An Introduction to The Pronunciation of English* (London, Edward Arnold, 2nd edn., 1970). An excellent example of the sort of information about pronunciation every language teacher should have. Unfortunately nothing really comparable on languages other than English.

L.M. Hyman, *Phonology: Theory and Analysis* (New York, Holt, Rinehart and Winston, 1975). Not in any way intended for teachers, this book provides a wide-ranging introduction to phonology. Indicates clearly the gap between the academic study of phonology and the phoneme-based practice of many language teachers.

J.D. O'Connor, *Phonetics* (London, Penguin, 1973). An introduction to phonetics including elementary discussion of phonology.

C. Grammar and linguistic theory

J.P.B. Allen and P. van Buren (eds.), *Chomsky: Selected Readings* (London, Oxford University Press, 1971). Selections from Chomsky's writings with linking and introductory sections by the editors. Too difficult in parts for the non-specialist, but can be read for accounts of generative phonology, non-behaviourist view on language acquisition and Chomsky's view of the relation between linguistics and language teaching.

J. Lyons, *Introduction to Theoretical Linguistics* (London, Cambridge University Press, 1968). Principally concerned with theory. Excellent on grammatical units, structure, categories and functions. Good on semantics too. Written for the student of linguistics.

J. Lyons (ed.) *New Horizons in Linguistics* (London, Penguin, 1970). Collection of articles specially written by prominent scholars. Intended to survey the state of the art for the general reader, but probably too difficult for the reader with no previous knowledge.

F.R. Palmer, *Grammar* (London, Penguin, 1971). Written specifically for the general reader. First half largely a corrective to traditional attitudes to language and notions of language structure. Second half tries to explain non-technically the contrast between post-Bloomfieldian and transformational-generative linguistics.

R.H. Robins, *General Linguistics: an introductory survey* (London, Longman, 2nd edn., 1971). A fairly technical and rather difficult introduction to general linguistics. Good on different approaches to phonology and on British linguistics.

D. Semantics and lexical structure

J. Lyons, *Semantics I* and *II* (London, Cambridge University Press, 1977). The most comprehensive and authoritative account of semantics yet to be published. Intended for the specialist. Not an introductory book.

F.R. Palmer, *Semantics* (London, Cambridge University Press, 1976). A readable introduction to approaches to semantics written for the beginning student of linguistics and the non-specialist.

B.L. Whorf, *Language, Thought and Reality*, edited by J.B. Carroll (New York, Wiley, 1956). Discussion of the linguistic relativity hypothesis, i.e. that the way we see the world is determined by the structure of the language we speak.

E. Stylistics and sociolinguistics

D. Crystal and D. Davy, *Investigating English Style* (London, Longman, 1969). The most practical study of non-literary varieties of language. Good for detailed analysis of texts, some of which will be of interest to the language teacher and useful for the chapter on stylistic analysis.

J.A. Fishman, *The Sociology of Language* (Rowley, Mass., Newbury House, 1972). An introductory text more concerned with wider issues of language in society than with linguistics but touching on questions of interest to the language teacher.

M. Gregory and S. Carroll, *Language and Situation* (London, Routledge and Kegan Paul, 1978). An introductory student text providing a framework for the description of language variety and referring particularly to work inspired by the ideas of M.A.K. Halliday.

P. Trudgill, *Sociolinguistics: an introduction* (London, Penguin, 1974). An introduction for the general reader, particularly strong on experimental approaches to sociolinguistic research.

F. Psychology of language

C. Burstall: Factors affecting foreign language learning: a consideration of some recent research findings. In *Language Teaching and Linguistics Abstracts* 8 (1) (1975). A useful survey of recent research into factors associated with motivation and age.

N. Chomsky, review of B.F. Skinner, 'Verbal Behaviour' (*Language* 35/1, 1959). Reproduced in many collections, including L.A.

Jakobovits and M.S. Miron, (eds.), *Readings in the Psychology of Language* (Englewood Cliffs, Prentice-Hall, 1967). Detailed critique of empiricist approach to the study of language. First modern formulation of an alternative view.

V.J. Cook, Second language learning: a psycholinguistic perspective. In *Language Teaching and Linguistics Abstracts* 11 (2) (1978). A survey article dealing with the psycholinguistic bases of language teaching methodology.

L.A. Jakobovits, 'Implications of recent psycholinguistic developments for the teaching of a second language' (*Language Learning* 18, 1968). An interpretation of the significance of the mentalist view for foreign language teaching. Reproduced in L.A. Jakobovits, *Foreign Language Learning: a psycholinguistic analysis of the issues* (Rowley, Mass., Newbury House, 1970). A collection of the author's previously published articles. Interesting but by no means as comprehensive as the title suggests. Useful bibliography.

W.E. Lambert, 'Psychological approaches to the study of language' (*Modern Language Journal* 47, 1963). Reproduced in H.B. Allen (ed.), *Teaching English as a Second Language* (New York, McGraw-Hill, 1965). A review of the literature. A little dated but still useful.

P. Pimsleur and T. Quinn (eds.), *The Psychology of Second Language Learning* (London, Cambridge University Press, 1971). A collection of papers given at the second International Congress of Applied Linguistics.

W.M. Rivers, *The Psychologist and the Foreign Language Teacher* (Chicago, Chicago University Press, 1964). A critique of current language teaching practices claiming to apply the results of behaviourist research to language teaching. Itself accepting the validity of basing accounts of language learning on the results of experimental psychology.

B.F. Skinner, *Verbal Behaviour* (New York, Appleton-Century-Crofts, 1957). The most complete behaviourist account of language acquisition and use.

G. Error analysis and contrastive analysis

J.E. Alatis (ed.), *Report of the Nineteenth Annual Round Table Meeting on Linguistics and Language Studies* (Monograph Series on Language and Linguistics No. 21, Washington D.C., Georgetown University Press, 1968). Collection of papers from a conference devoted to contrastive linguistics.

S.P. Corder, Error analysis, interlanguage and second language acquisition. In *Language Teaching and Linguistics Abstracts* 8 (4) (1975). This article surveys work carried out in the last few years in what is probably the most rapidly developing area of research into second-language acquisition.

R. Lado, *Linguistics Across Cultures* (Ann Arbor, University of Michigan, 1957). First formulation of value of contrastive analysis in language teaching. Good examples. A little oversimplified, but well worth reading.

G. Nickel (ed.), *Papers in Contrastive Linguistics* (London, Cambridge University Press, 1971). A collection of papers given at the Second International Congress of Applied Linguistics.

J. Richards (ed.), *Error Analysis* (London, Longman, 1974). A collection of papers including some of the most influential articles arguing for an emphasis on error rather than contrastive analysis.

U. Weinreich, *Language in Contact* (The Hague, Mouton, 1953). The classical study of bilingualism. Laid the ground for the interest of applied linguists in mother-tongue interference.

H. Linguistics in relation to language teaching

(1) *Books on applied linguistics:*

J.P.B. Allen and S.P. Corder (eds.), *The Edinburgh Course in Applied Linguistics*, vols. 1–4 (London, Oxford University Press, 1973–7). Consisting of contributions specifically written for this publication by appropriate specialists, the course provides a thorough survey of current thinking in applied linguistics and language teaching. Volumes 2 and 3 are likely to be of particular interest to practising teachers.

S.P. Corder, *Introducing Applied Linguistics* (London, Penguin, 1973). In contrast to the present volume, this book attempts to present the field of applied linguistics as a unified and coherent discipline with its own aims and methods of research.

K.C. Diller, *Generative Grammar, Structural Linguistics and Language Teaching* (Rowley, Mass., Newbury House, 1971). Discusses the recent and the more distant history of language teaching in the light of the view of language associated with transformational generative linguistics.

E. Roulet, 'Linguistic theory', in *Language Description and Language Teaching* (London, Longman, 1975). An historical and thematic

treatment of the development of linguistic theory and its contribution to the development of language teaching methods.

(2) *Conference papers:*

A major international congress is held every three years under the auspices of the Association Internationale de Linguistique Appliquée (AILA). The papers provide a useful indication of the directions being taken by research in the field of applied linguistics.

Proceedings of the Second International Congress of Applied Linguistics (London, Cambridge University Press, 1971).
Proceedings of the Third International Congress of Applied Linguistics (Heidelberg, Julius Groos Verlag, 1974).

For several years a colloquium has been held at the University of Neuchâtel to which a small group of European and North American scholars has been invited. The themes taken up by the colloquium have proved to be major influences on thinking in applied linguistics.

S.P. Corder and E. Roulet (eds.), *Theoretical Linguistic Models in Applied Linguistics* (Brussels, AIMAV and Paris, Didier, 1973).
S.P. Corder and E. Roulet (eds.), *Linguistic Insight in Applied Linguistics* (Brussels, AIMAV, and Paris, Didier, 1974).
S.P. Corder and E. Roulet (eds.), *Some Implications of Linguistic Theory for Applied Linguistics* (Brussels, AIMAV and Paris, Didier, 1975).
S.P. Corder and E. Roulet (eds.), *Theoretical Approaches in Applied Linguistics* (Published as Vol. 1 no. 1 *Studies in Second Language Acquisition*, edited by A. Valdman, University of Indiana Linguistic Club).

(3) *A number of important articles and books have appeared within the last few years arguing for a new approach to language teaching based on insights gained from linguistics and sociolinguistics:*

J.P.B. Allen and H.G. Widdowson, Teaching the communicative use of English (*International Review of Applied Linguistics* 12 (1) (1974).
C.N. Candlin, 'The status of pedagogical grammars', in Corder and Roulet (eds.) 1973.
T. Jupp and S. Hodlin, *Industrial English* (London, Heinemann, 1975).

R.V. White, 'Communicative competence, registers and second language teaching' (*International Review of Applied Linguistics* 12 (2) (1974).

H.G. Widdowson, 'The teaching of English as communication' (*English Language Teaching Journal* 27 (1) (1972).

H.G. Widdowson, 'Directions in the teaching of discourse', in Corder and Roulet (eds.) 1973.

H.G. Widdowson, *Teaching Language as Communication* (London, Oxford University Press, 1978).

D.A. Wilkins, Grammatical, situational and notational syllabuses, in *Proceedings of the Third International Congress of Applied Linguistics*, 1974.

D.A. Wilkins, *Notional Syllabuses* (London, Oxford University Press, 1976).

Index

(Page numbers in bold refer to sections explicitly devoted to the topic concerned.)